Out of Chaos:

REFOUNDING

RELIGIOUS

CONGREGATIONS

Gerald A. Arbuckle, S.M.

Paulist Press
New York · Mahwah

Geoffrey Chapman
London

Paulist Press gratefully acknowledges use of: Excerpt from *The Jerusalem Bible,* copyright © 1966 by Darton, Longman & Todd, Ltd. and Doubleday, a division of Bantam, Doubleday, Dell Publishing Group, Inc. Reprinted by permission; extract from *The Gospel Path* by J. M. Tillard, published by Lumen Vitae Press, is used with permission of Editions Lumen Vitae; extracts from *Four Quartets* by T. S. Eliot reprinted with permission from Faber and Faber Ltd. and Harcourt Brace Jovanovich.

Published by Paulist Press
997 Macarthur Boulevard
Mahwah, New Jersey 07430

Published in Great Britain by
Geoffrey Chapman, an imprint of
Cassell Publishers Limited
Artillery House, Artillery Row
London SW1P 1RT

ISBN 0-8091-3004-1 (Paulist Press)
     0 225 66549 2 (Geoffrey Chapman)

Library of Congress Cataloging-in-Publication Data

Arbuckle, Gerald A.
    Out of chaos : refounding religious congregations / Gerald A.
    Arbuckle.
        p.   cm.
        Bibliography: p.
        1. Monasticism and religious orders.   I. Title.
    BX2440.A73   1988
255—dc 19
                                                                88-11969
                                                                CIP

Book design by Nighthawk Design

Printed and bound in the
United States of America

Contents

For Mary, Dan, Jack, Bernie and Nico:
exemplars of apostolic, creative, imagination.

Acknowledgements

I am indebted to several hundred people with whom I have shared the basic thesis of this book at workshops or conferences in many parts of the world over the last few years, particularly in the United States, Australia, New Zealand, Britain and parts of Asia. Their questions and comments have helped to confirm the importance of the book's basic thesis for religious today. I hope I have done justice to the stimulating aid they have given me.

In particular, I thank Benedict Groeschel, O.F.M. Cap., Brian Hall and the late Dan Meenan, S.J., former editor of the *Review for Religious*, Kevin Lynch, C.S.P. and Don Brophy of the Paulist Press, for their encouragement to write the book. I thank the editors of the *Review for Religious* and *Human Development* for permission to use some material I had published in these reviews.

Very specially, I thank Tom O'Gorman, S.J., and the staff of the East Asian Pastoral Institute, who generously gave me the time and the fine research facilities for writing the book.

East Asian Pastoral Institute,
Ateneo de Manila University,
Manila,
Philippines   *8 December 1987*

Introduction

"The future of the Church cannot be planned and built up merely by the application of generally recognised Christian principles: it needs the courage of an ultimately charismatically inspired, creative imagination."

Karl Rahner[1]

Many religious congregations today are in chaos. They are not sure about the meaning, contemporary relevance or mission of religious life and, on the practical level, they find it difficult to cope with often rapidly declining numbers, few or no vocations and the rising average ages of membership.

Some congregations acknowledge that they are in chaos and are seriously concerned about wanting to do something about it. Others struggle to deny it, thinking it is just like a bad dream and very soon it will all disappear and "things will be normal once more." Other congregations, perhaps because they are still receiving vocations, e.g., in the Third World countries, think they are not in chaos. They may in fact be deep in chaos, because they complacently refuse to search for the inner meaning of religious life and how it must respond with apostolic vitality to the pastoral needs of people today. They cannot at some point in the future escape the consequences of their prolonged denial.

Chaos, however, can be a blessing from God. If ackowledged and rightly used, it can be the foundation out of which a new religious life creativity could emerge under the leadership of refounding persons, who have "the courage of an ultimately charismatically inspired, creative imagination."

Recently, I wrote briefly on the need for religious congregations to face the challenge of refounding in the midst of this chaos.[2] The reactions to these publications, together with an ever-increasing demand from many parts of the world to lecture on the theme of refounding, encouraged me to research more deeply into this theme. People find the insight of refounding highly relevant, challenging, even exciting. This book, therefore, is the result of the growing felt need for a more thorough, extensive and practical reflection on refounding religious congregations from within. In this introduction I clarify the book's theme and explain how the chapters are structured.

1

Clarification of Theme

At the beginning of *The Divine Comedy,* Dante Alighieri describes chaos and its effects:

Midway upon the journey of our life
I found myself within a forest dark,
For the straightforward pathway had been lost.
Ah me! how hard a thing it is to say
What was this forest savage, rough, and stern,
Which in the very thought renews the fear.
So bitter is it, death is little more.[3]

Many religious congregations can identify today with these lines. Despite the many positive changes in religious life since Vatican II, e.g. the search for a more authentic spirituality, a new understanding of and provision for the uniqueness of the individual,[4] they still feel "within a forest dark," in chaos, and uncertain about how to get out of the confusion. We have enthusiastically tried everything: chapters, more and finely worded documents in neatly bound covers, surveys, renewal programs, and, more recently, congregational mission statements and newly approved constitutions. Yet, nothing seems to be working: "so bitter is it, death is little more."

Certainly, the death of provinces, or of even entire congregations, is now a very real possibility for many of us. Congregations cease to exist historically for several reasons. Governments or the Church have suppressed institutes, e.g. Clement XIV in 1773 decreed that the Jesuit congregation be completely dissolved (though his edict was never fully put into effect). Some institutes just fade away because they have fulfilled the reason for which they were founded, e.g. a medieval French order, committed to the construction of bridges in order that roads could be opened to areas of evangelization, disappeared once secular governments had the facilities to do this.* Some die because their chronic denial of chaos, and of its positive challenges to conversion and refounding, eventually leaves them uninspiring and apostolically irrelevant. Others die because, though aware of their chaos, either they do not know how to get out of it or they are not prepared to do anything about it.

In this book I argue, however, that our experience of chaotic disorder can be positive, if in humility we turn to the Lord to help us to rediscover the innovative purpose of religious life and to discern the presence

---

*Information provided by John Padberg, S.J.

within our congregations of refounding people. If they exist and we use them wisely, they have the charism of leading us out of chaos to a new integration of Gospel values and the world. My hunch is that a refounding congregation will inevitably attract suitable candidates, because they are inspired by the quality of the Gospel life of its members and by the sharply defined apostolic relevance of the congregation's goals.

Our experience of chaos does not automatically lead to creativity nor to the discovery of refounding persons. It only disposes us to be open to growth from within by stripping away from us all the false securities that have accumulated within our congregations over generations. Personally and corporately we must decide whether or not to use this potentially productive climate of religious life confusion. If we refuse the opportunity given us, then apostolic paralysis and slow death must surely occur. If we accept the challenge, however, then we turn to God fully acknowledging our own chaotic weakness. And St. Paul tells us that this is where God acts most powerfully:

> So I shall be very happy to make my weaknesses my special boast so that the power of Christ may stay over me, and that is why I am quite content with my weaknesses, and with insults, hardships, persecutions, and the agonies I go through for Christ's sake. For it is when I am weak that I am strong (2 Cor 12:9f).

In salvation history, God permits chaos to develop that people may rediscover that he must be at the very heart of their lives (e.g. see Dt 8:1–4). Amos, at one point, vividly describes what happens when the Israelites suffer the crippling confusion of chaos and have no prophet (i.e. covenant refounding person) to lead them out of it:

> See what days are coming . . . a famine not of bread . . . but of hearing the word of Yahweh. They will stagger from sea to sea, wander from north to east, seeking the word of Yahweh and failing to find it (Am 8:11f).

Yahweh's response to this "staggering" experience of chaos is to raise up prophets to direct his people to reapply the values of justice and love to the world around them: "But Yahweh brought Israel out of Egypt by a prophet, and a prophet looked after Israel. . . . I will speak to the prophets, I will increase the visions and through the prophets I will deal out of death" (Hos 12:13, 10).

Without prophetic leadership of refounding persons our congregations will stagger, as did the leaderless Israelites, from crisis to crisis, drifting aimlessly from the closure of one house or apostolate to the withdrawal from another. Dante writes that "after I had reached a mountain's foot . . . which had with consternation pierced my heart, upward I looked. . . . Then was the fear a little quieted."[5] As we look at our own congregations, it is like confronting a huge mountain at its base. Consternation, fear and sadness can grip us. If we look up, however, our fear may be a little quieted, for there may be among us the necessary refounding persons, prophets to our institutes.

As with the founding persons of our congregations, refounding people are shocked at the sight of the chasm between the Gospel and the world. They see with the same spirit and drive of the founding persons just how this gap can be bridged and they proceed to do so, inviting others to join them. The inescapable truth is that every society, whether it be secular or religious, faces a joint task: it must inspire conformity to the existing order, but, far more difficult and crucial, it must permit to emerge and flourish those "heretics of each age," the people with outlandish ideas and ways of acting, who have often become the heroes and heroines of the next.

I do not underestimate the difficulties of finding such rare people in our midst. Theologian Johannes Metz, reflecting on the problems of discovering the right kind of Church leaders, asserts that "as regards the kind of model leaders who would manifest the meaning of reform, my feeling is that we are so poor in the church today that we not only do not have such figures, but in addition we do not even know what they should look like."[6] I think Metz is too pessimistic. I believe that with the aid of Scripture, history and the social sciences we are able to construct a reasonably accurate profile of what refounding people should look like. I also believe, *provided* we go about it in the right way, that we may well find in many congregations these necessary refounding people that God is offering us.

Structure of the Book: An Inter-Disciplinary Approach

The book is divided into two parts. In the first part the emphasis is on the theory of refounding religious congregations. In the second part there are practical suggestions about how to refound religious life institutes.

Contemporary research in cultural anthropology and management studies have here much to teach us. Cultural anthropology offers us rich insights into the creative potentiality of chaos and the need for innovative people to lead us out of it. Research into corporate business cultures helps us to define the qualities we should normally expect to find in refounding persons. It also assists us to pinpoint the enormous tensions, and their causes, that commonly exist within post-Vatican II congregations between refounding persons on the one hand and administrators and other religious on the other.

Back in 1963 Edward Schillebeeckx wrote: "One may say that the integration of sociology into Catholic thought is today a fact, even though, in some Catholic circles, not all reserve and suspicion have been overcome, due mainly to a misunderstanding of the real nature of sociological thinking."[7] I think he was too optimistic. The reserve, suspicion and misunderstanding remain, despite the fact that Vatican II said we must use in evangelization relevant insights and methods of the social sciences, including management studies.[8] It was St. Thomas Aquinas who said that every partial truth can contribute to the total truth and can therefore be important for grasping what the Holy Spirit wants of us. Yet to many theologians of his time, St. Thomas appeared to be a "dangerous rationalist, infected with the spirit of Averroes, a most unspiritual iconoclast."[9] Theologians and evangelizers, who today search through the findings of even "the marketplace social science" of management studies for insights into how the Gospel is to be better lived today, are being wrongly attacked as "dangerous rationalists and unspiritual iconoclasts". As in the time of St. Thomas, such critics are insensitive to the dynamic interrelationship that should exist between the world and the spiritual.

Religious life is an adventure in faith; its ultimate meaning is to be found in the mystery of the Trinity itself. However, religious life is incarnated within a human situation. To this extent, therefore, a religious congregation is very much a human product, and in fact each congregation forms a culture in its own right. For this reason a religious congregation can be examined and aided in growth in part by the insights of the human social sciences, e.g. cultural anthropology, management studies, whose specific task is to analyze cultures.

Also to help illustrate the theme of this book, I draw on the findings of contemporary Scripture studies. From these analyses we are able to grasp the importance and richness of chaos in salvation history. And in the lives of the prophets we see many of the qualities we would expect to find in contemporary congregational refounding persons.

In Part Two an attempt is made to answer the practical question: How are congregations refounded? In light of the theoretical insights of the earlier chapters, the key roles of refounding persons and major superiors are defined, potential tensions and conflicts between them are analyzed, and practical suggestions are offered for constructively resolving them. General and provincial chapters have been since Vatican II significant events for congregations attempting the process of renewal or refounding. I believe, however, that we have often expected far too much from chapters; hence, there is a need to refine precisely their function in the refounding experience of congregations. In the last chapter, I offer a case-study of a congregational province that I believe is actively attempting the process of refounding. The case analysis illustrates much of the theory and advice given in previous chapters.

Refounding: A Faith Journey

Finally, a word of caution to readers. Creativity and innovation, which are at the heart of any refounding action, are as elusive as they are complex in all human organizations. Just as business leaders need to be suspicious of any kind of proposition or gimmick that pretends to propose magically and instantly successful ways to creativity and innovation, much more so will wise religious hesitate before accepting any new proposal that claims to over-simplify the process of congregational revitalization and refounding.

So this book offers readers no dramatically simple or rapid way to begin and sustain refounding. In fact the road to refounding is a humanly complex and a spiritually painful one, for Christ calls us to a more intimate, privileged relationship with himself, which means being invited to share deeply in the purifying experience of his own suffering. What Simeon foretold of Mary, she who assisted at the Church's founding, can also be applied to those who are sincerely committed to congregational refounding: "and a sword will pierce your own soul too" (Lk 2:35). They experience the paradox of the Christian life, as Mary did: in the poverty of the cross, through detachment and mortification, we possess all things; in nothing—all things. Those who yearn, or "groan inwardly" (Rom 8:23), for the re-creating of their religious congregations instinctively make the prayer of St. Paul their own: "All I want is to know Christ and the power of his resurrection and to share his sufferings by reproducing the pattern of his death" (Phil 3:10).

Thus, we need to guard against a purely human way of looking at the refounding of religious congregations. On this point our secularist cultures can aid and frustrate refounding at the same time. Take, for example, the stirring exhortation of essayist Ralph Emerson in which he praises the rich spirit of courageous individualism, the vigorous confidence in human self-reliance and the enthusiasm for social, political and economic experimentation emerging within the American frontier world during the last century and still highly valued today:

Trust thyself! . . . Great men have always done so . . . redeemers and bene-
factors . . . advancing on Chaos and the Dark.[10]

A secular culture that in any way fosters a spirit of apostolic experimentation in religious life is to be praised. Similarly, we can be grateful to
creative management experts, anthropologists and Scripture scholars for
what they can teach us about the qualities of refounding persons and
how they are to be used to their best advantage.

Ultimately, however, we must realize that the gift of refounding is a
grace of God, demanding of us a prayerful journey into a world of
Gospel faith, on-going conversion to the Lord and at times discernment
in the midst of agonizing darkness and chaos. No amount of *merely*
human effort or experimentation on our part will bring about the refounding of any religious congregation. Our best prepared planning
may be of little or no value, for we relate to a God who is humanly
inconceivable and unpredictable in his ways, but who is at the same time
all-loving, merciful and compassionate. Readers, earnest for refounding,
should take to heart the advice of the fourteenth century author of *The
Cloud of Unknowing:*

So set yourself to rest in this darkness as *long as you can, always crying out
after him whom you love.* For if you are to experience him or to see him at all,
insofar as it is possible here, it must always be in this cloud.[11]

PART ONE

Understanding Refounding:
Practical Reflections

Chapter 1

From Chaos to Creativity: The Mythology of Regeneration

"By myths we mean the value impregnated beliefs that men hold, that they live by or live for. Every society is held together by a myth system, a complex of dominating thought forms that determines and sustains all its activities . . ."

R.M. MacIver[1]

A myth is a story of tradition which claims to enshrine a fundamental truth or inner meaning about the world and human life. Contrary to popular belief, myths are not childish stories or mere pre-scientific explanations of the world, nor are myths to be equated with falsities or fantasies. Myths are deeply serious insights about reality. Without myths we are unable to determine what things really are, what to do with them, or how to relate to them.

The role of myths in the revitalization of a religious congregation is increasingly acknowledged. For example, in a recent significant reflection on the future of religious life it is said: "Central to the project of revitalization is the need to deepen the mythic roots of one's own life and those of one's community."[2] However, the nature of myths, their relationship to culture and chaos and their precise function in revitalization (or refounding) are poorly researched. Hence, the aims of this chapter are to explain:

- the nature of culture, cultural chaos and change;
- the nature of mythology, especially regenerative mythology;
- how refounding people draw on regenerative mythology.

Culture, Symbols, Myths, Ritual and Chaos: Examples

A personal experience will help introduce these sometimes confusing terms. In the summer of 1959 I traveled from Rome to Forli to visit a

11

New Zealand war cemetery. I arrived at the Forli rail station weary, confused, suspicious of everything Italian and angry because people could neither understand me nor even, I thought, be polite: "If only they could speak English, as every decent person does, and there should be laws to make conductors on Italian trains polite," I kept saying quite unreasonably to myself. Worse was to come! For two hours taxi drivers ignored me. When I finally reached the cemetery as the sun was setting, I suddenly noticed a national New Zealand emblem, the fern leaf, on a gravestone. Without thinking I immediately fell on my knees and quite unexpectedly and a little embarrassingly broke into tears. In the midst of my feeling of confusion and chaos the symbol reminded me of all that is dear and familiar to me. Memories of great culture heroes flooded my mind, memories even of the hundreds of unknown New Zealand soldiers buried around me, rich in creativity and courage when confronted by seemingly impossible challenges.

Quite suddenly, my self-pity and sense of being lost in an unfamiliar cultural world disappeared. If these culture heroes had triumphed in the face of incredible difficulties, then so could I. With that I stood up determined to respond with the same courage, self-reliance and resourcefulness to the demands of the strange culture in which I found myself. I would not fall victim to the deadly chaos of self-pity and unjustifiable anger.

In this simple event we find described many elements of critical importance to this study: culture, symbol, mythology, ritual and chaos. Culture is an historically transmitted pattern of *meanings* embodied in symbols, myths and rituals by means of which people communicate, perpetuate, and foster their knowledge about and attitudes toward life.[3] Culture is a response to our fundamental needs for identity, meaning in life, security or order, a sense of belonging. Now to explain briefly the key elements of culture.

I reacted to the fern leaf in the above incident because it is a powerful symbol for New Zealanders. A symbol is any reality that by its very dynamism or power leads to (i.e. makes one think about, imagine, get into contract with, or reach out to) another deeper (and often mysterious) reality through a sharing in the dynamism that the symbol itself offers (and not by merely verbal or additional explanations). Symbols relate primarily to the hearts of people, to their imagination. While not denying the role of logical or conceptual knowledge, the real key that unlocks the door to reveal the power of symbols is the imagination. A symbol is not merely a sign, for a sign only points to the signified. Symbols *re*-present the signified. They carry meaning and values in themselves that permit them to articulate the signified rather than merely announce it.[4] The fern leaf did not just point to New Zealand; it brought my nation imaginatively alive and present to me in a way that restored my sense of belonging.

Symbols are multivocal, that is, they accumulate layer upon layer of meanings over time. The fern leaf reminds me now not just of New Zealand, but also of my experience at Forli and of a friend who played football for my country with a fern leaf emblazoned on his jersey. A symbol has also the ability to attract or absorb meanings around two semantic poles, one having affective or emotional value and the other attracting cognitive or moral norms. Between the two poles of meaning occurs an interchange of qualities. In the interaction they strengthen and enhance each other. The social norms and values gain greater force through saturation with emotion, and the basic emotions evoked by the sensory referents are ennobled through contact with social values or norms. For example, the cross I wear was worn by my friend when he died. This evokes a feeling reaction in me, but the feeling reaction is ennobled through reference to Christ. His death has meaning through Christ's death. There is also a polarization of meaning in a symbol, that is, a symbol can enshrine opposite meanings at precisely the same time, e.g., the cross symbolizes both the death *and* resurrection. Finally, there is a timeless quality to symbols. I had to check the actual year of the incident in Forli, despite the fact that the event is still very vivid in my memory. Because of their affective dimension, symbols have the power to grip the allegiance of people over a long period of time. Logical attacks on symbols do not necessarily destroy them.

All cultures have some forms of repeated symbolized behavior that is tied to their fundamental way of understanding the purpose of human existence. The repeated symbolic behavior we call *ritual;* the explanatory verbalization is *myth.* A myth provides a framework for comprehending phenomena outside ordinary experience; ritual offers a way of participating in it. At the cemetery the fern leaf restored my feeling of belonging, but the awareness of creative and self-reliant culture heroes linked me with my nation's primal creation mythology. New Zealand's productive agriculture economy was built on the ingenuity and rugged individualism of migrants to the then inhospitable land early last century. Identification with these people gave me renewed vigor; as they, and their successors, had triumphed over the impossible with such limited resources, so could I. The physical action of actually standing up, with a revitalized sense of determination, was the ritual expression of my identification with the founding mythology. Of course my regenerative experience of identifying with the creation mythology would not have occurred, if I had not first suffered the culture shock or chaos. Culture shock is the experience of disorientation and frustration that occurs when an individual is among people who do not share his or her familiar symbols, myths and rituals.

Culture, Chaos, Change and Innovative People

I now explain culture and its implications more in detail. In summary, culture, which sociologist Peter Berger calls *nomos*, protects us from the awesome insecurities of chaos (anomy). *Nomos* is "an area of meaning carved out of a vast mass of meaninglessness, a small clearing of lucidity in a formless, dark, almost ominous jungle."[5] When a culture dramatically disintegrates, therefore, people experience the darkness of meaninglessness, a crushing taste of chaos. We are confronted with this abyss of darkness often in life, when the ordinary supports of cultural security just no longer function, e.g. at the death of a dear friend, a mid-life crisis (i.e., the culture of early adulthood is no longer meaningful and the culture of middle adulthood has yet to be interiorized), the sudden and unprepared exposure to a significantly different culture as occurred to me in my Forli example.

Though experiences of this kind can be confusing, even terrifying, paradoxically contact with chaos or the world of the unpredictable or the unknown is critical *if* there is to be creativity in life or culture. Innovative scientists, poets, philosophers, artists, refounding people of cultures or organizations, all have one thing in common: they venture into the unknown, into the unpredictable, into chaos, in search of new meanings or new ways of doing things.

We are ambivalent toward these people. On the one hand, we can appreciate them for offering us through their initiatives and inventions better ways of doing things. On the other hand, especially until we have become used to the interesting things they provide us with, we fear them simply because they venture into the unknown world, the world of disorder and insecurity, the chaos of non-meaning. Berger expresses our fear of the innovator in this way: "the individual who strays seriously from the socially defined programs can be considered not only a fool or a knave but a madman."[6] (See figure 1.1)

Not only individuals, but also entire cultures or sub-cultures can experience confrontation with chaos, for example through contact with more dominant forces. To prevent chaos from undermining their way of life people often resort to new laws or rules, believing that such authoritative action *alone* will prevent disintegration. More than laws are required; there must be individual and corporate revitalization from within. Un-

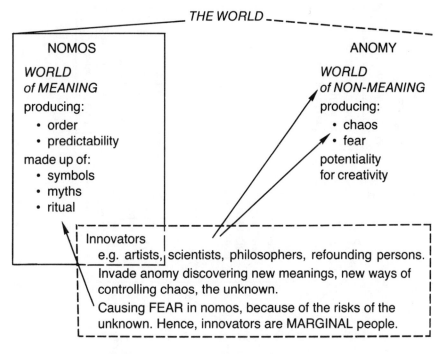

Figure 1.1 Culture, Chaos and Innovators

less this happens the onslaught of chaos is inevitable. Even when chaos emerges there are people who will refuse to admit its existence. They build walls of denial. As I write this the Philippines is slipping more and more into political and economic chaos. Yet people continue to deny the chaos and expect that government decrees, rather than internal individual and corporate self-discipline and revitalization, will effect stability and growth.[7] I initially fell into a similar trap of denial myself on the way to Forli, because I imagined that politeness for guards in Italian trains could be imposed by laws, whereas in fact the real problem lay within myself though I vigorously denied it. (See figure 1.2)

A culture cannot remain in the escapist denial stage of chaos indefinitely. Eventually, it either dies or is led to a new stage of adjustment to a world of change. If the latter, then the process of adjustment is led by innovative leaders or refounding people, but they can only do so *if* there are a sufficient number of people who have come to hope in the possibility of the new adjustment. Usually it takes a bitter, protracted experience of the confusion or malaise of chaos before some people begin to yearn for individual and corporate revitalization under the leadership of an

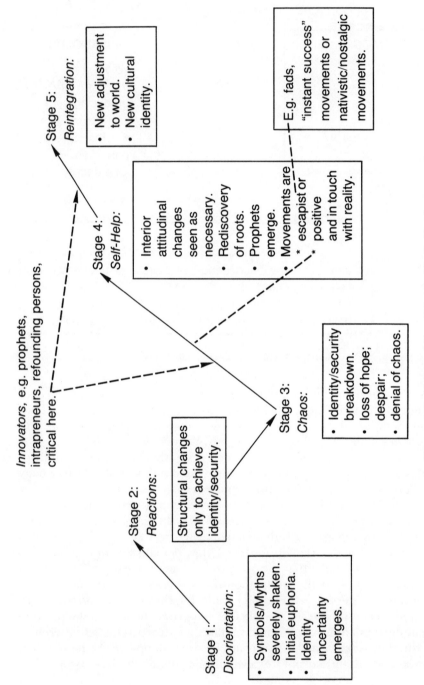

Figure 1.2. Cultural Breakdown: Revitalization

Stage 1:
Disorientation:

- Symbols/Myths severely shaken.
- Initial euphoria.
- Identity uncertainty emerges.

Stage 2:
Reactions:

Structural changes only to achieve identity/security.

Stage 3:
Chaos:

- Identity/security breakdown.
- loss of hope; despair;
- denial of chaos.

Stage 4:
Self-Help:

- Interior attitudinal changes seen as necessary.
- Rediscovery of roots.
- Prophets emerge.
- Movements are
  * escapist or
  * positive and in touch with reality.

Stage 5:
Reintegration:

- New adjustment to world.
- New cultural identity.

E.g. fads, "instant success" movements or nativistic/nostalgic movements.

Innovators, e.g. prophets, intrapreneurs, refounding persons, critical here.

innovative person. Charismatic leaders sense this yearning, articulate it and call people to face the future positively by drawing strength from their creation mythology. Effective leaders, like de Gaulle and Churchill, are able to do this with consummate skill.

Some innovative individuals, however, can play on people's fears of the unknown and their desire for an instant experience of order and meaning in their lives. They encourage people to withdraw from the world through membership in fundamentalist secular or religious cults or sects that give them an unreal and temporary sense of belonging and self-worth. Some cults romanticize an imagined former golden age; they seek to restore old symbols *intact*, e.g. the Lefebvre movement or the Shi'ite Iranian revolution. Millenarian cults, e.g. nazism and Soviet communism, offer their followers the assurance of an immediate protection from the threatening world of chaos and the promise of an exclusive peace in the future.[8]

By way of summary, there are several key cultural anthropological insights about change in the above analysis:

1. As anthropologist Mircea Eliade says, cultures are apt to experience cyclic regression to chaos as a prelude to a new creation or cultural integration; cultures, like individuals, can, however, deny in a variety of ways the creative potential in chaos and escape into an unreal world.[9] (See figures 1.2 and 1.3)
2. Innovative people are crucial for creative action; they are both feared and respected because of their contact with the world of chaos and uncertainty.
3. In order to be able to move out of chaos, the retelling of one's personal or cultural creation mythology is of critical importance in providing the necessary creative energy to act. Innovative leaders, with imaginative memories of creation mythology, tap the regenerative power of these mythologies in order to draw and energize followers.

Myths, Revitalization and Refounding of Cultures

Because mythology is so critically important in any revitalization or refounding of a culture or group of people, I will analyze more fully the nature and functions of myth. We need to know how myths relate to truth and history, how myths are to be interpreted, the important types of myths and how myths change or die out.

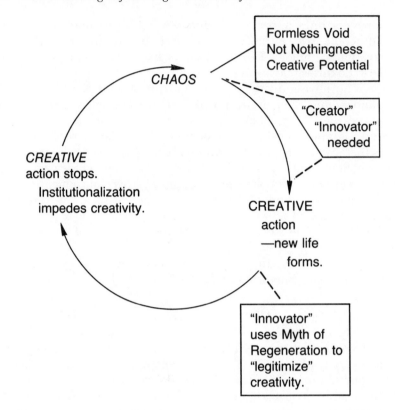

Figure 1.3. Eliade's "Culture of Cyclic Return to Chaos as Preface to Creativity"

Myths, Truth and History

Like sacred icons, myths are the "medium of revelation rather than of man's self-expression," says Thomas Fawcett. "They are accepted . . . as handed down from the gods themselves."[10] Sometimes individuals, e.g. Old Testament prophets, are seen as the agents of the revelations of the gods in the establishment or revitalization of myths. But the myths remain as the revelations of mysteries rather than clever illustrations or educative entertainments on the part of mere human persons.

As myths are made up of symbols, they can evoke deep emotional responses and a sense of mystery in those who accept them, simply because they emerge out of the very depths of human experience of birth, life, the need for meaning, death. No matter how hard we seek to deepen our grasp of the meanings of myths, they still remain somewhat ambiguous and mysterious because they attempt to articulate what cannot be fully articulated.

Myths are about *reality*. They are efforts to explain what usually is beyond empirical observation and to some degree or other outside human experience. They speak of reality and experience *other* than the physical world. This is an important point that needs to be understood if confusion is to be avoided. Myth and empirical truth do not contradict one another. Myths, after all, reveal truths that cannot be grasped through empirical observation.

Myths are about values in life; they do not go into details about how those values are to be reconciled when they appear to be oppositional. For example, the American mythology does not tell us how the stress on individual rights is to be reconciled with the need to work for the common good.

Though myths can contain or have solid foundations in historical realities, the purpose of myth and history differ; myth is not concerned so much with a succession of events as with the moral significance or evaluation of these happenings. A myth is a "religious" commentary on the beliefs and values of society. For example, Abraham Lincoln can be viewed historically or mythologically. If the former, then he is described as fitting into a definite time period, influencing and being influenced by events around him. If, however, he is evaluated as a person who exemplifies the virtues of zeal for the rights of the individual, inventiveness in the face of difficulties, hard work and honesty, then we are measuring him by the foundation mythology of the American nation.

Functions of Myths

Myths, as Joseph Campbell points out, provide meaning in response to four needs.[11] We need a satisfying reason for existence, a coherent cosmology, that is, we need to know where we fit in within a comprehensible and hopefully safe world; we need a social organization, together with supportive attitudes, so that we can work together in some degree of harmony and thus avoid chaos, and we need an inspirational vision that inculcates within us a sense of pride.

Take the example of the creation mythology of the United States. As the Great Seal of the nation reminds us, God, or some extraordinary destiny, calls us to participate in a new exodus, a new journey, from the poverty and oppression of other nations, in order to participate in the building of a new promised land. This gives meaning to our lives; it fits us into a coherent cosmology. The Constitution, and its supportive sentiments of equality, freedom, respect for the rights of the individual, provide the system of social organization that guarantees my rights to participate in this journey into the promised land. The fact that I and others have been called by God to participate in this work of building, "while others remain struggling in poverty and oppression elsewhere," is a vision that instills within me a sense of nationalistic pride.

Interpretation of Myths

Commentators generally interpret myths in one of three different ways: functionally, psychologically, or structurally. Sometimes authors blend aspects of two or all three ways of interpreting myths. This blending is invaluable, for myths are too rich to allow only one method of interpretation.

According to the *functional* theory, myths exist primarily to justify existing social institutions or ways of acting.[12] Myths act as "charters" for social rules or structures. This view is limited because it over-stresses the cultural role in the evolution of particular myths and the common elements in all myths are neglected. Psychological interpretations assume that mythology is a poetic way of communicating; the meanings of myth are to be found beneath the surfaces of stories. Carl Jung believes that "the primitive mentality does not invent myths, it experiences them."[13] There is a "collective unconscious," the psychic background which is common to all people, though at the same time supra-personal. There are archetypes, "forms or images of a collective nature," which have been transmitted by traditions, migrations and heredity. These archetypes are identical with the themes of myths. Jung concludes that myths are not charters to legitimate cultural institutions, but psychological realities or expressions of the archetypes or primordial images of the collective unconscious. Myths give a "local habitation and a name" to these primordial images.

Freud uses this insight to explain the universality of the Oedipus complex, believing that there was an actual historical event of father-killing and mother-son incest taboo. He holds that myths and dreams are the projections of frustrated desires which the conscious mind suppresses, so that they eventually surface in distorted imagery.[14]

Anthropologists consider the psychological interpretations to be oversimplistic, as they force complex realities into simple, pre-structured patterns. And, moreover, there is no way to disprove them since assertions about the unconscious are hard to verify objectively. In addition, the role of culture in mythology is unnecessarily ignored or downplayed.[15]

Today anthropologists generally prefer the *structural* approach to interpretation according to which myths are the product of both conscious and unconscious elements. One group of structuralists, led by anthropologist Claude Levi-Strauss, build their theory particularly on the insights of linguistics and psychoanalysis. Myths are logical structures of binary oppositions, e.g. order/disorder. They express oppositional relationships that the conscious mind will not face; myths seek to resolve the contradictions logically and imaginatively.[16]

More recently, a more modified version of this structural approach has become popular, under the leadership of anthropologist Victor Turner, because Levi-Strauss underestimates the cultural impact in the evolution of mythology. Myths for Turner are *liminal* phenomena; they are recounted frequently at a time or in a state that is "betwixt and between" (technically called *liminality*), that is, when people are confused or without their traditional cultural supports. Myths recount a period in which the uncertainties and tensions of being in a state of confusion or chaos do not exist.[17]* For example, the psalmist in the midst of desolation turns to the mythical expression of God's abiding concern for Israel. The recounting of the myth gives him consolation, energy or a renewed sense of purpose and drive: "I remember the deeds of the Lord; yes I remember your wonders of old. . . . You led your people like a flock under the care of Moses and Aaron" (Ps 77:12, 21). Though not denying that other interpretations contain helpful points for understanding myths, I personally favor Turner's approach; it is especially helpful in understanding why the retelling of myths is important in times of personal or group chaos.

Types of Myths

Among the many possible types of myths I explain five that I consider particularly important if we are to grasp the inner heart of cultures and how they are able to be refounded out of chaos. In my analysis I will give most attention to creation and regeneration myths.

1. Creation and Regeneration Myths

While all cultures have specific myths through which they respond to questions of identity, it is in their creation myths that the most basic answers are to be found. Not only are creation myths the most all-embracing of mythic proclamations, addressing themselves to the widest range of questions of meaning and values, but they are also the most profound. Take, for example, the New Zealand Maori myth of creation. *Being-Itself* evolves from "the conception" through thought, spirit and

*See below, Chapter 3, pp. 48ff.

matter to the great peak, the "blaze of day from the sky."[18] Creation myths like this speak about *first causes;* in them people express their primary understanding of the world and their own role within it.

Many ancient creation myths place an *absolute* reality as the very foundation of all life. This reality is both transcendent, i.e. true for all times and places, and immanent, i.e. true in the here and now. To be both transcendent and immanent, the reality is believed to be eternal. While this *absolute* reality, in whatever way it is defined, is behind all major myths, it is most obviously so in strict creation myths. They are concerned about the relation of the unknowable to the known, e.g. in the American foundation myth the relation between the deity and the people he has called to establish "a new order of things" through the world's "greatest experiment in democracy." Often the original reality out of which the *absolute* created the world is considered to be primal chaos, i.e., the "new promised land" of America for the early Pilgrim fathers. Rather than being *something* negative, chaos is here vigorously positive inasmuch as order can emerge from it.

Mircea Eliade believes that there is a creation dimension within every kind of myth. Myth, he says, "is always the recital of a creation; it tells how something was accomplished, began to be. It is for this reason that myth is bound up with ontology; it speaks of realities, of what really happened."[19] For him *reality* means *sacred reality* and the latter belongs to sacred time, that is, the time when creation took place. In profane time people carry on the ordinary business of daily living. It is sacred time which gives meaning to life; sacred time breaks into people's lives through rituals in which people re-enact, relive the holy or the original creation, their emergence out of chaos. In short they relive the founding myths of their cultures.

The reliving of the founding myth, in which people lock into the power and dynamism of the primal creative act, is called a *regeneration* ritual. It is especially relevant when a people's cultural identity seems to be falling into, or is threatened with, chaos. People feel the need to relive their original founding, and thus win back their identity. At the Forli cemetery I regained my identity and balance by reliving my nation's founding myth; the myth thus became regenerative.

Regenerative rituals are not *commemorative;* they are always *re-creative* in their demands on people. That is, people are expected to undergo a deep interior and exterior change or revitalization; they must experience a new creation out of chaos. They are to be passive *and* active in the presence of the revealing absolute: passive in being open to the myth and active in interiorizing its inner energizing heart.[20] To use Eliade's language, in regeneration rituals sacred time breaks into profane time;

sacred time is ritual time, the brief transcendence through festival. It consists of those rites in which people re-enact the holy, aboriginal events of their culture. By journeying into sacred time one is rescued from the world of non-meaning or chaos.

2. Charter Myths

These myths legitimate actions in the present and the future, e.g. the American political system of checks and balances is legitimated in the Constitution myth.

3. Identity Myths

These myths, intimately related to creation myths, provide individuals and cultures with a sense of belonging, e.g. the Exodus narrative for the Israelites. In identity myths there are often heroic persons who symbolize this identity and whose lives indicate how this identity is to be achieved or restored, e.g. Old Testament prophets.

4. Eschatological Myths

These myths are about the end of an age or the end of time. They speak about key issues of life, death and resurrection, future rewards and punishments, even an apocalyptic insight into a future age of peace and plenty.[21] They often tell of a former age of peace that was lost but is to be restored if people act rightly. They are the driving force behind the way people live their morality and initiate revolutionary movements. Communism, for example, offers its golden age of the classless society, one to be shared by those who battle against oppressors. The collective culture hero in this myth is the proletariat which struggles against and, eventually overcomes, the bourgeoisie.

5. Dominant, Supportive and Directional Myths

In the narrative story of a people, different myths may be interconnected into what is called a mythology. Generally, one myth will stand out over the others in the mythology and this is called a *dominant* myth; the other myths complement or support this dominant myth. Some myths, which I call *directional* myths, indicate *how* the foundational or creation myth is to be lived out, though these myths will not go into concrete details and may in fact be somewhat ambiguous. The written American Constitution, which established the political system, could be considered a directional myth.

Myth Management

New myths are created and old ones are maintained in existence, are constantly revised or die out, because of a variety and flow of forces, changing needs and new perceptions. The creation, revision or disappearance of myths I term *myth management,* and it occurs through such processes as myth extension, substitution, drift and revitalization. I will briefly describe the first three, but explain at greater depth myth revitalization because this process is especially integral to the refounding of any type of human group.

Myth Extension

When people ransack the past to find legitimation for present intentions or actions, there is myth extension. For example, politicians are apt to quote great culture heroes of the past in order to legitimate what they are saying about the present situation. In the process of extension the myth is applied to new needs. Sometimes revision or extension occurs if only the *meaning* of the specific myths, not the words themselves, is changed. For example, the American foundational myth—which includes the "revelation" that "all men are created equal"—is still vigorous, even though we have come to include blacks and all women in an originally restrictive assertion. Although the meaning of the myth is much extended, the "fact" of equality is still considered to be unchallenged.

Myth Substitution

Myth substitution is a difficult and often painful process. Marxist Russian leaders seek to manipulate their people, often under the threat of violence, by inventing new myths to legitimate their power and supremacy.[22] Sometimes a new myth becomes acceptable through a process of patient education, persuasion and example. Paul VI deliberately used ritual experiences to help people grasp Vatican II mythology. For example, in order to stress the servant role of the papacy he put aside the use of the regal tiara. For his funeral he willed that he be buried in a simple wooden casket.

Myth Drift

Drift occurs when myths change, degenerate or disappear without deliberate planning on the part of individuals or groups. Fairy tales and legends are sometimes secularized myths; they have lost their original sacredness because over time they have ceased to be important to people in answering key questions about life and its meaning.

The vigorous technological emphasis within our cultures encourages the dangerous tendency to equate "literalness" always with "truth." When this happens the power of myths is undermined. If the Genesis creation story is claimed to be literally true, then when this interpretation is questioned the *inner meaning* of the myth is also in danger of being discarded. The religious symbols of myth cannot be reduced to purely factual or intellectual terms. Truth, as poets know so well, is bigger than what can be empirically dissected.

Sometimes the dominant myth is distorted because a secondary or directional myth assumes an exaggerated position. This has happened to the Genesis creation myth. Extreme capitalism, with its emphasis on individualism, displaces the original stress in the myth on our responsibility as co-creators with God in this world. Social consciousness thus is downplayed in what has become a distorted myth. Marxism, with its emphasis on the future golden age, is a secularization and vulgarization of the same creation myth; for, remove God and individual dignity is unprotected.[23]

One of the most powerful barriers to an understanding of myth, and its survival, is the fact that people may no longer share the kind of faith which had originally given it birth. For example, a person who has lost faith in the mythology of democracy will no longer have any use for, or even appreciation of, the American or British parliamentary systems of government.

Myth Revitalization

Myths are narratives that aid us to feel at home with ourselves and with the world in which we live. They articulate how "chaos became cosmos."[24] As we have seen, when people are threatened with chaos, and especially when they are weary of experiencing chaos, they are more open to the need to rediscover and relive their original creation myth. In the reliving of the myth, they seek to regain their self-worth and energy to survive and grow.

Examples

To illustrate this point, consider Prime Minister Margaret Thatcher who was able to rally Britain to support the Falklands War by promising her people with Churchillian oratory the chance to relive the imperial creation myth that "Britain rules the waves." Take the example also of the American foundation myth, which exalts the potential of the human person to grow in strength and human perfection. During the late 1960s and 1970s the nation experienced cultural turmoil. Anti-heroes abounded: people burned the sacred flag, presidents failed to live up to the American spirit of pride in the nation's prestige, the nation suffered a disastrous war in Vietnam and was humiliated in Iran. There was needed, said *Time* magazine, "a reassertion of man as shaper of the world rather than the '70s model as victim or passive partner."[25] The 1984 Olympics at Los Angeles gave many Americans the chance to relive their founding myth: "The belief was reborn that Americans can do, well, anything."[26] There were other events also in that year: "It was a year of ceremonies. . . . Some of the rites played a kind of sacramental role . . . conferring a healing reassurance."[27] And there were the cultural heroes, cultural revitalizers or refounding people: the organizer of the Olympic Games, the participants themselves, the country's actor-president. The refounding process would not have taken place without them.

The foundation myth in the revitalization process can be updated, distorted or purified. The actor Sylvester Stallone in the films *Rambo* and *Rocky* is an updating of the American mythic hero; he is the modern cowboy, now dressed for contemporary deeds. In the light of the Gospel, and indeed of the creation myth of America itself, this updated mythic hero is a moral distortion of what the hero *should* be because of the senseless use of violence.[28] Notice, finally, that for revitalization of foundational myths to occur in ways that touch the new needs or the changing views of people, either the myths should be expressed in new symbols, e.g. in the American Olympics through the "Games Extravaganza," or old symbols must be allowed to have layers of new meanings added, e.g. the symbol "equality" in the American Constitution now connotes *all* peoples and *both* sexes. If this does not happen, then the supposed revitalization can be a regressive and fundamentalist movement, such as happened in the Iranian revolution. There is a failure to adjust to the realities of change.

Archetypes, Ritual and Cultural Refounding Persons

We have said that in a culture the repeated symbolic behavior is called *ritual* and *myth* is its explanatory verbalization. As a myth sets out what *should* be by way of behavior in a culture, it is termed an *archetypal* directive for people. In ritual, people "own" or interiorize that directive and it thus provides a way of participating in the myth experience. The key word is *archetypal,* a term used by Jung but here substantially modified, as I now explain.

The absolute—in whatever way culturally it is defined—is immanent as well as transcendent in every creation myth. That is, the absolute is *here* as well as everywhere; it is *now* as well as always. The absolute achieves transcendence and immanence through *archetypes,* that is, they give shape and form to this or that. Archetypes are always valid, never change, because they are the absolutes and belong to sacred time. Archetypes break into profane time through ritual, thus giving people the chance to experience sacred time. Jesus, *the* archetype, rises from the tomb and transcends his relativity at all times; thus he is with us now as he was with those who saw him on the resurrection day.

One further clarification. The archetype is not a *prototype.* The latter connotes the first of a line and may or may not continue to influence subsequent events. Yet the archetype has a universal application, for it is timeless, it guarantees authenticity, it is the representation of the absolute of the myth in the here and now. Adam has relevance to us, not just because he is considered the first man, i.e. prototype, but because he represents the essential man. Since he is an archetype, his original sin is therefore ours. It is inherent in the human condition and we inherit the sin to the degree that we inherit our humanity.[29] This is an example of what we mean when we say that a myth is an *active* force or is saturated with power.

For that power or active force to have an effect, people must acknowledge its existence. They must *own* it by allowing the myth to "come alive" in profane time. The archetypal spirit of the Pilgrim fathers becomes a power in me, if I assent in my life to the abiding value of hard work, initiative and trust in God. The cultural refounding person enters into the sacred time of the original founding, rediscovers the archetypal power of that moment, identifies with it and reapplies its vision to a changing world. He or she invites others to enter into the same experience, that is, to undergo a conversion to the reality and power of the myth. In conversion we accept the reality and the force of *sacred time* within our lives. We allow the transcendent absolute of the myth to become immanent.

Summary

Culture, which consists of symbols, myths and rituals, gives us a vital sense of meaning and belonging. Myths, especially creation myths, which are at the heart of every culture, tell us that we form a unique group in the world, with a particular destiny. Anthropologist Bronislaw Malinowski tries to describe the integrating role of myths in this way: myth "is not merely a story told but a *reality lived* . . . not an idle tale, but a hardworked *active force*."[30] Eliade believes myth is a "sacred history" and hence "saturated with being . . . and *power*."[31] They are right. These two experts in the study of mythology are speaking of the "eternal" relevance and dynamism of myths for those who accept them.

When a people's culture is dramatically undermined, they lose their sense of meaning and belonging and thus experience chaos. The only way out of chaos is for people to enter again into the sacred time of their founding in order to relive their creation mythology. Through this experience they are reinvigorated. But for this to occur, they must want to move out of chaos and they need refounding culture leaders who have the ability to articulate the creation mythology and express it in ways that relate to the changing world around them. The original creation mythology then becomes regenerative, a process well described by Malinowski as "a narrative resurrection of a primeval reality."[32]

Chapter 2

Chaos and Refounding:
Lessons from Corporate Cultures

"The true objective is to take the chaos as given and learn to thrive *on* it. The winners of tomorrow will deal *proactively* with chaos. . . . Chaos and uncertainty are . . . opportunities for the wise."

Tom Peters[1]

"But cultures can be changed if the managers who would change them are sensitive enough to the key cultural attributes—heroes, values, rituals—that must be affected if the change is to succeed."

Terrence E. Deal and Allan A. Kennedy[2]

There is a precedent for religious leaders turning to management experts for advice on how they are to fulfill their duties in the service of the Lord. Jethro, the father-in-law of Moses, had "observed what labors he (Moses) took on himself for the people's sake" and how tiring this was for Moses and the people with him. The father-in-law, the forerunner of today's management experts, then taught Moses the value of the principle of subsidiarity or delegation: "But choose from the people at large some capable and God-fearing men . . . and appoint them as leaders of the people . . . so making things easier for you and sharing the burden with you. . . . Moses took his father-in-law's advice" (Ex 18:14, 21, 24). So, with the same critical judgment of Moses, we also turn to management experts—the Jethros of the contemporary world—for advice on refounding religious congregations. We might, with their help, "be able to stand the strain" a little better "and all (our) people (may) go home satisfied" (Ex 18:23).

The emphasis today in management studies is to view business firms as corporate *cultures* with their own symbols, myths and rituals and so subject to all the stresses and strains of culture change and the risks of chaos.[3] The consequences of this approach are especially relevant to the theme of this book, because, despite the radically *fundamental* differences in aims and values between corporate business and religious congregational cultures, there are some common characteristics.

29

For example, management research shows that, *first,* continuous innovation is essential for survival and growth; the more constant and rapid the change in society, the more important is the need for on-going creativity. *Second,* there are powerful cultural forces within existing corporate cultures that inhibit or frustrate innovation. *Third,* many corporate cultures are in chaos and are in urgent need of revitalization.[4] *Fourth,* corporate revitalization is possible only through myth purification and the fostering and correct placing of refounding people. Given these features, which corporate cultures share with contemporary religious congregations, I believe that, by studying how corporate cultures approach the challenge of revitalization from within, we will obtain invaluable insights that can be used in the refounding of religious congregations.

Hence, taking into account the theory presented in the previous chapter, I will here:

- clarify what we mean by corporate "myth purification";
- define the nature and qualities of corporate culture refounding persons ("intrapreneurs");
- describe what management must do to encourage the development and survival of corporate refounding persons;
- summarize the cultural obstacles to the effective action of refounding persons and management.

Corporate Myth, Purification and the Intrapreneur

In a recent study Harold J. Leavitt pointed out that historically three categories of people are involved in the process of corporate culture development:[5]

> *pathfinders,*
> +
> *problem solvers,*
> +
> *implementers.*

The pathfinders are visionaries, future-oriented persons because they can see entirely new ways of doing things, or how new products can be made, that no one has ever thought of before. They are intuitive and imaginative people prepared to move ahead, refine their insights as they go along, and remain stubbornly at the task until they achieve the break-through. Because planning details are not always clear, especially at the beginning, they find it difficult at times to communicate their intuitions to others.

Problem solvers, on the other hand, are highly rational and organized people, committed to logically analyzing problems and producing solutions for *existing* programs of production. Their task is not to invent entirely new products or ways of doing things, but to make sure that the present action is being done as efficiently as is possible after careful and thoroughly systematic analysis. Unlike the pathfinders, who are *proactive* because they anticipate new needs, the problem solvers are *reactive* people since their task is to react to problems as they emerge in existing programs.

The implementers are the doers; they take the solutions given them by the problem solvers and make sure the job is done according to the specifications passed to them.

The primal creative myth of contemporary industrialization is this: industrialization developed through the imaginative, stubborn, creative and inventive individualism of certain pioneers. For example, there were individuals who dreamed of how to replace horse power with engines and they proceeded to invent such machines. In the early stages of industrialization such individuals were the culture heroes; problem solvers and especially the implementers, the uneducated factory workers, were purely the servants to the pathfinders. They were not expected, and were rarely asked, to offer advice to the pathfinders, so the model of production and organization was very hierarchical with the power very firmly in the hands of the pathfinders.[6]

As mass production developed, with its standardized products, the process of myth extension took place and in the first decades of this century the problem solvers moved into the dominant place. Radically new inventions were not seen as important, so the role of the pathfinders declined. This was the age when the "role or bureaucratic culture" model of corporate organization became popular. Each of the three categories had clearly and rationally defined roles in production. Implementers were to continue to do what they were told to do without question by their superiors, and managements, with problem solving mentalities, could see little need for people with "dangerous visionary ideas."

After World War II both the roles of the problem solvers and implementers were revitalized, the first category by the invention of the computer which improved the quality of the analysis and solution of the day to day problems of production, and the second category through the emphasis on the values of the human relations movement. Implementers in the

1960s and 1970s were encouraged to participate in wide consultation and decision-making procedures in close cooperation with management.

Values like teamwork and consensus were highlighted and problem-solving managers knew they dare not ignore them. Thus the the original creation myth was now scarcely recognizable, with the implementers equal, or even ahead at times, to the problem solvers in pragmatic importance. The model of the corporate manager during these years, and still very much in fashion in business schools, was of the person who equates professionalism in management with hard-headed rationality, one who "seeks detached, analytical justification for all decisions."[7] Pathfinders had definitely moved to the lowest position in this vigorously person-oriented, and at the same time highly rational, corporate culture model. (See figure 2.1)

Myth Purification and the Intrapreneur

As Western economies moved increasingly into chaos in recent years, the mythology of corporate cultures, as extended and modified, has come under severe scrutiny and criticism. While not denying the importance of computerization in problem solving and the value of implementer participation, it is now recognized by several management researchers, and corporate culture practitioners, that the creation myth of production in the process of extension has drifted perilously away from acknowledging the primary role of the visionary pathfinder.[8]

Attempts are now being made to purify the myth to allow the imaginative pathfinder to take his or her rightful role as the one who *alone* can dynamically grasp the original corporate creation myth and adapt its

19th Century	PATHFINDERS +	Problem Solvers	+	Implementers
c. 1900– c. 1950	Pathfinders +	PROBLEM SOLVERS	+	Implementers
c. 1950– c. 1980s	Pathfinders +	Problem Solvers	+	IMPLEMENTERS
Future Trend?	PATHFINDERS +	Problem Solvers	+	Implementers

Figure 2.1. Changing Roles within Corporate Cultures

power to the present world, for without such people there is no way out of chaos. As Leavitt notes: "We've become so skillful at analytic thinking, and so busy exploiting its huge potential, that we've let our imaginations get rusty. Now we're trying to get those old creative engines humming again."[9] Expressions like "leadership," "change-masters," "entrepreneurs," "intrapreneurs," "values," "vision," "mission," "proactive" and "creative" are now to the fore.[10]

The *intrapreneur*[11] is a person whose task is to revitalize an existing business or corporate culture, whereas the *entrepreneur* is a term best used of people who establish new ventures outside the existing businesses. The intrapreneur has the visionary and creative qualities of the pathfinder, but his or her role is yet more extensive. He or she is not just a person with a good idea or invention, but is one who, energized by the creative power of the corporate culture founding myth, sees *how* ideas can be put into practice and *actually* moves to do so. The intrapreneur recognizes the archetypal directive of the corporate culture's foundation myth: creativity is at the source of the survival and growth of the culture. The intrapreneur identifies with the myth and invites others to relive with him or her the sacred time of the culture's creation, thus breaking into profane time with new ways of acting/producing adapted to the needs of a changing world. Identification with the founding myth is not for the intrapreneur and followers a nostalgic escape into the past, but a force prepelling them into the future.

The intrapreneur, in his or her task of making sure the vision is put into concrete shape, assumes a vigorous leadership role in the categories of problem solving and implementing. In terms of the theory explained in the last chapter, the actual implementing of the visionary insight is the *ritual act,* that is, the visible expression of the revitalized corporate myth. In brief, the intrapreneur personifies by his or her vision, and its realized ritual expression, the values at the heart of the foundational corporate myth: creativity and action for survival and growth.

The Intrapreneur in Action: Tensions

The most significant theories of management from the 1960s to the early 1980s emphasized the need for management to foster worker participation in decision-making through a variety of techniques, and the ability rationally to analyze and react to various kinds of corporate crises.

But it is now increasingly recognized that the emphasis on worker participation, with its egalitarian and consensus qualities, is not the atmosphere most conducive for the emergence of dynamic, creative-mission-oriented pathfinders. Frequent meetings, especially if the gatherings take the form of quasi-encounter sessions, whose primary concern are the details of personal growth of individuals and consensus, are suffocating experiences for pathfinders whose immediate and imaginative interest, if the corporate culture is to survive and grow, is beyond the group to a world of rapidly changing needs. A stifling atmosphere can develop even in the most distinguished businesses—for example, the "top management of Bank of America got so deeply into consensus building that it neglected banking for a time."[12]

On the other hand, implementers see the pathfinder/intrapreneur as a threat to their own security and so move out of fear of chaos to marginalize the non-conformer. Little wonder that many would-be-intrapreneurs, to escape frustration, wastage of energy, rejection of their ideas and the fears of marginalization, opt out of existing businesses and either go to more favorably disposed firms or start their own enterprises where they are entirely free to act as they wish.

There are tensions also between the problem-solver type, who in recent decades has come "to terms" with the consensus-oriented implementers, and the pathfinder/intrapreneur. The former demands detailed planning from the latter and considers anything that is not thoroughly rational and predictable as dangerous and crazy.

Contemporary managers, therefore, must discover ways in which "both pathfinding individualism and cooperative implementing"[13] are fostered and positively interact. Intrapreneurs must be allowed to be involved, not just with pathfinding, but with problem-solving and implementing. The challenge is an enormous one, especially since the emphasis has for so long been in favor of consensus implementation with its distrust of the pathfinder's "strange and rather vague new ideas," but unless it is met and successfully resolved, Western corporate cultures will slide further into chaos. The success of Japanese enterprises is largely due to their ability to reconcile all these tensions without loss of creativity.[14]

Qualities of Intrapreneurs

Let me reiterate the two major conclusions of contemporary research into corporate cultures:

- First, as two authors put it: "Individuals, not organizations, create excellence. With their unique skills they lead others along the pathway to excellence, carefully cultivating those who will later assume the controls."[15]
- Second, if existing corporate cultures are to be revitalized they need

a particular type of individual, the intrapreneur; he or she sees the opportunity for creative growth, is able to create a response and moves to implement the insight.

We now specify more precisely the qualities of intrapreneurs, who, given the nature of the gifts required, will be rather rare people:

1. Ability to Listen/Creative Imagination/Action-Oriented

The innovator's most significant gift is a creative imagination but it can function only if people are prepared to listen to hear what is happening within and outside themselves. Popular definitions of imaginative creativity could include statements like: creativity is "daring to differ," "having another go," "doubting the doubters," "trusting daydreams," "turning down a side road."[16] But we need to venture further into the nature of this important, fascinating, albeit perplexing, gift.

Creative persons have the capacity to be surprised, that is, they have an unconscious alertness to see that some aspect of everyday life differs from the normal pattern and that the difference is significant. There is a driving curiosity to look beyond the conventional wisdom on any topic, to let go of the predictable and the safe in the search for new insights or meanings. Everything is open to questioning; the frontiers of experience and rational knowledge can never be static, they must be constantly pushed back. With even the poetic language of symbols, myths and rituals creative people in all spheres of life will struggle to express the findings of their journeys into, and out of, the chaos of the unknown.[17]

The creative aspect of their imagination is the ability to jump afield from a starting point, to see relationships or links which others fail to see. Take the example of Dr. Glenn Conroy, a specialist in physical anthropology, who on visiting a supermarket noticed on the cover of a magazine a three-dimensional image of a person's head with the flesh removed. Built up from computer-tomograph scans by Dr. Michael Vannier, the image had permitted a plastic surgeon to plan surgery to correct deformities of the face and skull. Before Conroy had finished paying for his food supplies, he realized that the same technique might also be particularly helpful in his own area of research. If it could electronically "dissect" stone-embedded fossil skulls and show their hidden features, it would solve a long existing problem of how to analyze rare fossils without fracturing or even destroying them in the process. Both scientists have since had considerable cooperative success in their task.[18] Thousands of other people must have noticed the cover of the magazine, but lacked creative knowledge to see the necessary relationships.

Creative imagination involves two kinds of mental activity. First, there is the skill to use an interesting, stimulating or unsatisfactory situation as a springboard from which one's imagination moves, apparently in an uncontrolled and undirected way, freely searching all kinds of associations of images or ideas. The imagination then returns to the issue of concern, either with a workable insight on how to resolve the unsatisfactory situation, or with some new analytical model or pattern that puts into order the observed facts. In the above incident, Conroy was concerned with a thoroughly unsatisfactory situation: the inability to research fossils without breaking them apart. While not engaged with anything scientific, he nonetheless allowed his imagination consciously to roam without control freely seeking some intuition that might solve the problem. It worked!

The second kind of mental activity is the ability to permit one's purely unconscious processes to act *without* any knowing awareness or control of the action, then permitting the outcome to pass into consciousness. Though there is no agreement about the exact nature of this process, nonetheless the role of the unconscious in creativity is regarded as of considerable, if not decisive, value. The permitting of the unconscious processes to work is what we might call the incubation or mulling-over stage, because the processes can take some time to be effective. The insight, or newly found way of looking at reality, rises to the surface sometimes dramatically, e.g. when one is walking or relaxing with a novel.[19]

Take the example of my culture shock at the Forli war cemetery referred to in the previous chapter. I was able to rise out of my feeling of chaos by identifying with the creation/regeneration myth of New Zealand. At the time it happened, however, I did not consciously realize I was actually doing this. I do recall that I was a little surprised, even puzzled, about my sudden surge of self-confidence and determination to rise out of the chaos of my self-pity. My feeling of puzzlement must have remained in the unconscious, because years later, when studying the power and nature of mythology, I suddenly understood why I had acted the way I did. This discovery has remained a powerful and creative experience in my life and has certainly influenced both the writing of this book and its emphasis on the regenerative force of creative mythology.

People with this gift of creative imagination are somewhat detached from themselves and from the societies in which they live. It requires a certain detachment, and personal sense of security, to allow the imagination to roam freely in a world of chaos and uncertainty, searching unconsciously, with little or no control of the intellect, for possible patterns that can make sense of one's experience. The results of this journey of the imagination could be threatening as it might mean that one must give up what one has held dearly for years. One must be able to live with the consequences of a creative imagination. With detachment goes of course flexibility, versatility, patience and vision. If there is no vision there is no drive to allow the imagination to search for significant relationships in one's experiences. In view of this analysis, therefore, I would agree with Paul Ricoeur's incisive assertion that the imagination "has a prospective and explorative function in regard to the inherent possibilities of human beings"; it is "par excellence, the instituting and constituting of what is humanly possible; in imagining possibilities, human beings act as prophets of their own existence."[20] Strong words, but realistic.

In Western cultures which exalt youth and fear the aging process, the popular image is that creative imagination begins to die about the age of twenty-five. Though research suggests that the thirty to forty age category is the most creative, in fact inventiveness is possible at all ages. Galileo, the sixteenth century controversial physicist and inventor, was still creative in his seventies, the artist Picasso into his nineties. My own father on the day before he died at eighty-seven was still searching to discover how to make crossword puzzles more interesting . Readers, take heart!

Finally, the person with the type of creative imagination needed in the business cultures is action-oriented, that is, he or she sees a need, imaginatively shapes a response to the need, and then *acts* to put it into effect, unless obstructed by external obstacles, e.g. management officials. There are often many people with ideas of what should be done, but the rare people are those who take imaginative ideas and shape them into a reality.

2. *Passionate Commitment to Refounding*

Without being fanatical there is in the intrapreneur a passionate commitment to the project, a creative stubbornness in clinging to standards of excellence, derived ultimately from an identification with the regenerative power of the corporate culture's creation myth.

3. *Acceptance of Hard Work*

Authors are thoroughly united on this point: there can be no intrapreneuring without hard slogging. "They expect the impossible from themselves, and consider no sacrifice too great," writes Gifford Pinchot.[21] Innovations are rarely the result of "flashes of genius," but rather the result of hard, systematic and painful activity. Mick Jagger, one of the most long-enduring and creative rock musicians in the entertainment industry, once expressed contempt for the rock groups that appeared unrehearsed claiming to depend on instant inspiration and spontaneity for creativity. They produced "rubbish" because, he said, there can be no spontaneity without craftsmanship, no expressiveness without hard work.[22]

4. Little Need for Affirmation

The task of intrapreneuring can be an intensely lonely one, for intrapreneurs must endure at times being pushed to the margins of their corporate cultures because of their non-conforming views. To survive they derive self-confidence and self-esteem from their passionate belief in their own ability to create. They survive without the affirmation of others.[23]

5. Commitment to Small Beginnings

Even though intrapreneurs may be dreaming of vast new projects, they know the wisdom of beginning with small steps, for then they can more readily make changes if their experiments are not working out.[24]

6. Team Builders

The reference to intrapreneurs as team builders may at first sound out of place. The popular image of the intrapreneur is of a dogged and dramatic loner. On the contrary, contemporary agents of group change must become masters directly or indirectly in fostering the participation of problem solvers and implementers if their projects are to succeed. In today's complicated technological world of corporate enterprises, they cannot do everything by themselves even though, especially in the early stages, they must personally be intimately involved in the tasks of problem solving and implementing.[25]

This need to obtain the cooperation of others is fraught with enormous difficulties. As we will see, management must come to the aid of the would-be intrapreneurs in helping to choose problem solvers and implementers who are ready and capable of working with them. Those who join the intrapreneur need to realize that it is the latter who has the original vision and often he or she cannot always articulate the practical details of the vision; they are to be members of a team to assist and energetically to challenge, but not to obstruct, the intrapreneur.[26]

The Role of Management in Supporting Intrapreneurs

"If a society hopes to achieve renewal, it will have to be a hospitable environment for creative men and women."

John Gardner[27]

When the insight into the need to foster pathfinders/intrapreneurs for the refounding of corporate cultures first came out a few years ago, it initially received enthusiastic managerial support. People saw the idea as a way to solve complex problems quickly and painlessly without thorough strategic thinking and planning by management; but with such a faddish and unrealistic approach to intrapreneuring, it was inevitable that disasters occurred and managers lost patience with the insight.[28]

In practice, intrapreneuring is a slow and difficult process demanding of management sensitive and *informed* cooperation with intrapreneurs. The overall task of management is to foster the growth of a corporate culture that is open to the creative power of the foundation myth, or, in other words, their duty is to foster a culture that is consistently favorable to on-going creativity or intrapreneuring. I set out below what is required of management if corporate cultures are to emerge favorable to intrapreneuring.

1. Personal Conversion to the Corporate Creation Myth

The myth says that for survival and growth one must opt continuously for tomorrow, so, therefore, management must be prepared to free a culture's creative resources for this purpose. If management is not converted to the myth and its consequences, he or she will eventually give way to the pressures of maintenance rather than stressing consistently creativity to ensure that there is a tomorrow.[29] One consequence of management's conversion to creativity will be that management will allow itself time for reflection or for the imaginative exploring of corporate chaos. They cannot support intrapreneurs if they are consistently bogged down with excessive and exhausting work.

2. Discover Would-Be Intrapreneurs

This cannot be done by sitting in an office and waiting for them to knock on the door, but concerned management will be out in the field looking for them. It could happen that they will not be found; then management must struggle to entice such people into their enterprises. This search for intrapreneurs is a key function of contemporary management, an example of what has been aptly termed the "hands-on, value-driven" approach,[30] a form of management that will be described more fully below.

3. Structurally Support Intrapreneurs

Intrapreneurs need sponsors who can structurally free them from tasks that inhibit their creativity. Sponsorship is the function of management who alone have the political corporate power to support the intrapreneur with structures conducive to creativity. One author says that the most general formula for effective innovation is: an idea, initiative and a *few friends*.[31] Converted managers are the "few friends." This rule, I discovered, was effectively used by Jesuit Marion Ganey to foster village change from *within* through credit union development in the Fiji Islands. He deliberately acquired the effective political backing of the then colonial governor, who cut through government red-tape to prevent paternalistic official interference in the village change process. He refused to act until this structural support had been obtained.[32]

4. The New Belongs Elsewhere

To permit the intrapreneur to have the required freedom, the new venture should normally be established as separate from the existing operation. This will protect the intrapreneur against unnecessary on-site interference from members of the dominant organizational culture and from having constantly to justify his or her actions. Accountability—yes, but to a limited number of people designated to receive it.[33]

In my research into village revitalization in Fiji, I found that Fr. Ganey quite deliberately declined to attempt revitalization within existing socioeconomic or cultural organizations, for he correctly judged that the pressures in these groups against the rising village intrapreneurs would be overpowering. So he initiated new programs, with their own internal organization and values favoring intrapreneuring.

5. Let Unproductive Projects Go

Innovation is "first, the systematic sloughing off of yesterday," to release resources to allow the intrapreneur to function.[34] This is bound to meet with vigorous resistance.

6. Cultivate Chaos

At times the only way to break through rigid conservatism obstructing necessary growth is to permit corporate culture chaos to develop, for example by refusing to prop up what is obviously a dying section of a corporate enterprise though the people involved remain blind to this fact. People may then eventually be better disposed to listen to and follow intrapreneurs and their creative values. Recently, a Japanese professor of industry and economic research told his listeners that "introducing chaos is one way to combat stagnation and regimentation" in Japanese industry.[35]

7. *"Hands-On, Value-Driven"*

If management wishes to encourage the emergence of corporate cultures that are constantly oriented to fostering the development and support of intrapreneurs, they need to have what is called the "Hands-On, Value-Driven" approach. This approach requires that the central management personnel have the ability to articulate and transmit to others the essential values of their companies, e.g. quality, creativity, flexibility and the critical role of the intrapreneurs (and all creative people) in responding to the changing needs of consumers. "Clarifying the value system and breathing life into it are the greatest contributions a leader can make," declare two management experts.[36] Leaders do not have to be intrapreneurs to do this, in fact in all likelihood they will not be, for their management duties will be sufficiently demanding of their time and energy.

In order to transmit these values management personnel must themselves be mobile, constantly in touch with the grassroots of the enterprise if the people in the field are to be challenged to accept and interiorize the message. Letters or exhortatory newsletters are no substitute for the person to person approach at the site where values are to be inculcated and problem solvers and implementers are to be reconciled with intrapreneurs. Research shows that in order to keep the leadership team active and unhindered by bureaucratic pressures at the center, the leadership at the top must be kept surprisingly small, lean; increase the central staff and it will multiply reasons why it cannot be regularly out in the field of action.[37]

8. *Reward Creativity*

While intrapreneurs may not always require special recognition, nonetheless other members of the corporate culture need reminding that creative innovation is an esteemed value and intrapreneurs are the cultural heroes.[38]

9. Encourage Several Intrapreneurial Efforts Simultaneously

All innovative actions are risky. Hence, the need to have several innovative efforts underway at the same time lest one or more fail.[39]

Corporate Culture Resistance to Change

Intrapreneurs, actively supported by management, aim to bring about
culture change within *existing* corporate cultures. However, they can be
confronted with enormous resistance, as anthropologists have discovered in their analyses of obstacles to change within cultures. The following is a summary of the major reasons why people resist change.

1. Preference for Order over the Chaos of Change

While the human person is achievement-oriented, a striver who looks
for progress and so theoretically is open to change, and may even assent
to an "orgy" of creative rhetoric in position or vision papers, in fact the
basic need for order, predictability and stability is so much stronger,
because change threatens to expose us to the dreaded unpredictability of
chaos. Anthropologist Clifford Geertz concludes: "One of the most significant facts about us (human beings) may finally be that we all begin
with the natural equipment to live a thousand kinds of life but end in the
end having lived only one."[40]

2. Ethnocentricism inhibits Change

Cultures have an addictive quality like tobacco or drugs. Most often
without realizing it, we believe that our ways of doing things are the best
and we become blinded to their deficiencies. This cultural blindness or
addiction is generally termed ethnocentrism.

3. Denial of Chaos

Despite the fact that chaos can be the catalyst for new creative leadership and action, nonetheless a common human tendency is to deny that
chaos exists at all; denial can be so powerful that it can take hold of an
entire culture. One observer writes somewhat cynically, but with more
than a touch of truth, that "the last act of a dying organization is to get
out a new and enlarged edition of the rule book."[41] Denial of chaos can
continue to the very end! Ernest Becker aptly comments: "The idea of

death, the fear of it, haunts the human animal like nothing else; it is a mainspring of human activity . . . (which) is designed largely to avoid the fatality of death, to overcome it by denying in some way that it is the final testing of man."[42] To give up the old ways of doing things demands of us a kind of death, but we seek to avoid at all costs facing death and its consequences.

5. Fear of Losing Power

There is a yearning in most people to want power over others and, once they have it, they struggle to hold on to it for fear of the chaos that will result for themselves if they lose it. In corporate cultures, people fear change lest they lose their position of status or control over others, so they are apt to resist whatever threatens the status quo that benefits them.

6. Group Pressure Develops Neutralizing Mechanisms

Because of group pressure, the tendency is for individuals rarely to rise much above or fall much below the level of their groups; usually the group is a conservative influence maintaining the status quo.[43] Most often the pressure to conform to the status quo is expressed with so little fanfare, but generally effectively, that it is not recognized by those who are not on the receiving end.

That shrewd social critic of the eighteenth century, satirist Jonathan Swift, describes in story form what happens to a person to dares to have innovative ideas in his day. Gulliver, in *Gulliver's Travels,* wakes to find the little people of Lilliput doing their very best to stop him from daring to move: "I attempted to rise, but was not able to stir; for as I happened to lie on my back, I found my arms and legs were strongly fastened on each side of the ground."[44] Anthropologists have uncovered all kinds of subtle, and not so subtle, methods whereby people struggle to tie down would-be-innovators, or to neutralize "dangerous, chaos-threatening" qualities of would-be intrapreneurs, just as the little people surrounding Gulliver tried to do.

These methods of control, or of "tying down," are called *rituals of control* and they are to be found in all cultures, including corporate cultures, unless there are constant and effective counter-actions or revitalization movements. The non-conformist must contend with threats of ridicule, spiteful gossip and social ostracism (even directed to include the "deviant's" family) by the threatened group. Still worse things can occur. When a culture (or sub-culture) is in chaos, people are unsure of their collective values or identity and are uncertain about the cause of their confusion. They are then disposed to participate in "witch-hunts" in order to discover the "deviants" whom they believe are undermining the unity and identity of their society, e.g. Senator McCarthy's flailing away at supposed communist saboteurs in the early 1950s fits this category. The process of searching for scapegoats and forcing them to conform or withdraw becomes in itself a way to clarify traditional values and assert unity, thus preventing the onrush of chaos.[45]

An organization, however, can ostensibly acknowledge and even praise a would-be innovator by referring his or her insights to a review committee. In this ritual of control the committee is expected to so modify the innovator's creative ideas that they will be rendered harmless to the group, or else the non-conformist becomes so tired of waiting for the committee's results, or of having to send in more and more details of the proposed plans for the project, that he or she withdraws the project in disgust or retires completely from the group. One further form of restraint is to have the would-be intrapreneur "domesticated" by appointing him or her to a demanding administrative post. It appears to be a promotion or recognition of creative gifts, but in fact the posting is so burdensome and exhausting that the individual has no time for intrapreneuring or threatening the group with "outlandish ideas."

Summary

In corporate business cultures three categories of people can be distinguished: pathfinders, who are the visionaries or future-oriented people; the problem-solvers, who are concerned with rationally analyzing and resolving present production problems; and the implementers, who are primarily involved in putting into practice what is presented to them by the pathfinders and the problem-solvers. Industrialization was spearheaded primarily through the imaginative action of the pathfinders, who were driven by the corporate myth of "creativity for survival and growth." These culture heroes personally and in action embodied the very heart of the corporate myth.

Increasingly, in this century, the foundation myth has been positively and necessarily extended to involve both the problem-solvers and the implementers, but to the degree that pathfinders have been dangerously forced into a very inferior role. The chaos in Western corporate cultures today is due to this dramatic marginalization of the creative pathfinders. This harmful drift in the foundational myth of the corporate culture must be reversed *if* business companies are to survive and grow. Revitalization is ultimately dependent on imaginative corporate pathfinders. There is no escaping the truth of what John Gardner says: "Renewal springs from the freshness and vitality of individual men and women."[46]

Today we refer to the pathfinder as the intrapreneur; he or she not only creates, but at least initially is intimately involved in both the problem-solving and implementing categories in order to guarantee the success of the project.

Management's role is to discover these rather rare would-be-intrapreneurs, place them to the best advantage and support them. Their task is also to inculcate the values of creativity, flexibility and mobility within the corporate cultures; without these values it is impossible to maintain an atmosphere supportive of intrapreneurs—in which case corporate death is inevitable.

Corporate cultures, especially long-established ones, like all cultures have their insidiously negative "rituals of control," that is, people so fear security-shattering new ideas, even if they are themselves in chaos, that they seek to neutralize the effectiveness of would-be-innovators. Recently, a biologist, P.B. Medawar, bluntly stated the negativism in this way: we humans are apt to treat "a new idea the way the body treats a strange protein; it rejects it."[47]

Chapter 3

Biblical Calls to Refounding Out of Chaos

"In the beginning God created the heavens and the earth. Now the earth was a formless void, there was darkness over the deep, and God's spirit hovered over the water." (Gen 1:1f)

A revitalization or refounding movement is "a deliberate, organized, conscious effort by members of a society to construct a more satisfying culture,"[1] out of a state of chaos under the leadership of a refounding person. The Old Testament in particular offers us many well-documented examples, or attempted efforts, of such refounding movements: Yahweh is *the* refounding person and the prophets are his instruments.

In the previous chapter we reviewed how refounding movements take place *within* existing corporate cultures. In this chapter we study refounding movements particularly within the Old Testament. Anthropologists have devoted much time researching revitalization movements in many cultures, but there has been a tendency to neglect the prophetic leaders themselves.[2] Fortunately, there is no neglect by Scripture scholars of the prophets or covenant refounding people in the Old Testament, so we can draw on their findings.

In this chapter, I describe:

- the notion of *chaos* in the Bible;
- the Israelite regenerative mythology and its degenerative drift;
- the role and qualities of the prophets as Yahweh's refounding agents.

The conclusions of this chapter, together with the insights of previous pages, will provide us with a very adequate background for understanding the role and qualities expected of contemporary refounding persons within religious congregations.

The Biblical Notion of "Chaos"

The word "chaos" was used by the ancient Greeks to describe the amorphous state of primeval matter prior to creation. This concept of a murky and watery primitive world-mass, found also in Egypt and Mesopotamia, is the biblical creation myth; the earth prior to God's creative act is depicted as formless and void, and concealed deeply under dark waters (Gen 1:2f). Quite aptly for us, the Genesis chaos, in the mind of the book's writer, is also describing the state of the people in the Babylonian exile—wanderers lost in despair, malaise, depression, hurting, benumbed and burdened with guilt. To negate this state, God decides to breathe, and with that, chaos begins to give way to cosmos, order, meaning or hope.[3]

The same word "chaos" is found several times in the Bible. In its particularly concrete meaning, it connotes a barren wasteland (Dt 32:10), emptiness, nothingness in general, e.g.

> All the nations are as nothing in this presence,
> for him they count as nothingness and emptiness. (Is 40:17)

> Taken altogether they are nothing;
> their works are nothingness,
> their images wind and emptiness. (Is 41:29)

However, the emptiness or nothingness is itself potentially creative, as is the case also in the Genesis story of creation. It is not once and for all "dead matter" or "sterile nothingness." Chaos, which is described in terms of confusion, darkness, emptiness, nothingness, carries with it the notion of indeterminacy and potentiality. The primary motif, or symbol, in the mythological use of these expressions is that through God's creative power, his mercy, and with human cooperation, new and vigorous life can spring up, new order and meaning can return to life. Take the moving Psalm 88 in which the author describes the feeling of absolute abandonment at the time of his grave sickness: "You have plunged me into the bottom of the pit, into the dark abyss . . ." (v. 7). To this day one can feel the terror of the author in the midst of his agony. Yet there is hope in his cry. Yahweh will answer, for the psalmist admits his absolute dependency on him, and Yahweh will in his mercy breathe new life into the afflicted man.

However, the experience of the Israelites in the desert or wilderness is a fundamental and most vividly powerful symbol for them of chaos. For the period in the wilderness after leaving Egypt and becoming a people (Ex 16–18) is the *archetypal* experience of what chaos means: travelers without a sense of direction, bickering with one another, angry at Yahweh and Moses his spokesman, hungry, a prey to all kinds of diseases and attacks from enemies, without landed roots that would give them an abiding sense of belonging. They yearned for land they could call their own and for the chance to grow their own good tasting food. In such misery even the oppression of Egypt seemed heavenly, as they complained to Moses: Why did we not die at Yahweh's hand in the land of Egypt, when we were able to sit down to pans of meat and could eat bread to our heart's content! As it is, you have brought us to this wilderness to starve this whole company to death" (Ex 16:3).[4]

In the previous chapter I referred to Victor Turner's "betwixt and between" ritual periods in the lives of people; social statuses and roles that are important before and after these periods (often referred to as liminal stages) are temporarily suspended and people interact at the level of "raw humanity." And the experience of pure brotherhood relations (called by Turner *communitas*) provides an enduring bond that persists beyond the ritual and can enrich post-ritual relationships.[5]

For example, persons undergoing a rite of passage in an initiation rite usually have any signs of social distinction external to the ritual removed and the expected behavior particular to the situation is normally passive or humble. "It is as though they are being reduced or ground down to a uniform condition to be fashioned anew and endowed with additional powers to enable them to cope with their new station in life."[6] Part of the purpose of this stripping process, or the temporary return to the state of chaos, is to dispose people to be more open to influence by the sacred, by the creative forces now present that are greater than those encountered in the ordinary, structured, everyday life in the world. They suffer the uncertainty and insecurity of chaos, but in so doing, unprotected by cultural roles, they are disposed to experience key truths about themselves, the meaning and purpose of life.

In summary, *liminality* is an intrinsically unstable and uncertain condition, involving the embracing of meaninglessness (anomy), or chaos, for the sake of the expanded creative possibilities it can provide and for the experience of existential *communitas* or pure brotherhood.

This was surely the case per excellence with the Israelites. Despite their many faults they discovered, in the chaos of their initiation into the promised land, that Yahweh remained creatively faithful and protective even though he seemed at times to be distant and uninterested in them: ". . . you of all the nations shall be my very own for all the earth is mine" (Ex 19:5). The choice of the Israelites by Yahweh was something unique: "You alone, of all the families of earth, have I acknowledged" (Am 3:2). The memory of this exodus chaos and the abiding presence of Yahweh would be for the Israelites at the time of the exile a dramatic source of consolation: life can emerge out of the most traumatic experience of chaos. (See figure 3.1).

Walter Brueggemann[7] explains that for the Israelites the experience of chaos, the antithesis of rest, is often described as "weariness." They are weary when they want to live an ordered life in a way that takes no account of Yahweh's plans for them: "Here is rest; let the weary rest." But they were condemned to remain weary because "they would not listen to" him (Is 28:12). In the Lamentations weariness is being the slave to a false master, while rest connotes service to the one true Lord: "The yoke is on our necks; we are persecuted; we are worked to death; no relief for us" (Lam 5:5). After examining many other texts, the author comments that "it is clear that *weariness* refers to a time of misery and trouble of drastic proportions and *rest* means a context of security and well-being." The texts show that only Yahweh's powerful intervention or that of his agent can remove the state of chaotic weariness: "these texts play upon an old mythological pattern of chaos and creation."[8]

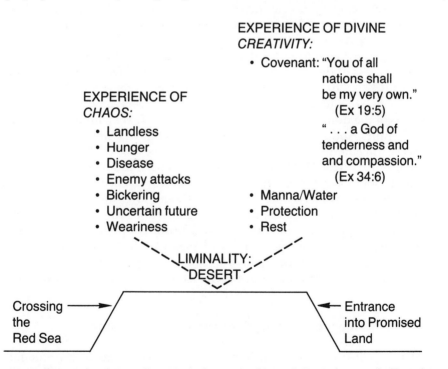

Figure 3.1. Primal Israelite Mythology: Archetypal Experience of Chaos/ Creativity

Brueggemann also reflects on the use of the two words "weariness" and "rest" in Matthew's Gospel: "Come to me, all you who are overburdened, and I will give you rest. Shoulder my yoke and learn from me . . . and you will find rest for your souls" (Mt 11:28f) The "yoke" is a reference to the call to repentance, if rest is to be achieved. And what Yahweh was offering his people Jesus has the same authority to offer: rest for those who move out of chaos through repentance. He concludes that since "weariness is only dealt with by a return to the God of rest," this "has enormous implications for contemporary society"[9] and, I might add, for the refounding of religious congregations.

Throughout the Bible God is pictured as actually *allowing* chaos to develop as the preface or catalyst for a marked creative faith response from his chosen people. The Israelites experience all kinds of plagues, famines, floods, exiles, wars, political treacheries; even their Savior is crucified in the presence of his mother Mary (Jn 19:25). The two disciples on the road to Emmaus, symbols of countless others who had come to know Jesus in the years of his public ministry, are thrown into a state of chaotic confusion and desolation, because the security they had sought was not what Jesus had promised: "Our own hope had been that he would be the one to set Israel free" (Lk 24:21).

They had failed to grasp that Christ should be allowed to enter into the darkness of the tomb so that they might themselves be brought out of chaos (Lk 24:26). Despite the enormity of these "tragedies" throughout the long Israelite history, the basic motif or archetype of the creation myths of the human race and of the chosen people remains the same as it was in the exodus: God's love is overwhelming; new and dynamic life/power will emerge out of chaos, provided "we believe the full message of the prophets" (Lk 24:25). That message is: repent and trust in the Lord's power alone. Every time the Jewish people experience chaos or weariness and then resurrection to rest in Yahweh's love, they relive the primal events of their creation in sacred time. We see then the richness of the biblical application of anthropologist Bronislaw Malinowski's conclusion, recorded in the first chapter of this book, that every myth is "a narrative resurrection of a *primeval* reality." I explain more fully in the following paragraphs the nature of the Israelite regenerative mythology.

The Regenerative Myth of the Israelite People

The Israelite creation myth is this: Yahweh has a special love for his chosen people; this love is evident very particularly in times of chaos when they are more disposed to acknowledge their own sinfulness and their utter dependence on Yahweh. On those occasions they retell the incidents, e.g. the exodus, Yahweh's saving presence, and the recounting of these deeds gives them new life and hope. They must dynamically express this new hope in works of love and justice to Yahweh and to one another. Often the founding myth drifts and is corrupted wherever the people try to legitimize their own injustices and over-attachments to things of this world. They become over-confident that God will abide with them forever, no matter how evil and forgetful they are of him. Now to illustrate these points.

Recall first the invitation to Abraham: "Leave your country, your people and your father's household and go to the land I will show you. I will make you into a great nation" (Gen 12:1f). Abraham's journey into the wasteland of unknown temptations and trials with the Lord becomes creative only because in faith he said "yes" to God. Yahweh's promise is irrevocably associated with Abraham's willingness to enter into a wilderness or to push back the frontiers of the unknown. Poor Abraham! He is surely tested. And he falls; he gives way to fear at one point in his journey (Gen 12:10–20). He succeeds in his journey only as long as he cooperates in faith with Yahweh, and it is this faith that so dramatically supports him in his time of especial testing—the preparation to sacrifice his son: "My son, God himself will provide" (Gen 22:8).

During the time of Moses the Israelites are challenged over and over again to recognize the creative potential of chaos and its visible expression, the desert or wilderness, and to respond in faith and action to Yahweh's presence. The following text describes the frustrations of years of journeying in the desert and also the ultimate reason for their sufferings: if through the experience of chaos they lose excessive cultural supports, attachments and securities, then they might be better disposed to turn back to Yahweh:

> Remember how Yahweh your God led you for forty years in the wilderness, to humble you, to test you and know your inmost heart—whether you could keep his commandments or not. He humbled you, he made you feel hunger, he fed you with manna which neither you nor your fathers had known, to make you understand that man does not live on bread alone but that man lives on everything that comes from the mouth of Yahweh (Dt 8:2f).

When the Israelites do at times acknowledge that they are utterly confused and overwhelmed with their suffering and that they desperately need Yahweh's help, then they retell the myth of his creative love for them shown in former times, when they were also lost. So, we read:

> Loudly cry to God, loudly to God who hears me.
> When in trouble I sought the Lord. . . .
> Remembering Yahweh's achievements,
> remembering your marvels in the past,
> I ponder all your achievements (Ps 77:1f, 11f).

To recognize one's own chaotic condition—one's human weakness and fragility—and one's constant need for God is to discover the creative love of him, who leads us "out of darkness into his wonderful light" (1 Pet 2:9). This the Israelites did, but they frequently forget the desert and his love and are seduced by the good things of this world. They acculturate themselves with ease to the pagan religions and pervasive materialism around them. Then, prophets like Amos forthrightly demand, in the name of Yahweh, their return to detachment and the acknowledgement that God alone is the source of all their security and joy.

Jeremiah is *the* prophet of creativity out of chaos, of life through death. He sees the political breakdown of his beloved country and participates in its complete disintegration. He even encourages his people not to resist the Babylonian invader, because the people have so drifted away from the authentic demands of the nation's creative myth that there is nothing worth holding on to (Jer 5:30f). To him, it seems that the Israelite culture is to be reduced once more to the "primeval chaos from which God had originally redeemed it":[10]

> I looked to the earth, to see a formless waste;
> to the heavens, and their light had gone. . . .
> I looked, to see the wooded country a wilderness (Jer 4:23, 26).

The pivotal symbols of the national culture—Jerusalem, the monarchy, the temple—to which they are overly attached are to be destroyed:

> I am setting you over the nations and over kingdoms,
> to tear up and to knock down,
> to destroy and to overthrow (Jer 1:10).

What frightening words! The people believe that no matter how unfaithful they are Yahweh will never withdraw his presence from such sacred symbols of their identity and security. This is a corruption of the myth. They have lost the detachment of being pilgrims and they have allowed their culture to become too static, too institutional. They no longer hear the call of Yahweh to be ever creative as pilgrims in this world in justice and love.

Yet, the Lord is merciful. In the midst of the people's shattering grief and despair, Jeremiah foretells signs of revitalization, of the *refounding* of the nation: "I am setting you . . . to build and to plant" (Jer 1:10). A new covenant between God and the revitalized culture will succeed the previous one (Jer 31:31ff) and it will be a richer one, since it will be adhered to in the hearts of believers, not just obeyed out of a sense of duty. The destroyed city would be rebuilt, secure forever (Jer 31:38–40), and the gift of personal and intimate union with God will be a sign of the authenticity of his people (Jer 31:34). Even in the exile's darkness significant pastoral creativity emerges; the people learn to pray in small supportive groups without the presence of the temple and traditional religious practices are updated in light of the changed situation, for example, circumcision becomes no longer so important as an initiation rite, but rather it develops as a new symbol of cultural identity.[11]

Second Isaiah takes up the promise of a regenerated people and culture, calling them away from despair and nostalgic/escapist dreams of past glory. He depicts the return of the exiles in grandiose terms; it will be an even more dramatic event than the exodus: "Prepare in the wilderness a way for Yahweh. Make a straight highway for our God across the desert" (Is 40:3) The author, in the midst of the exile crisis, recounts the mythology of re-creation. After telling the story of Yahweh's creative power at the beginning of the world, when he transformed chaos into cosmos or order, he narrates once more the incredible victory over the Egyptians at the beginning of the exodus:

> Yes, Yahweh has pity on Zion,
> has pity on all her ruins;
> Turns her desolation into an Eden,
> Her wasteland into the garden of Yahweh. . . .
> Did you not split Rahab in two,
> and pierce the dragon through?
> Did you not dry up the sea,
> the waters of the great Abyss . . .
> for the redeemed to cross? (Is 51:3, 9f).

From chaos to order: from weariness to rest, from suffering to joy, from sinfulness to justice—the theme runs constantly through the Old Testament. The prophets arise to remind people and their culture that this is the message of the Lord, and each time they respond positively they relive the primal myth of God's creation of his chosen people and are energized by the experience.

And, finally, the mystery of God's regenerating love reaches its perfection in the humanly inconceivable *re*-creating love of Christ's life, his death and resurrection and the new covenant relationship foretold by the prophets. (See figure 3.2) The people of God of the new covenant, because of their unique relationship with the Father through Christ, do not despise the world, they only fear it. They acknowledge their mission to improve the world, for in it the kingdom of God begins; and they receive their inner strength to permeate the world of cultures with Christ's love and justice from repeatedly reliving the new covenant's re-creating myth: the life, death and resurrection of Christ.

This myth measures not only the quality of customs and aspirations of cultures "out there," but also, just as the Israelites were charged to do in their day, the Gospel authenticity of the Church's own cultural institutions, the lives of its members (and of course religious themselves): "While the Church is bound to give witness to justice, it recognizes that anyone who ventures to speak to people about justice must first be just in their eyes. Hence we must undertake an examination of the modes of acting and of the possessions and life style found within the Church itself."[12]

Re-Creating Mythology Demands Radical Conversion

While the term "conversion" is rare in the Bible, its synonyms are frequently used, e.g. "repentance," "regeneration," "being born again." No matter what expression is used the meaning is the same: all human faculties—rational, volitional, and affective—are involved. Jeremiah, speaking the words of Yahweh, insists on this: "I will be their God, for they will return to me with all their heart" (Jer 24:7). Ezekiel is of the same mind: "Repent, renounce all yours sins . . . make yourselves a new heart and a new spirit" (Ez 18:30f).

The covenant relationship with God, which demands the constant reliving and reapplying of the founding myth of the nation, is possible only if there is this total turning to him. The fundamental principle is: attachment to God alone will bring security and authentic identity; no building, no sacred site, no official or sacred office, no attachment to this or that piece of ancestral land, will of itself bring one's family, culture or nation, or oneself, into union with God.

Conversion of people—individually and corporately—must result in creativity in the service of the Lord. Only if there is on-going innovative action will justice and love be constantly applied to new and changing situations. The prophets repeatedly condemn their people for their failure to be creative in responding to newly developing unjust situations,

Mythology of Chaos/
Creativity: Biblical

CHAOS ⟶ AGENT OF ⟶ LIFE
CREATION

1. *Old Testament*		
Primal chaos: formless void	Yahweh	World
Flood: return to primal chaos	Yahweh/Noah	New world
Abraham on journey: desert	Yahweh/Abraham	Chosen people
Exodus: into unknown	Yahweh/Moses	Promised land

Exile: destruction
  of symbols:Jerusalem
        temple
        kingship
	Yahweh/Prophets:
	Jeremiah
	Second Isaiah
		New covenant
		  promised

2. *New Testament*		

Birth of Christ:
  destruction of worldly
  king image
	Holy Spirit/Mary	Christ: Light
		  to "little people"

Message: life through death to self	Christ/followers	Union in Christ
Death of Christ: tomb/cross	Christ	Resurrection
3. *Religious Congregations*		
Founding: purification of founding person	Holy Spirit/founding person	New congregation

Refounding:
  • destruction of symbols
  • purification
	Holy Spirit/refounding
	person
		Refounded
		  congregation

Figure 3.2.

e.g. usury, the oppression of the poor. Liturgical reform without conversion to the demands of social justice is hypocrisy, as Amos records in his his usual refreshingly blunt and down-to-earth way:

> I hate and despise your feasts,
> I take no pleasure in your solemn festivals. . . .
> Let me have no more of the din of your chanting,
> no more of your strumming on harps.
> But let justice flow like water,
> and integrity like an unfailing stream (Am 5:21–24).

This understanding of conversion is carried through into the New Testament; one must admit one's complete dependence on God by dying to oneself and embracing the Lord in faith: "Anyone who finds his life will lose it; anyone who loses his life for my sake will find it" (Mt 10:39). Without the Lord, one has within oneself nothing but an unproductive chaos, a desert. This the Pharisees refused to acknowledge, and it inevitably brought them into conflict with Jesus. They had developed their own ways to live a life faithful to Judaism, and in a sectarian way they had drifted away from the inner heart of the founding myth of the Israelites. They self-righteously claimed that the detailed observance of external rituals relating to such things as food and washing would ensure friendship with Yahweh. Inner conversion, leading to the creative expressions of love and justice adapted to a changing world, made no sense to them; their Judaism had become fossilized in externals. For this Jesus condemned them (Mk 7:1–23; Mt 6:1–18).

St. Paul, reflecting on the experience of his own journey away from a formalistic Judaism, emphasizes the creative potential of his acknowledging inner chaos: "So I shall be very happy to make my weaknesses my special boast so that the power of Christ may stay over me. . . . For it is when I am weak that I am strong" (2 Cor 12:9f). I particularly like the following description by St. Paul in which he contrasts the chaos of his own experience with the overwhelming power of God:

> We are only earthenware jars that hold this treasure, to make it clear that such an overwhelming power comes from God and not from us. We are in difficulties on all sides, but never cornered; we see no answer to our problems, but never despair . . . always, wherever we may be, we carry with us in our body the death of Jesus, so that the life of Jesus, too, may always be seen in our body. . . . So death is at work in us, but life in you (2 Cor 4:7–8, 10, 12).

We lock into the regenerating mythology of Christ by acknowledging our utter dependence on him; then there is oneness with him to the degree that we can say with Paul, "I live, not I, but Christ lives in me" (Gal 2:19). From our nothingness we become one in Christ, in his power, in his love. It takes the courage of faith, born of love, to confront our own inner darkness. The urge to escape this inner journey can be overwhelming; we can turn in desperation to various artificial or purely human lights to aid us, but the real inner darkness or chaos remains as it was. Only in Christ do we have "a light that darkness could not overpower" (Jn 1:5). (See figure 3.2)

Converted to the Lord and strengthened by his light within us that darkness cannot overpower, we are prepared to labor with others to build and refound communities of love, justice and worship, thus witnessing to "the new heavens and new earth, the place where righteousness will be at home" (2 Pet 3:13).

The Prophets: Covenant-Culture Refounding People

The major initiative for the refounding of the Israelite culture according to the three fundamental values—total dependence on God, justice and love—did not come from the people. It came from Yahweh himself who acted through his personally selected prophets: "Then Yahweh . . . said to me: 'There! I am putting my words into your mouth' " (Jer 9:9). They are "prophetic intrapreneurs" whose hearts and lives are totally committed to Yahweh and to the refounding of the Israelite way of life according to the values of the covenant. For their task they are given special qualities. (See figure 3.3)

1. Memory

They are Israel's creative, dynamic and questioning memory. They repeatedly return to the creation myth of the nation: Yahweh loves his people and they must respond with sincerity of heart, worship, justice and love. And the special objects of their concern must be the poor and defenseless ones. Feel the penetrating power of memory and condemnation in these stinging words of Amos:

> Listen, sons of Israel, to this oracle Yahweh speaks against you, against the whole family I brought out of the land of Egypt. . . . I sent you a plague like Egypt's plague . . . filled your nostrils with the stench of your camps; and yet your never came back to me (Am 3:1; 4:10).

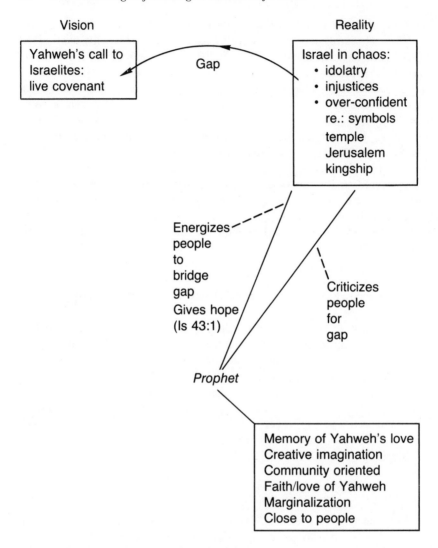

Figure 3.3. Role of Prophets as Refounders

Through their repeated, and unpopular, reminders about the purpose for which Israel was created, the prophets provide unity and sharpness of thrust to its many journeyings, crises and experiences of chaos.[13]

2. Creative Imagination and Listening

The prophets reject the distorted culture in which they live, for they measure it against the vision they know can and should be realized, if their creation myth is taken seriously. Though each prophet calls for the same conversion, each directs his words to the particular needs of the time, e.g. to *this or that group* of poor or oppressed. Each used different imaginative and innovative expressions that the people of their times could readily understand. They break through the chaos of confusion, of numbness and denial, by pointing out the way the people must go in order to return the culture to Yahweh-centered foundations.[14] Their exercise of creative imagination is possible, however, only because they are compulsive listeners, that is, they are listening at the same time to Yahweh's covenant requirements and to the sinfulness and the cries of the people.

Like all people trapped in cultural disintegration, the Israelites are tempted at times to escape nostalgically in order to hide within the comforting memories of Yahweh's past achievements, not to be energized by them for creative action now and in the future. So in Second Isaiah there is the warning: "No need to recall the past. . . . See, I am doing a new deed. . . . Yes, I am making a road in the wilderness" (Is 43:18f).

The prophets are optimistic people, full of hope, and for this reason they are so imaginatively creative about how the people are to return to their pilgrim road in the presence of Yahweh. No matter how dark and chaotic the world may be, God loves us.

3. Community-Oriented

Prophets are not loners, even if they are marginalized or threatened with death by the people for whom they work; they earnestly seek to summon the people into the deep covenant communion with one another and with Yahweh. His mind becomes their mind. The oneness with Yahweh on the one hand, and the sight of the people's rejection of communion with him on the other, leads at times to experiencing the disappointment and sorrow of Yahweh himself. Jeremiah, despite the people's often cruel treatment of him, deeply grieves over their sinfulness and their stubbornness of heart: "The wound of the daughter of my people wounds me too, all looks dark to me, terror grips me" (Jer 8:21).

So deep is the commitment of the prophets to being with the people they criticize and condemn for their evil ways that they are prepared to suffer persecution, even death, by remaining with them. They know that they would have to cease being prophets if they flee the community which they are called to serve.[15]

4. Men of Faith, Love and Prayer

There are times when the prophets are tempted to run away from their burdensome tasks (Jer 20:9), and even to fall victim to the people's desire to be flattered with lies to avoid having to tell the hard truth: "Do not prophesy the truth to us, tell us flattering things; have illusory visions, turn aside from the way, leave the path, take the Holy One out of our sight" (Is 30:10f). Yet they do not fail the Lord, because they themselves are radically converted to him and to his service in faith and love. They are "trapped" or "seduced" (Jer 20:7) by the friendship they share with Yahweh: "The close secret of Yahweh belongs to them who fear him, his covenant also, to bring them knowledge" (Ps 25:14).

The faith, love and extraordinary courage of the prophets is sustained and constantly nourished through their listening and talking with the Lord. We see dramatically presented in the prophetic autobiographies that prayer raises the prophet's consciousness to the primal experience of being grasped by Yahweh. Authentic prayer, which is a deep awareness of God who speaks out of the depths, requires of us that we acknowledge our own inner and outer chaos, and thus our need to be completely dependent on him. Psalm 130 begins with the words:

> From the depths I call to you, Yahweh,
> Lord, listen to my cry for help!
> Listen compassionately to my pleading (Ps 130:1f).

One can still feel the agony of Jeremiah as he pleads with the Lord from the depths of his own inner emptiness, when he becomes increasingly aware of his own sense of inadequacy and the enormity of the personal suffering his work will involve:

> A curse on the day when I was born . . .
> for I have committed my cause to you. . . .
> Why ever did I come out of the womb . . .
> and to end my days in shame. . . .
> But Yahweh is at my side, a mighty hero . . .
> for I have committed my cause to you (1 Jer 20:14, 18, 11f).

This frightening cry of feeling utterly abandoned, similar to that cry from the cross of suffering centuries later, is not a curse on God nor the refusal by Jeremiah of his vocation, but a prayerful confirmation of his trust in God; he sees the depths of his own misery and need. In a spirit of total openness he offers himself to Yahweh who alone can make up for his weaknesses.[16]

5. *Patient in Hard Work, Marginalization and Suffering*

The prophets work hard, are often marginalized, verbally and physically abused and at times murdered, because their message describing the conditions necessary for the refounding of the nation committed to Yahweh is not acceptable to a people enthusiastically enjoying worldly values. It is not just the evil people who are rejecting of the message, but the mediocre feel affronted and annoyed that they should be told to be better:

> Let us lie in wait for the virtuous man,
> since he annoys us and opposes our way of life. . . .
> Before us he stands, a reproof to our way of thinking;
> the very sight of him weighs our spirit down. . . .
> Let us test him with cruelty and with torture (Wis 2:12, 14, 19).

Of Hosea the people cry: "The prophet is a fool. This man of the spirit is crazy" (Hos 9:7) Yahweh's special heroes intensely suffer at times for their "craziness"; in fact, suffering is a mark of their authenticity as messengers of Yahweh. Take Jeremiah, who testifies to his faithfulness to Yahweh not only in his private spiritual agony, but also publicly through a life of ostracism and persecution. He is rejected by his family and friends (Jer 11:18); nor can he marry and enjoy a comforting family life, so he knows the loneliness of marginalization from what is dear and familiar to him: "I for my part was like a trustful lamb being led to the slaughter-house, not knowing the schemes they were plotting against me, 'Let us destroy the tree in its strength, let us cut him off from the land of the living, so that his name may be quickly forgotten' " (Jer 11:19).

In speaking with Jeremiah, Yahweh uses the symbolism of clay in the hand of the potter to illustrate the need to return to pristine chaos if there is to be new growth:

> And whenever the vessel he was making came out wrong, as happens with the clay handled by potters, he would start afresh and work it into another vessel, as potters do. . . . Yes, as the clay is in the potter's hand, so you are in mine" (Jer 18:4, 6).

While Yahweh is primarily referring to his relationship with Israel, his prophets recognize that they must also became primal clay in his hands if they are to be his authentic refounding voice to the drifting Israelites. This inevitably involves personal suffering for the prophets.

Summary

The culture history of the Israelites exemplifies the significant characteristics of most traditional cultures: powerful symbols, vividly expressed mythology and, at times of significant culture stress, there are revitalization/ refounding movements most often being led by God's chosen leaders, the prophets.

One of the most powerful symbols in the Bible is chaos. "Chaos" in its many different expressions, like all symbols has many, even oppositional, meanings. On the one hand, it connotes confusion, darkness, emptiness, nothingness, loss of meaning. On the other, it carries with it the notion of indeterminacy and potentiality. Yahweh, if the Israelites are willing to cooperate, can create a new people out of chaos into which they have fallen.

The exodus from Egypt is the core religious experience for the Israelites and it forms the creation myth or story of how they were initiated as a people. And in the wilderness they encounter not just the confusion of chaos, but also dramatically repeated contact with Yahweh himself. Thus the painful experience of the desert is at the same time remarkably creative, because a new and intimate relationship emerges between the people and Yahweh. That relationship had to be expressed on the people's part by their conforming to the values of righteousness, the centrality of God in worship, humility, trust in God, love and justice toward their neighbor (Is 1:16f; 7:9; 30:15). The Israelite culture and nation had to be built on these values.

Often the people forget these values. They fall into chaos, e.g. by suffering under foreign enemies or by being dragged into exile, by accepting the values of idolatry and materialism. The prophets are named by God to call the people back to the original covenant, that is, to be his instruments as the refounders of the God-centered culture. If the people repent, they retell their creation myth and from this retelling they are energized with hope and courage to submit to the sovereignty of Yahweh. Among the key qualities of the prophet are the memory of Yahweh's mercy to his people and a vivid creative imagination to aid them in challenging the people to return to the Lord in the ways of justice and love. Frequently, these prophets harshly suffer for their loyalty to Yahweh, e.g. through social ostracism, physical pain and even death.

These reflections on the notion of biblical chaos, the call to be completely at the disposal of the Lord and the role and qualities of the prophets, will be helpful in articulating the role of refounding persons in religious congregations.

PART TWO

Refounding Religious Life

Chapter 4

Into Chaos: Religious Life Since Vatican II

Put yourselves on the ways of long ago,
inquire about the ancient paths:
which was the good way? Take it then,
and you shall find rest
                                        (Jer 1:16).

Make us come back to you, Yahweh,
and we will come back.
Renew our days as in times past
                                        (Lam 5:21).

To summarize our approach so far, this book rests on three significant and interconnected insights into culture and culture change, now reinforced through our biblical reflections. First, symbols are inescapably double-edged in their meanings. The symbol of night implies at the same time the light of day; the more we come to appreciate and feel the power of night the more we come to grasp the significance and necessity of daylight. Think of chaos and one also thinks of its opposite—order, creativity; reflect on sin and one is drawn then to its contrary—graced union with God. The more we seek to grasp in fact the notion of chaos or disorder, the richer becomes our insight into its opposite.

Second, all traditional myths, in Mircea Eliade's opinion, have a cyclic dimension. That is, they involve regressions to chaos in order that a new creation can be born, just as Zeus came after Chronos or the New Jerusalem will be the substitute of the old, developing out of the disorder of Armageddon.[1]

Third, for the new creation to arise out of the chaos there is needed a certain type of person, the cultural refounding person, who has definite qualities of leadership. However, he or she can exercise their remarkable gifts only if other people support them. One basic quality of the refounding person is an openness to be energized by the power of the original creation myth and to be inspired to apply this power adapted to the demands of the new age. This quality is to be found, despite their widely different value systems and diverse functions, in political charismatic leaders, in corporate culture intraprenuers and the prophets of the Old Testament. For example, a most pervasive quality of the 1960s' counter-culture was its dramatic attack on political boundaries of all kinds. Out of this experience of political chaos, there emerged charismatic leaders like Martin Luther King, who effectively grasped the power of the American creation myth that "all peoples are equal" and demanded that it be applied to blacks.

Of course, the most basic symbol of our concern is *chaos*. Chaos is "subversive" in any culture, because it disposes us to ask questions like What values should form any new culture? Who should lead us out of our confusion? How should we cooperate? Though there are many positive experiences in religious life since Vatican II, a feeling of chaos remains, for we find ourselves, as John Lozano says, "somewhat without moorings."[2] If we are to ask more and more relevant "subversive questions" about religious life, then we must dig deeper into our chaos and how it has developed. In this chapter, therefore, I will explain:

- that creativity in the service of the Church is at the heart of religious life mythology;
- that chaos in religious congregations had emerged well before Vatican II because of mythological drift and distortion;
- why chaos remains in many religious congregations after Vatican II and the various ways we deny it exists.

The Mythology of Religious Life

We believe as Christians that the absolute in the Genesis creation myth is God himself and that Jesus is the absolute in the regenerative myth of the Gospels. We come to these insights through the power and presence of the Holy Spirit: "The Spirit we have received is not the world's spirit but God's Spirit, helping us to recognize the gifts he has given us" (1 Cor 2:12). The life, suffering, death and resurrection of Jesus is the re-creation myth; through Jesus we have a more profound understanding of God and his designs for us.[3]

The Christian becomes one with the re-creation myth by accepting the same mission that the Father gave the Son, the mission to go out into the world and creatively, under the inspiration of Holy Spirit, bring the good news to all. The call by the Father to mission with the son is the *creation myth* of religious life. The life purpose of religious is to give themselves undividedly to the living out of this creation myth in the service of the Church. Religious are to be contemporary prophets.⁴ From within the very heart of the Church's inner union with Christ, they are to pronounce that God loves us in Christ, that union with him and with one another is possible, that commitment to the false gods of wealth and power obstruct this love. Religious are to be prophets who with the clarity, energy and daring of their Old Testament predecessors point out the new roads of justice and love that we must follow.⁵

While all people are committed to evangelical perfection and mission with the Son, religious for their part publicly commit themselves in faith to be *unconditional* in their response to the Father's call, in their love of him and members of their own communities, his Church and the world he wants to be saved. They openly dedicate themselves not to this or that demand of the Lord at this or that particular time and place, but to be totally available, as other Christs, for the Father's work. They are to strive to take seriously always the command of the Lord: "Be converted and believe in the good news" (Mk 1:15). This requires of religious an enduring identification with Christ, an act of love that must govern all their actions. This describes the *identification myth* of religious.

Religious are drawn by the power of the *eschatological myth* also, that is, the myth of the promise of new heavens and a new earth where . . . the justice of God will reside" (2 Pet 3:13). They seek to reveal this new world of justice and love *now,* particularly through their special option for the poor and the powerless, that through their example others may discover the saving power of the Lord, his mercy and compassion. So crucial is this issue of justice for the poor that the revitalization of religious life cannot be considered today, if there is no concern for the exploited and the "little people" of this world. Religious are to be more radical Christians, in the sense of struggling to live the life and holiness of the Church in all its radicalness and integrity. There can be no radicalness without concern for the poor.⁶

The commitment to the Lord through the vows logically flows from the earnestness of religious to be without reservation available to the Lord and to his Church. On the one hand, the vows testify to the fact that religious believe that the Lord is the ultimate and totally sufficient center of their lives and, on the other, that they are totally at his service. The vows form a *supportive myth* in religious life, that is, they aid religious to fulfill the purpose for which they exist.

As religious commit themselves to be in the forefront of revealing the mythical mystery of the Lord's redemptive love for the world, the Church rightly expects of them an enduring quality of apostolic creative dynamism for searching out new and better ways of preaching and living his message. They are to be noted for their "boldness of initiatives" in the apostolic life,[7] and these initiatives give ritual flesh to the myths that motivate them. I like the way that the theologian Johannes Metz identifies the role of religious, indicating that religious are to be the descendants of the Old Testament prophets:

> (Religious are to be) a kind of shock therapy instituted by the Holy Spirit for the Church as a whole. Against the dangerous accommodations and questionable compromises that the Church as a large-scale institution can always incline to, they press for the uncompromising nature of the Gospel and of the imitation of Christ. In this sense they are the institutionalized form of a dangerous memory within the Church.[8]

The two words "dangerous memory" concisely summarize the task of religious in relating to the church. As the prophets of old did, religious are to be to the Church and the world the "subversive" or "dangerous memory" of what God is requiring of us, and they are to have the creative imagination to blaze new and apostolic pathways through a world of secularism, injustice and materialism so that the rest of us can follow. Norbert Lohfink recently referred to religious as "God's therapy for the Church" or as a life-giving force to challenge us not to identify with the worldly symbols of power, consumerism, and secularism.[9]

Once religious cease to be a *dangerous memory* or *God's therapy* within the Church, they stop being identified with the distinguishing mythology of religious life.

Ultimately identification with Christ the Redemptive Myth comes through faith, nourished in prayer, and for this reason religious are to be known as personally experienced specialists in prayer. The day-to-day struggle of the religious to be uncompromising in mission will at times fill him or her with fear and distress, such as Jesus experienced in the garden before his passion, for "the spirit is willing, but the flesh is weak" (Mk 14:38). Their fervent prayer is: "My father . . . if it is possible, let this cup pass me by. Nevertheless, let it be as you, not I would have it" (Mt 26:39). Zeal without prayer cannot survive. In prayer we discover the precipitous depths of our own poverty and at the same time the saving presence of Jesus the Myth. With him we speak confidently for strength to the Father.

Mythological Drift and Distortion before Vatican II

Individual religious congregations develop in the Church because founding persons are deeply shocked, sometimes suddenly or over a long period of time, to see the gap existing between the Gospel and the world.

They see people who do not know the mercy and healing power of Christ or who have heard but now compromise with worldly values. In other words, they see chaos around them and are confused about what to do about it and in a spirit of faith this feeling of inadequacy acutely annoys them. Not only do they want to do something about chaos, but founding persons begin to recognize how the gap between the Gospel and the world can be bridged through particular apostolic strategies and with the spirit of the Gospel. Like all good myth-makers, founding persons formulate organizational structures, eventually enshrined in constitutions, to facilitate the realization of these strategies. And inspired by the Holy Spirit, they invite others to join them in living out their vision. Thus the seeds are sown for a new religious congregation to emerge.

Each congregation, then, has its own distinctive way of living out the basic religious life mythology, which is usually referred to as the congregational charism.[10] The myth-maker is the dynamic, creative founding person who acts in cooperation with the Holy Spirit. The root symbol in the dominant myth will be the special aspect of the redemptive myth of Christ as seen to be especially applicable at a particular time and place in the Church's life, e.g. the poverty of Christ, Christ as evangelizer. A religious congregation, when it is true to its mythology, is a medium of God's revealing and redeeming presence in the world.[11]

The fervent attachment to the original congregational myth, as history shows, is very rarely sustained, even at times by the second generation of the congregational membership. Our analysis of myth management in Chapter 2 helps us to understand how this winding down of enthusiasm occurs. Through a process of "myth drift" religious congregations, even without realizing it, can accommodate their apostolic work and way of living too much to ambient secular values and customs. They neglect the uncompromising nature of the original mythology.

In the Middle Ages the Benedictines in Europe went into decline. "No one (any longer) looked to them for new ideas and new forms of spiritual life," comments historian Richard Southern. "Rather they looked to them for stability, pageantry, involvement in the aristocratic life of the upper classes."[12] Gone was the inner commitment to the founding myth of creative obedience through a vigorous spirit of self-abnegation. In today's pastoral jargon, they became "lost in maintenance and forgot mission."

Historian David Knowles, reflecting on the decline of the quality of the lives of monks, religious and clergy in the early Tudor period in England, comments: "Monks and clergy alike were children of their age and country; it was this that made the Dissolution (of the monasteries under Henry VIII), and indeed many of the religious changes of the reign, not only possible but relatively easy of accomplishment."[13] They had accommodated themselves so comfortably to the worldly values of the time that they were indistinguishable from the socially and economically well-off they claimed to be evangelizing. Through the neglect of their founding mythology that committed them to on-going evaluation of their way of life in light of the Gospel, religious had drifted to a point of spiritual and innovative enfeeblement or stagnation. Their extinction was then inevitable, even if Henry VIII had not himself acted with such speed.

Sometimes a secondary or directional myth can be substituted for the creation and/or identity myths as a result of unchecked drift on the part of the religious congregation. For example, a congregation established for the pastoral needs of the poor through education found itself eventually running large-scale educational institutions for the well-to-do. Members of the congregation "justified" this movement away from the poor on the grounds that the institute was founded "for education through schools." The mythology of the congregation was being misread. Concern for the poor belonged to the creation and identity myths; the establishment of schools pertained *only* to a directional myth and not to the identifying heart of the congregational charism. A direction myth merely indicates how the charism is to be lived out in this or that particular historical circumstance and so it is subject to change. As the poor, in the country in which the congregation worked, were being neglected, this congregation in loyalty to its founding mythology should have withdrawn from the schools and created other pastoral structures to guarantee the education of the poor. The congregation had definitely moved away from its authentic mythical roots.

Raymond Hostie believes that a myth substitution through the imposition of a semi-monastic model of religious life affected many congregations for several centuries prior to Vatican II.[14] There were several reasons for this. For example, in its defense against the effects of the Reformation and an emerging secularism, the Church turned in on itself. Its "narcissistic preoccupation," as Avery Dulles phrases it, discouraged experimentation.[15] The changing world had to adapt to the Church and not vice versa. Women's congregations were more affected than men's as the Council of Trent reintroduced for them the obligation of enclosure. Because of this inward-looking emphasis of religious life, the vows were seen not as forming a supportive myth but as the dominant myth itself. As J.M. Tillard notes:

> One becomes a religious for the sake of the Gospel, not strictly for the sake of the three classical vows. Although the vows represent elements that are specific to the religious life and therefore indispensable to whoever feels

called to that life by the Holy Spirit, they are not the primary elements in the concrete life of grace of the religious.[16]

Congregations certainly grew numerically and spread geographically, but the originally creative insights of founding persons, which should have led to radically new forms of religious-life witness and pastoral action, were unable to be realized. A frightening amount of creative energy and time was turned inward just to maintain extraordinarily structured, unchanging rules and dress codes. It is not surprising, therefore, that the models of religious life in non-European lands even now remain Western. Religious congregations were planted even in tropical countries with practically no adaptation whatsoever to the diversity of cultures and climate.[17]

Another pastorally crippling assumption was the elitist belief that religious life was in some way or other superior to the lay vocation. Back in 1092 Pope Urban II had issued a Bull in which he asserted that "from the beginning the Church has always offered two types of life to her children: one to aid the insufficiency of the weak, the other to bring to perfection the goodness of the strong."[18] The elitist view of religious life remained officially unchallenged, though questioned by a growing number of people, right through until Vatican II, and it helped to maintain pastorally unnecessary barriers between religious and laity. Religious were considered within the Church as being "perfect, as close to God" as the human person could possibly be; therefore, they could never be expected "to understand the ordinary human problems of the laity who were called to a much lower level of Gospel life."

Case Study of Mythological Distortion: The Marists

In this case study I will first describe the mythology system of a particular religious congregation; then I will summarize what has happened to this mythology after the congregation was formally approved. The case study shows how the above theory can be applied so that readers may be better able to reflect in turn on their own congregational experience.

Mythology of the Society of Mary

The Society of Mary (Marist Fathers and Brothers) was founded by a priest, Jean-Claude Colin, in Lyons, France, and formally approved in 1836. Its aim is to carry on Mary's work in the world. "She is," he writes, "the refuge, the defense, the support, the advocate . . . the recourse of the militant Church." The creation (and dominant) myth reveals Mary as supporting the apostles at Pentecost or at the beginning of the Church, but with an added dimension. That support is to be continued *now* in and through Marists and other people committed to her service. She is believed to have said to the one who had the first inspiration to establish the congregation: "I upheld the Church at its birth; I shall do so again at the end of time." Mary herself, through the Holy Spirit, decides to found a congregation which is to take her name. Her human instrument in this founding, according to Colin, is Colin himself. She remains the first and perpetual superior of the congregation, which is itself committed to be her presence within the Church "at the end of time."

The key symbol in the creation myth is Mary herself, Mother of Mercy. And it is from this symbol that Marists receive their identity. Marists are to "be Mary" to the world; they are to think, judge and act as Mary does. So the vision presented by the myth's vision is precise and inspiring: they are to be instruments of the Divine Mercy, called to the service of the Church "by a gracious choice" of Mary herself.

There are several directional myths indicating how Marists are to *be* Mary as the support of the Church. As instruments of Divine Mercy, Marists are to stress qualities of forgiveness, tenderness, compassion. A second direction myth is summarized in the phrase "hidden and unknown." In the early Church Mary acted quietly, aiming all the time to inspire people to grow in Christ. So also Marists are to encourage people to develop their own gifts in the Lord. Hence, Marists must be prepared to withdraw from involvement as those they serve discover their own potential for self-growth. A powerful symbol of this action-principle, "hidden and unknown," is Nazareth. No one can act in a hidden, self-effacing way unless he or she has the humility, the detachment that comes from deep union with Christ in prayer. Nazareth symbolizes these key virtues. Only through these virtues will a Marist avoid selfishness and the desire for power that are the obstacles which would obstruct Mary's work in the Church. To be Pentecost people, Marists must be firmly rooted in the contemplative virtues of Nazareth.

A further directional myth is devotion to learning. Marists are to be concerned for any kind of learning that would make them better instruments of the Divine Mercy: "Learning there must be, and a great deal of it. The age we live in . . . will listen only to those it considers to be on a par with it. So, in order to do good for it, to bring it to virtue, to lead it back to God, we must study, but not for our own sake—for the glory of God and the salvation of souls. . . . Without knowledge I would have no faith in the Society, without knowledge it will be ruined."[19]

There is also a vigorous eschatological myth within the Marist mythology. "The Society of Mary," declares its founder, "must begin a new Church over again." By this he means not an arrogant claim to reform, but rather a challenge to "re-create the faith of the first believers." As the early believers were of *one mind* and *one heart,* so there will be the same kind of communion in the fullness of Christ's kingdom. By living in one mind and in one heart in the presence of Mary, Marists will help transform the Church, aiding it to be now what the world will be in the perfection of the kingdom to come.

This eschatological myth affected the founder's vision of how Marists are to relate to lay people and to worldly symbols of power. Colin had the vision of a family, a family of Mary, in which there would also be lay people who commit themselves to *be* Mary in the world in which they live. Because he stressed the notion of Mary's family, Colin reacted to the evils of clericalism or ecclesiastical elitism and of attachment to worldly distinctions evident among clergy in Colin's time. On the practical level, therefore, Marist priests and brothers are to live together without distinction, showing to a world in which distinctions and unequal differences of lifestyles are commonplace that such behavior patterns are foreign to the kingdom that is to come.

The particular object of Marist apostolic concern are those who are the most abandoned, the "little people" of this world, those with whom no one else is pastorally involved. The concern for the "little people" belongs to the identity myth of the congregation.

Anthropologist Levi-Strauss, whom we referred to in Chapter 2, speaks of "binary oppositions" within myths (as there are within symbols). Such oppositions exist in Marist mythology. And they are dialectical in quality or tension: Pentecost versus Nazareth, identification with the local Church versus the congregation's right as an independent institute to go anywhere in the world where the apostolic needs are the greatest. Take the latter tension. Colin says that bishops must consider Marists "as if they were their men." On the other hand, he insists in word and action on areas of independence from bishops. How are the two to be reconciled? As in all myths, no detailed instructions are given on how such tensions are to be reconciled in practice. It is assumed that their resolution is possible only through people identifying thoroughly with the mythology. Marists in a spirit of faith will discover ways in which the tensions are to be worked out in reality, thus revealing that people *can* live together with one heart and one mind.

In summary, Colin founded a congregation committed, through its stress on Pentecost, to a service within the Church that is to be pastorally creative, flexible and mobile, depending on the priority of need. He strongly detested any apostolate that would prevent the congregation from acting according to these qualities. Hence only in very exceptional conditions did he allow Marists to staff parishes, e.g. in pilgrimage centers or if there are absolutely no other priests available. "If the Society can do good only by accepting parishes, it must come to an end, it must be wiped out, because it has no goal, no longer anything to do in the Church," he wrote.[20] He feared that parishes would prevent Marists from being available for works of greater need. Colin believed that the nineteenth century had ushered in the age of Mary. He felt chaos on all sides, both in the civil and in the ecclesiastical spheres. Mary established her congregation to be one instrument of mercy to people caught in this chaos. To respond adequately to this chaos, Marists must possess the creativity of Pentecost and the hidden, contemplative virtues of Nazareth.

Implementation of Marist Mythology: Myth Management

Did Colin's dream of Pentecostal creativity take place in the congregation he founded? For a variety of reasons, the actual interiorization and living out of Marist mythology (as revealed through Colin) up to Vatican II have been very hesitant indeed. Certainly, as with many other congregations founded in France during the nineteenth century, the institute expanded numerically and geographically at great speed. Marists, with extraordinary courage and faith, left for remote and dangerous mission fields.[21] The congregation has loyally served local churches wherever it has been established. But, as with many other congregations over the last two hundred years, the institute has rarely shown any above-average pastoral creativity, mobility or flexibility—at least if we take the founder's Pentecostal symbol as the measure of analyses.[22] Powerful internal and external factors militated against the type of pastoral and religious life creativity that should have been expected from such a dynamic founding charism.

Internally, myth management through drift and substitution particularly dulled the impact of the founding charism. The founder's successor as superior general had not adequately interiorized the founding mythology. He had a far less exalted vision of what the congregation should be and so he proceeded to impose his own mythology on the young institute. He believed that the congregation should be nothing more than a pious association of dedicated people and for a long time he received considerable support for this view. With the exception of the founder, the growing congregation accepted this myth imposition almost without question.

Many years later the founder had his own vision concretized into approved constitutions. But in practice the institute rarely lived the rich insights of the creation and dominant myths. What was the directional myth—the Nazareth symbol—became instead the dominant myth. Instead of the Nazareth myth ("hidden and unknown") remaining as an action-principle, that is, indicating *how* Marists are to act apostolically, it became an end in itself. Now Marists were to do nothing apostolically that would in any way attract attention to themselves. This was a tragic distortion and it has negatively affected the life of the congregation ever since. It legitimated mediocrity and dullness. It reinforced the already existing nineteenth-century image of religious life, namely, that it be semi-monastic in structure, inward-looking and a vigorous supporter of the status quo.

The distortion also effectively killed another key directional myth, namely the concern that the founder had for learning as an essential means for the living out of the creation myth. Few people were encouraged to research and publish their findings for fear that they would draw attention to the congregation and to themselves. Inevitably the distortion influenced the initial formation programs of the institute, so that it thus became perpetuated from generation to generation.

The overall failure of the congregation to grasp the founder's insights is evident in a review of the general and provincial chapter decrees or legislation from the 1870s to Vatican II. For example, the 1873 general chapter of the Marists established the aims of the provincial chapters: to promote religious discipline according to the Rule and to inquire into the financial administration of houses. No mention was made of the need to foster new forms of religious life witness or pastoral action. The 1893 provincial chapter of one of the provinces directed that religious (including pastors) were "prohibited from going out after the evening meal for unnecessary visits." The assumption was that a Marist house is a quasi-monastery; people should respect this, and anyone in need pastorally should be discouraged from approaching Marists "after the evening meal," unless in exceptional circumstances.

An examination of provincial visitation reports reflects the same concern for the maintenance of religious discipline and respect for the Rule, but again there is no interest in the evaluation of pastoral effectiveness or creativity. For example, just prior to the Japanese invasion of New Guinea in World War II, a provincial reported on the state of Marists in a particularly dangerous geographical section of that country: "The fathers, in spite of their poverty, must wear socks when saying Mass and be dressed decently, as respectable clergymen ought to be when appearing in public."[23] Nothing was said about the *enormous* pastoral and cultural challenges which confronted the men.

Educationally the congregation was affected deeply by the semi-monastic view of religious life referred to above. This model provided very little opportunity for the type of creative pastoral training envisaged by the original Marist mythology. It was assumed theologically that the world should adapt to the unchanging Church, not vice versa. Marist seminarians lived isolated from the world, as did most seminarians prior to Vatican II. The curricula of seminaries rarely allowed space for positive social science subjects, e.g. sociology, anthropology, which aim to examine critically existing social structures and attitudes. These subjects were not seen to be necessary for the apostolate and were even considered infected with agnostic values, thus "dangerous" for seminarians to study. I once asked a Marist missionary in New Guinea what formation he had had before ministering in an extremely difficult apostlate, and his reply indicates the poverty of the training of those days so contrary to that at least implicitly demanded by the founder's vision:

> I arrived on a small island and asked the old priest for advice, for I knew nothing about the culture of the people, nor their language. The priest replied, "Kneel down, Father, I will give you my blessing." I knelt down and was blessed. "Stand up, for now you are a missionary ready to go to that island over there to evangelize the natives. The boat leaves this afternoon."

Concluding Reflections

The above analysis is given not to provide reasons to ridicule the past, but to illustrate the historical way in which this particular congregation, along with many others in the pre-Vatican II era, found difficulties in interiorizing the founder's vision. The analysis also assists in placing into perspective the adaptive efforts of the congregation since Vatican II.

In the 1950s, there began within the congregation an historical in-depth analysis of its mythology. Thus the institute was well prepared to take up the challenge of Vatican II that religious should rediscover their founding charisms. The richness of the original insights of the founder were already being exposed before the Council initiated this critically important move. Through the advances in Scripture and theological studies, the congregation was able to deepen yet further its grasp of the meanings of its myths.

Thus, through a process of myth extension, it is now possible for the congregation to embrace insights unknown at the time of the founder, e.g. insights into Mary as a symbol within the Church, the role of the local Church, confirmation about the creative role of religious life. Marists are now exposed to a mythology that was denied many previous generations. Little wonder that the comment is made today that the congregation, having rediscovered its original mythology, is set for *re-founding*; some say that it is in the process of being founded for the *first* time because the founder's original vision was, for the reasons I have explained above, never at any stage heard or realistically accepted by the congregation. I am inclined to the latter view, and I suspect that the same comment could be made of many other congregations especially of those founded last century.

Chaos and Reactions Since Vatican II

We are too close to Vatican II to have the objectivity that only the passage of time can provide, so I feel rather like Peter and John, who could only reply to the accusations directed against them by the court, that they could not "stop proclaiming what we have seen and heard" (Acts 4:20). So the reasons I offer for how chaos evolved following Vatican II remain necessarily subjective. I can only proclaim what I have seen and heard over many years of contact with religious congregations, though I do where possible seek the help of other commentators. I also adapt an anthropological model of change explained in Chapter 1 that helps to frame my own experience. The many hundreds of religious I have shared the model with so far find that it generally fits also the experience of their own congregations since Vatican II. (See figure 4.1)

Theologically there was a fundamental, and long overdue, mythological shift at Vatican II that produced profound value changes within the Church. In addition the nature of the shift, and the speed with which it was introduced into the everyday life of religious congregations, resulted in culture shock reactions for many religious.

At Vatican II, which had opened at a time when the Church considered itself to be necessarily unchanging in all aspects of its culture, there re-emerged an ancient symbol of the Church as "a tent of the pilgrim people of God, pitched in the desert and shaken by all the storms of history, the Church laboriously seeking its way into the future, groping and suffering many internal afflictions, striving over and over again to make sure of its faith,"[24] calling its people to face a world in revolutionary change in order to listen to its aspirations, sufferings, anxieties, hopes, that those in need may be better served in compassion and justice.[25] Gone was any official support for the maintenance of an inward-looking or ghetto triumphalistic Church.

It would take a little while before people recognized, not just in their heads but above all in their hearts, the dramatically practical consequences of this mythological shift. People, who like the Israelites of old

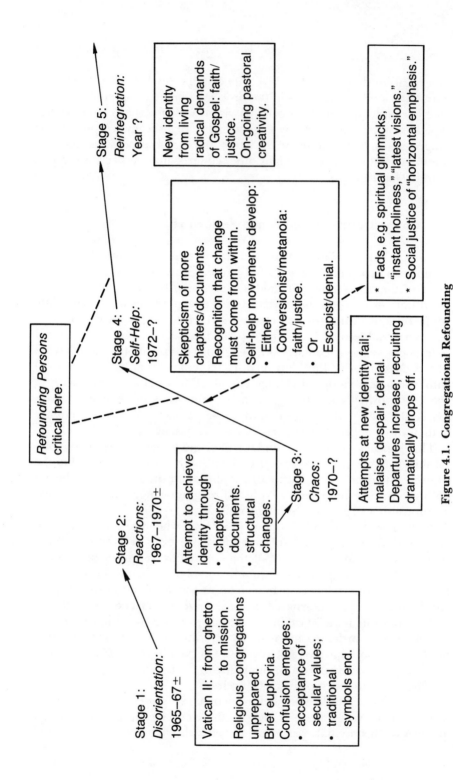

Figure 4.1. Congregational Refounding

Stage 1:
Disorientation:
1965–67±

Vatican II: from ghetto to mission.
Religious congregations unprepared.
Brief euphoria.
Confusion emerges:
• acceptance of secular values;
• traditional symbols end.

Stage 2:
Reactions:
1967–1970±

Attempt to achieve identity through
• chapters/ documents.
• structural changes.

Stage 3:
Chaos:
1970–?

Attempts at new identity fail; malaise, despair, denial.
Departures increase; recruiting dramatically drops off.

Refounding Persons critical here.

Stage 4:
Self-Help:
1972–?

Skepticism of more chapters/documents.
Recognition that change must come from within.
Self-help movements develop:
• Either
  Conversionist/metanoia: faith/justice.
• Or
  Escapist/denial.

* Fads, e.g. spiritual gimmicks, "instant holiness," "latest visions."
* Social justice of "horizontal emphasis."

Stage 5:
Reintegration:
Year ?

New identity from living radical demands of Gospel: faith/ justice.
On-going pastoral creativity.

had based their faith on what was considered quite wrongly ever-enduring symbols of God's presence, gradually began to feel lost and confused because the familiar cultural supports had suddenly disappeared. Often they needed time to grieve the loss of what had given warmth and meaning to their lives, e.g. the Latin liturgy, but unfortunately the space to mourn was rarely given them by those ever anxious to implement the changes based on the purified mythology. They were being called to place their faith in Christ alone, his life and teachings, not in ephemeral and accidental incarnations of this faith, e.g. traditional liturgies.

The world to be evangelized, with its new attitudes toward affectivity, intimacy, sexuality, freedom and authority, was for many Catholics, who had become used to the protective shield of Catholic ghetto culture, difficult to comprehend with the freedom they were expected now to exercise. This was the period of the Cultural Expressive Revolution when everything that was once thought to be culturally, morally and politically sacred and unchangeable was being turned upside-down and questioned.[26] It is not surprising, therefore, that ten years after the Council had ended, theologian Avery Dulles could conclude that many Catholics in most countries were finding within the Church "internal conflict, confusion, and disarray. The Church seems, for the first time in centuries, to be an uncertain trumpet."[27]

How did religious cope with all these conflicting and chaos-creating forces within and outside the Church? While a number of religious had prepared themselves through research and writing well before the Council for the changes, the majority were totally unprepared for the mythological reorientations and their consequences. They inevitably, I believe, suffered varying degrees of culture shock, and many, I feel, have not recovered.

I now explain the five stage model of how I think religious congregations have reacted, or continue to react, to the mythological shifts introduced by Vatican II. (Figure 4.1) Recall that a model is merely an attempt to frame complex experiences; key emphases are highlighted, but the details are overlooked. In reality also the stages are not necessarily as orderly in their sequence as I set them out, for parts of congregations or provinces can be in one stage while others are in different stages at the same time.

Stage 1: Disorientation Begins—1965–67±

If people over-identify with structures and symbols, then when these structures are seriously weakened or destroyed these people are apt to lose meaning and purpose in their lives. This happened with many religious. The reasons to exist evaporated overnight; they were left with a hollowness that the religious life as now presented to them could not fill.

The traditional mythology base, on which the structures of religious life had rested for centuries, was severely undermined in two ways. First, and the most potentially shattering, when the Council stated that *all*, including laity, are called to holiness in the Church,[28] those religious who believed that they alone had this vocation lost the meaning for an elitist existence. All the structures that had been built up to express this myth of elite holiness were no longer valid. Second, the call to religious to be in the forefront of creatively evangelizing a world in rapid change left many religious confused about how to understand and to respond to this world of cultures.

Directly after the Council many congregations initiated studies into the nature and origins of their charisms, and consequently into the relevance of traditional apostolates. It was an unnerving experience for some, but exhilarating and liberating for others. Many, on entering religious life, had never imagined that this radical type of reflection and analysis would happen within their congregation, for it was assumed that customs and apostolates would carry on and on into the future without need for major questioning or change in light of the founding person's charism.

Stage 2: Reactions: Disorientation Continues—1967–70±

However, the actual internal awareness that the traditional mythological bases for religious life had been dramatically shifted took some time to penetrate the hearts of many religious.

In the stage immediately after the Council there was considerable justifiable euphoria among religious, e.g. many structures and customs that were offensive, anachronistic or bore no relationship at all to the purpose of religious life were now legislated out, and religious began to feel the importance attached by the Council to human values in their lives like personal identity, growth and the need to be consulted by superiors in matters affecting one's life. The community and governmental structural changes were relatively easy to make, but in our understandable enthusiasm we often overlooked the far more difficult challenge to inner conversion to the Lord.

About this time, thousands of religious began to leave their congregations for a wide variety of reasons, and the sense of disorientation for the rest of us intensified. Forgetting that the religious person is "committed to the honor and service of God under a *special* title,"[29] some thought that adaptation to the needs of the world meant that we should so identify with the laity that we would not be distinguished from them. It was felt that the more we live like the people being evangelized, the better we would understand and serve them. One religious made this comment to me:

> Sure, I live like a middle-class person. Why not? I work in a middle-class parish and the people want me to be like this. So I enjoy the material things I have for the sake of the apostolate!

He, like many others who reacted the same way, left religious life. Lacking a vigorous interior commitment to the heart of religious life, they became so absorbed by the material things around them that they moved out.

Religious also left because their reasons for entering religious life, they thought, had gone: "If all are called to be holy, and holiness is possible even for lay people, what is the use of being a religious? One can be more effective for the Church as a married lay person!" Some pulled out because they felt that religious life had ceased to exist once the traditional structures had gone. Others thought the changes were not fast enough and, frustrated, they left in anger or despair.

Some withdrew because they thought their congregations were not committed enough to the cause of social justice, or because in their excessive zeal they had become so absorbed in an unrealistic and ruinous search for a totally perfect world here below that religious life lost all meaning for them. When religious, particularly those occupied in difficult social apostolates, failed to give themselves the much-needed nourishment of prayer, they then lacked a faith-oriented inner life to measure what was happening around and within them. Little wonder such people drifted out of their congregations. Others withdrew because the social stigma of leaving had now lessened; their commitment to religious life may have ceased years before, but now they could leave with some ease and still maintain long-established friendships.

The period about 1967–1970 was the time for the chapters of renewal; well phrased documents were written initially to update the old constitutions and rule books in light of Vatican II. We gave ourselves to this process with earnest seriousness. More and more community meetings, or encounter group sessions, were the in-thing, e.g. to discuss proposals for new constitutions, liturgies, for assignment to community responsibilities, how to get to know each other better and to build a more vibrant community. The thrill of being rid of so many oppressive rules and the pettiness of the traditional structures was still a time-absorbing and liberating experience. Somehow we imagined that all this activity would work a thorough revitalization of our lives and congregations.

However, we were beginning to feel the impact of the withdrawals from our congregations and the marked drop-off of vocation recruitment, so we sought to "close ranks," as it were, by writing/legislating in our chapters with increasing urgency about our identity, the need to respect the dignity of the human person in all decision-making procedures, personal fulfillment and responsibility, on the importance of participative/consultative government. We said all the "right things," so that many creative people initially responded with hope about the future in the light of the documentary changes, but so often attitudes remained unchanged that their frustration and cynicism grew.

We continued to write on mission, on the need for apostolic creativity and for communal and individual prayer, but as long as we lacked the interior conversion and the right leadership, the legislation and the magnificent renewal rhetoric alone did not effect the desired revitalization. Moreover, despite all our documents, the purpose of religious life still remained at heart unclarified; the Council had not provided a clear-cut vision of the religious life, but had challenged religious themselves to work at it.[30] Until this could be achieved by religious themselves, then the mere production of external supports, e.g. congregational documents, new governmental structures, would provide only temporary identity.

As the years slid by, and the finely printed and produced chapter documents gathered dust, that inner sinking feeling that all efforts at renewal were simply not producing their desired results was less and less able to be hidden from those deeply concerned about the future of their congregations.

Stage 3: Chaos—1970—?

This is the stage of "marvelously messy chaos." If it is rightly confronted, I believe, it could be the catalyst for a solid refounding movement within provinces or congregations. The Lord has allowed circumstances "to tear up and knock down, to destroy and to overthrow" (Jer 1:10), so that all our securities and visible symbols of power/congregational prestige are crumbling around us, sold—laicized or administratively still controlled though with a minimal congregational presence: "You dissolve like a cobweb all that is dear to him" (Ps 39:12). It is a hurting and grieving experience for many to see this all happening in so short a space of time.

This is the stage I estimate most religious congregations are now in, with individuals or groups struggling in different ways to enter stage 4, Self-Help and even beyond. This stage of chaos is marked by confusion, a sense of drifting without purpose. Nothing that has so far been tried is working; recruitment is either non-existent or down to a bare minimum; the average age of the membership is rising inexorably, causing financial problems in some instances of massive proportions as congregations struggle to care for the aging and sick membership.[31]

The sense of corporate belonging is weak. Though religious may still live together, they work at different apostolates. Members are weary of having community meetings to discuss their future or how to improve community life; they just want to be left alone to survive and do the best they can. After all, they say to themselves, to have more meetings merely provides the opportunities for old wounds and hurts of previous gatherings to be opened up; it is better to live in peaceful co-existence and avoid raising our deep theological divisions.[32]

So community life is shallow and apt to be more of the boarding house or "gentlemen's club" style—pleasant, but definitely not threatening, for real issues that might divide are avoided and individual independence is very carefully preserved. Questions like these become important to individuals: Can I hold on to my car in my retirement? Who will look after me if the old folks' home is full?

Despite all the signs of chaos some congregations or their provinces deny it exists. They delay planning for the future, e.g. how to house and responsibly care for their aging religious, how to use limited and declining resources for the best pastoral advantage of the Church. They dream that "something will turn up," or "those many vocations our congregation is getting in the Third World can come here until we return to normal," or "things are just not as bad as they might appear," or "it is wrong to speak of planning for withdrawal from apostolates or death, when we should trust in the Lord."

In a survey of one province, that was vigorously denying the slow development of chaos, one religious reflecting the views of many others less blunt than himself wrote: "There should be no insistence on the 'generation gap.' To do so is merely to create it. It is not evident until some fool (i.e. the researcher) starts looking for it. I am all for improving the seaworthiness of our boat, but I am entirely against rocking it! All we have to do is trust in the Lord!" Sadly, there was a very evident generation gap that effectively discouraged creative initiatives among the younger religious: some sixty percent of religious in the younger age bracket, compared with only seventeen percent above the age of forty-five, considered that their communities were "self-centered, self-preoccupied." One respondent summed up the situation like this:

> Many of us want to ask difficult questions about the relevance of our apostolates to the needs of this country. We are given frozen looks or we are told not to offend the older religious by such questions. We want also to

experiment with new apostolic ways, but are told that the old ways have served us well so there is no need for changes. Why should we change, we are told, when people keep telling us we are doing a good job.

This atmosphere of denial was not supportive of those with creative imaginations. The manpower study of the same province revealed that the aging process could be reversed only through a dramatic increase and better retention rate of new candidates into the congregation. The desired increase did not occur, but, since denial had become so deeply rooted in the province culture, nothing was done for years to confront constructively the crisis of how to care for the aging and how to utilize the remaining personnel resources to the best advantage of the local church and congregation.

Stage 4: Self-Help—1972–?

At this stage chaos begins to be seen by some as a liberation, a chance to put aside apostolically irrelevant symbols of the past, the chance to discover their inner desperate need of the Lord, with the cry of the psalmist on their lips and deep in their hearts: "To me, poor wretch, come quickly, God! My helper, my savior, Yahweh, come without delay" (Ps 70:5) They recognize deep within themselves their own personal and congregational desperate need of the Lord, just as Paul so eloquently testified:

> Yes, we were carrying our own death warrant with us, and it has taught us not to rely on ourselves but only on God, who raises the dead to life. And he saved us from dying, as he will save us again; yes, that is our firm hope in him, that in the future he will save us again (2 Cor 1:9f).

Generally, religious who have reached this stage have passed through some deep personal spiritual revitalization process, e.g. the Ignatian Exercises, in which they have confronted their own inner chaos and rediscovered the creative power of Christ in their lives. Some in this category may even be looking for refounding persons to lead them in some radically new expression of their congregation's charism. Some may themselves be refounding persons and may even have begun the task of revitalizing their congregations. The charism of their founding figure is no longer for them something contained in an historically well-researched book, but an experience they personally relive and identify with. They are open to new ways to preach and live the Gospel of charity and social justice.

At this stage also there are communities that enter into a deeply spiri-

tual and courageous discernment process and discover that God is allowing them to die; they are coming to the end of their mission within the
Church. They embrace death, but in a spirit of the resurrection, for they
recognize that in accepting cheerfully the will of God for them they
testify to what is at the very heart of religious life: union with Christ in
his death and resurrection. Their acceptance of congregational death
becomes salvific for themselves and for the Church.

Others, however, while recognizing that they must do something, escape into all kinds of proposed, but ineffective, quick/instant solutions to
overcome internal and external chaos. They know they must do something, provided it is not too personally demanding on them! There are
many available escape routes from which to choose. For example, they
may become intensely busy people apostolically in an effort to dull the
need to look too deeply into themselves and discover there what God
wants of them. They may give themselves *exclusively* to the cause of social
justice in *this* world ("horizontal social justice"), forgetting the God-
centered orientation that should mark this apostolate if it is to be Christian. They hope that this or some other absorbing social activity might
give them the much-desired feeling of relevancy as religious. By neglecting the Christian dimension, however, they find that anger begins to grip
their hearts, with a harshness and intolerance distorting their judgments
about people and their motives. The warmth of charity is nowhere to be
seen. Left unchecked, such religious end up burnt-out cases and/or out
of religious life.

Others become professional workshop participants particularly on
prayer, earnestly desiring to discover the latest "guru" who can lead
them into the promised land of a new identity as religious, with some
speed of course and without the long and tiresome task of reconversion
demanding radical responses in charity and justice. Course after course
takes on something akin to magic. If one has not done the latest, one is in
danger of missing out on the much-desired secret to peace and good will.

Others too escape into the latest cult movement, e.g. they become the
most avid devotees of the "most recently recorded visions of Mary" or of
some "newly discovered holy person." These spiritual escape movements
are frequently socially very conservative, for they can massage their adherents into thinking that concern for social justice is really only for the
"dangerous leftists."[33] All we have to do, they claim, is pray harder and
seek one's personal salvation. Then there are those who find their identity in nostalgic cult groups seeking to restore unchanged the symbols
and practices of the past: "We were happy in the old ways and we had
vocations then, so we will have them now if we return to the old ways of
doing things."

Stage 5: Reintegration—?

It is rather difficult to describe just what religious congregations will look like at this stage, since we are still too close to chaos and await the insights of refounding persons to guide us. However, it is certain that under the direction of refounding people, there will be apostolic social justice concern for the poor, but of a type that is not exclusively related to this world, that is there will be the faith "prophetic proclamation of a hereafter, the human person's profound and definitive calling, in both continuity and discontinuity with the present situation: beyond time and history, beyond the transient reality of this world . . . beyond the person, whose true destiny is not restricted to his or her temporal aspect but will be revealed in the future life."[34] The proclamation of the full Gospel will be accompanied in religious congregations by a life-style and way of acting in accordance with the beatitudes and the respective charisms of the congregations. In brief, one thing is certain: refounding religious congregations will be marked by the radicalness of the Gospel message. And the refounding process must forever be on-going; we will always be needing refounding people to help us relate to the rapidly changing pastoral needs of people.

Summary

Chaos is a thoroughly biblical image, beloved by Yahweh and his mouthpiece—the prophets and *the* prophet Jesus Christ. Religious congregations are today in chaos for a variety of reasons, e.g. because of the distortion over time of their founding myths, the hesitancy, confusion, even denial, of religious when confronted with the chaos, the lack of refounding persons with the gifts to lead people out of their confusion.

That brilliant eighteenth century satirist poet, Alexander Pope, wrote of chaos which he sees as the result of mere human activity; the search for human knowledge, human vanity, if left unchecked, will ultimately lead to a horrible mediocrity, dullness. Using Virgilian and biblical prophetic symbols and styles, which together form a parody of the Genesis *Let there be light*, he writes:

Lo they dread Empire, CHAOS! IS Restored;
Light dies before thy uncreating word;
Thy hand, great Anarch! lets the curtain fall;
And Universal Darkness buries all.[35]

The chaos we find within ourselves, in our congregations and in the world around us, is sterile, warns Pope, if we fail to grasp it through the eyes of faith. "Universal Darkness buries all" if we do not reach out in faith to the Lord as the Israelites did across the Red Sea, through the wilderness of the desert and into the unknown land beyond.

The chaos we face is of such depth that each congregation requires its own prophets, its congregational intrapreneurs, who, endowed with faith, creative imagination and a personalized experience and love of the founding gift, are able to call us to a new faith/justice conversion. They devise new Gospel strategies to bridge the gap they see between the Gospel and cultures and they can energize us to act with the driving spirit of the founding person. They are chosen by God, as were the prophets of old, and we, like the Israelites of old, can accept or reject them. The next chapter concentrates on the role and qualities of these rather extraordinary and necessary people.

Chapter 5

Out of Chaos:
The Role of Refounding Persons

"The Lord your God will raise up for you a prophet like me from among you, from your brethren . . ."

(Dt 18:15)

A revitalization movement generally occurs under three conditions: members of a particular society are experiencing the confusion and malaise of chaos; they acknowledge that they are suffering the stress of chaos and are unable alone to get out of the frustrating state; and finally there is a leader (or leaders), or cultural refounding person, who is able to articulate and implement a new satisfying cultural repatterning.[1]

In the previous chapter, we described the stages of chaos that many religious congregations are now experiencing. Our task here is to describe the third requirement for a revitalization movement, namely the refounding person of a religious congregation. Their role and qualities are akin to those found in the prophets of the Old Testament who are the exemplars of all authentic reformers in the Church. With memory and imagination they call us back to our founding mythology and invite us to join them in building strategies to confront the world around us with the Gospel message. There is a fire in these people, a Gospel radicality that inspires the converting, disturbs the complacent, the spiritually lethargic, those who deny chaos both inside and outside themselves and those who compromise with worldly values. They can be feared, like all innovators, because they dare to push back the frontiers of the unknown—chaos, a world of meaninglessness—in the name of Jesus Christ.

In this chapter I aim to reflect on refounding persons;

- who they are and their role;
- their qualities;
- the difficulties they can experience.

Prophets to the Prophets: Defining the Refounding Person

I define the congregational intrapreneur as follows:
   A refounding person,

   • in response to the inspiration of the Holy Spirit,
   • is one who, in imitation of the "faith shock" and reaction of the founding person who suddenly, or over a period of time, perceived the gap between the Gospel and the world of his or her time,
   • acutely sees the contemporary chasm between the Gospel and secularizing cultures,
   • and moves, through creative pastoral strategies, to bridge the chasm,
   • and at the same time restlessly summons others to faith/justice conversion—especially members of his or her own congregation—and to share in the vision to go out into the unknown in order to implement the Gospel strategies (Figure 5.1)

The working definition is tediously long, but I am seeking to be as exact as is possible. Readers themselves may over time wish to refine it further in light of experience. I will now explain key points in the definition.

The Refounding Grace: A Gift of the Holy Spirit

The grace of refounding is an *extraordinary* gift of the Holy Spirit. He can offer the gift to certain people and they can accept or reject it, for the Holy Spirit will not compel anyone against his or her will to become a refounding person. Similarly, a religious community or congregation can refuse to be led into the refounding stage.

By "gift" of the Holy Spirit, I mean that it is a supernatural grace which is given for the development of the Church of Christ and which comes from the Holy Spirit: it is "the work of one and the same Spirit, who distributes different gifts to different people just as he chooses" (1 Cor 12:11). The Spirit offers gifts in ways that reflect the spiritual/pastoral needs of the Church as a whole, the talents and abilities of the individuals concerned. The gift is "extraordinary" in this sense that it is not lightly offered; it involves something radically *new* within the Church.

The gift is for the service of the Church, "for a good purpose," writes St. Paul (1 Cor 12:7) and not for the private welfare of the one receiving the gift. The Holy Spirit is the source of such gifts, because he is "charged" to watch over and care for the disciples and the Church after the resurrection and ascension of the Lord: "When he ascended to the

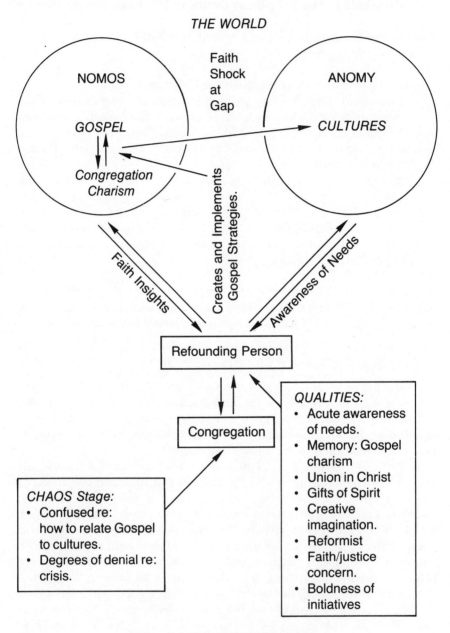

Figure 5.1. The Refounding Person

height . . . he gave gifts to men. . . . And to some, his gift was that they should be apostles; to some, prophets; to some, evangelists; to some, pastors and teachers; so that the saints together make a unity in the work of service, building up the body of Christ" (Eph 4:8–12). St Paul in his naming of the gifts of the Holy Spirit does not aim to be thoroughly exhaustive. Some gifts are constantly present within the Church, but others are active only at particular times according to the needs of the Church, e.g. the gift of "tongues" in the local churches established by Paul himself.

The gifts are not all of the same importance: "In the Church, God has given the first place to apostles, the second to prophets, the third to teachers; after them, miracles, and after them the gift of healing; helpers, good leaders, those with many languages" (1 Cor 12:28). Paul advises the people: "You must love more than anything else; but still hope for the spiritual gifts as well, *especially prophecy*" (1 Cor 14:1). And he tells them why prophecy is important in the community: "The man who prophesies does talk to other people, to their improvement, their encouragement and their consolation. . . . (The) man who prophesies does so for the benefit of the community. . . . (The) man who prophesies is of greater importance than the man with the gift of tongues, unless of course the latter offers an intepretation so that the Church may get some benefit" (1 Cor 14:3–5).

The gift of prophecy has a highly important function within the Church, just as it was in the days of the early Church. For example, we find that "Judas and Silas, being themselves prophets, spoke for a long time, encouraging and strengthening the brothers" (Acts 15:32). Prophets are expected to interpret, under the inspiration of the Holy Spirit, Christ's message to the world, a role stressed by St. Paul: "If you read my words, you will have some idea of the depths that I see in the mystery of Christ. This mystery that has now been revealed through the Spirit to his holy apostles and prophets was unknown to any man in past generations" (Eph 3:5).

Associated with the gift of prophecy is the grace of discerning spirits, for there must be within the Church certainty that what is being said or done comes from the Holy Spirit. Not everyone who calls himself or herself a prophet has the gift of prophecy, and the warnings given the early Christians remain true today: "It is not every spirit, my dear people, that you can trust; test them to see if they come from God; there are many false prophets now in the world" (1 Jn 4:1).

The refounding person is a prophet because he or she has the same ability as the founding figure, shares the same vision and is driven by the same burning desire to preach the Gospel of the Lord. Through their prophetic leadership the congregation is offered a fresh start within the world that is vastly different from that known to the founding person. The refounding leader has the prophetic gift of being able to lead the congregation into a new apostolic relationship with an increasingly secularized world. Only certain individuals have this gift, while others are graced by the Holy Spirit to *follow* these individuals. However, as gifts are freely offered by the Holy Spirit they need to be prayed for; and they also need to be responded to for they can quite easily be neglected or rejected by those who are offered them.

Prophetic congregational figures "restlessly summon" others to faith/justice conversion (metanoia), that is, the grace of responding to the call to follow demands an inner change of heart, and this is to be expressed in a faith/justice response. As action for justice is a constituent dimension of the Church's mission, conversion can never be reduced to something purely spiritual. It must be expressed in charity and justice.[2]

Alexander Pope, in a passage that is thought to have no equal in the literature on the human person because the expression is so powerfully incisive, describes the limitations of the person:

> Born but to die, and reas'ning but to err;
> Alike in ignorance, his reason such,
> Whether he thinks too little, or too much;
> Chaos of Thought and Passion, all confus'd. . . .
> Great Lord of all things, yet a prey to all
> Sole judge of Truth, in endless Error hurl'd.[3]

In our efforts to describe the need for congregational prophets, I have turned to the findings of anthropology, management studies and biblical reflections. These insights are helpful, but of themselves they cannot lead us out of the darkness of congregational chaos. While we are the "great lord of all things," without Christ, the Light of the World, we are prey to our human limitations. Without Christ we cannot walk out of the valley of darkness! We cannot be converted through our own resources. We may think, without quite realizing it, that we are the "sole judge of Truth," but without this Light we are "in endless Error hurl'd". Refounding is, and will remains always, an experience of faith both on the part of the refounding persons and on that of those who respond to their leadership.

The Reformist Role of the Refounding Person

There are three broad categories of religious communities: traditionalist, adaptationist or reformist.[4] People belonging to each type will have a quite different understanding of apostolic or religious life creativity.

Those who hold to the *traditionalist* type of community view the world as unchanging, so there is no need to alter one's apostolic methods; what was suitable for yesterday is equally apt for today and tomorrow. Creativity is fostered only to the degree that it helps to maintain the same type of apostolic approach that was used yesterday.

In the *adaptionist* community people recognize that changes are required if the community is to survive. For example, lay people are encouraged to assume responsibilities in schools usually reserved to the religious, not because of some new insight into the apostolic role of the laity, but simply because there are too few religious available to staff the schools. If religious vocations increase again, then the laity are to be replaced with the new religious. There is creativity here, but of a highly restrictive type, for there has been no attitudinal or conversion change to the theology of mission and lay involvement. Only pragmatism, based on the need for survival, has encouraged a "temporary" change.

At Vatican II it was said that "Christ summons the Church, as she goes her pilgrim way, to that *continual reformation* of which she always has need, insofar as she is an institution of people here on earth. Therefore, if the influence of events or of the times has led to deficiencies in conduct . . . these should be properly rectified at the proper moment."[5] The Church is calling for reformers, not *revolutionaries*. The latter aim to destroy through a process of militant confrontation what already exists and to recreate something totally different. They demand a complete break with the past.

In reform, on the other hand, there is both continuity and discontinuity with the past; reformers strive to get in touch with the founding myth and identity of the group, but at the same time put aside all those accidental accretions that hinder or obstruct this myth from being related to the needs of a rapidly changing world today. Paul VI highlighted the continuity and discontinuity dimensions of reform within the Church in this way:

> We should always wish to lead it (the Church) back to its perfect form on the one hand corresponding to its original design and on the other fully consistent with the necessary development that like a seed grown into a tree has given to the Church its legitimate and concrete form in history.[6]

Refounding persons within religious congregations are thus not to be revolutionaries. They are to be reformers. They assume that change to be deeply effective must be gradual and is the result of four kinds of discoveries or rediscoveries:

a. There is the *re*discovery of the power of Christ within oneself that comes from conversion (metanoia), that is, the reformer identifies again with the power of the founding myth of religious life itself and so with its emphasis on the apostolic virtues of mobility, flexibility, creativity.

b. The reformer discovers with a renewed vitality, and identifies with, the power of the founding myth of the congregation itself. For example, a Marist who is called to be a refounding person relives the powerful creating experience of the founder when the latter, in the presence of Mary, recognizes the spiritual poverty of the rural people in the mountains around Lyons, France, and is so shocked that he is determined to found a congregation to do something about it. The spirit of the founder becomes his spirit.

c. The congregational reformer *re*discovers with renewed freshness the role of religious life within the dynamic mission of the Church to the world; religious must be in the forefront of creatively responding to the needs of the Church.

d. The reformer discovers the spiritual or pastoral needs of people in the world and sees that something can be done. The reformer, experiencing the same kind of faith shock as did the founding person when he or she discovered the enormity of the chasm between the Gospel and people or cultures, prepares in practical ways to respond to these needs. A Marist reformer, true to the spirit of the founding mythology, would be extremely disturbed to see the present growth in secularism within Western cultures and he would see some entirely new way to respond to this, but according to the spirit (direction myth) of the founding gift, that is, he would refrain from telling people what to do but rather concentrate on fostering in them a strong motivation to respond to the challenge in their own lives.

Types of Refounding Persons

In brief, congregational prophets are those who strive to uphold the founding person's message in all its purity, but, at the same time, they are able to make it relevant to the contemporary world. It is possible to distinguish two types of congregational prophets with these characteristics: major and minor prophets.

Major congregational prophets are those who have the gift of the Holy Spirit to reorientate the congregation, or an officially recognized division of a congregation, e.g. a province, *significantly* to the contemporary apostolic needs of the world. I think personally that the former superior general of the Jesuits, Father Pedro Arrupe,* is such a person. He was able to grasp the heart of the founding myth—conversion, apos-

*See below, Chapter 8, pp. 163ff.

tolic creativity, flexibility, mobility in the service of the Church—and challenge the congregation to adapt this myth to specific needs of today.[7]

Throughout this book I speak of *refounding* persons, not the *refoundation* of the congregation, simply because the speed of change in the world is so revolutionary that a congregation can never be said to have finished the process of refounding. It is an on-going process of challenge and reaction. A congregation needs a "never-ending" succession of refounding people. The word *refoundation* connotes, however, that the task of refounding is only needed from time to time, that is, there are stages of dynamic refounding followed by lengthy static periods. That was possible prior to Vatican II, since it was assumed that religious congregations had to remain relatively static anyway. They needed to be creative in the traditionalist or adaptionist sense, but reformist creativity was considered unnecessary and in fact quite discouraged.

When the Holy Spirit offers the gift of refounding to a particular person, he may also extend to other people within the congregation the gift of responding to the congregational prophet. These people, whom I call *minor refounding persons,* are drawn freely to see in the message of the refounding person that which corresponds to their own deep yearnings. They group around the refounding person at his or her invitation, acting as a creative support in the refounding experience. Since their task is a supportive one, theirs is *not* the gift of the refounding person. Major and minor refounding people have two distinct gifts and they must not be confused.

The refounding person, after a period of discernment and with the consent of superiors, needs the freedom to invite those people he or she considers have the gift of minor refounding. The congregational prophet, who has the vision of what should be done, how it should be achieved and what qualities are required in those who have the gift of minor refounding, is the person who intuitively is able to discover those who are the authentic minor refounding people. The gift of minor refounding is a grace and not all people are offered it, even though they may claim that they have been chosen by God. Minor refounding persons must be aware of the limits of their supportive role, for when they consider themselves to have the gift of the major refounding person, then there is conflict and the refounding process is either held up or dies. They must be consulted, however, on issues, e.g. implementation of the project, that do not pertain essentially to the refounding insight.

The Qualities of the Refounding Persons

There are two qualities that are present in all founding people, according to John Lozano: the belief that God has called them to found a new religious group, and the effective ability to define the ends and lifestyle of the institute and provide it with a definite spirit.[8] Similarly, refounding persons do feel at some point in their journey that they are called to the task of congregational prophecy. And to be effective, they recognize that they must revitalize the goals and objectives of the institute in line with the needs of the contemporary world scene, its lifestyle and its spirit.

Is it possible to be more concrete in defining the particular qualities that we might normally expect in today's refounding persons? I believe so. As yet we cannot list a sufficient number of existing congregational prophets to see what is common to them. One reason is that we are still too close to the chaos stage to be completely certain that particular individuals are authentic refounding persons. However, it is possible to proceed in an *a priori* fashion by looking at the qualities in the prophets of old, at the personal histories of founders and at what is expected in the natural order from intrapreneurs in corporate cultures. I would not claim that all the qualities listed must be in every refounding person, though I think there are some that must be considered essential, e.g. creative imagination, gifts of the Holy Spirit, identification with the congregation founding myth, deep union with Christ in prayer.

To facilitate our analysis I distinguish, somewhat arbitrarily, between human, psychological/faith and spiritual qualities:

A. Human Qualities

1. Close to People

As with the prophets of old, congregational prophets are in close contact with what is happening to people; they have a special sensitivity for the sufferings of the poor. Because they are aware of people's needs, they are able to see where the congregation is out of touch.

2. Creative Imagination and Listening

As we have seen in Chapter 2, the creative individual has an above average capacity for imaginative innovation and original thought. Refounding persons are energized through their active listening to Christ's presence within them and the founding myth of their congregation. They hear and see people who are starved of Gospel values and, just as the founding persons did before them, they are able creatively to construct new ways to respond to this deprivation.

3. Commitment to Hard Work

This does not mean that reformers do not enjoy relaxing pursuits. On the contrary, they generally like periods on their own in order to relish the chance to ponder, to think things through. There may be a certain poetic or dreamer touch to them, while nonetheless being also pragmatic at the same time.

4. Commitment to Small Beginnings

As reformers they believe that a movement can be most effective if it is willing not to rush beyond the capacities of people to absorb what is happening, to give its energies to immediate and attainable goals and to utilize as far as possible existing "political" processes. Initial smallness does not unnecessarily threaten people; it also allows for space in which to experiment and change course if necessary without too much confusion.

Another reason why reformers commit themselves to small steps is that, even though they have a large vision of what should be done, they still are uncertain about the details as to how this vision is to be concretized. They often have to work intuitively or through trial and error; by moving in small steps they can evaluate better what they are doing in light of their vision.

5. Toleration of Failures

Reformers are open to learn from mistakes, temporary setbacks. If they were to take failures personally, they would rarely have the resilience to bounce back and try a new way of approaching the challenge.

6. Community-Oriented

A basic assumption in this analysis is that it is highly unlikely that an original idea can come from a team, although the team is often useful in acting as a catalyst for an individual to be creative, expanding and applying the original insight once it emerges and developing structures through which the idea is applied to practical purposes. So the reformer needs other people.

Moreover, theologically the congregational prophet cannot be a loner, for even though he or she may be rejected or marginalized by the group because of their prophecy, the reformer yearns to foster Gospel community within their institution as a witness to Christ's loving presence in its midst.[9] The example of Christ himself is both poignant and powerful:

"Jerusalem, Jerusalem, you that kill the prophets. . . . How often have I longed to gather your children, as a hen gathers her brood under her wings, and you refused" (Lk 13:34).

B. *Psychological/Faith Qualities: Insights of Fowler*

James W. Fowler is a seminal figure in the psychology of religion and he has produced a faith development theory of considerable help to evangelizers concerned with the various stages of faith conversion. As the theory also provides helpful insights into the qualities required of refounding persons, I will first explain his approach and then draw out relevant conclusions.

Faith for Fowler is close to what St. Thomas Aquinas refers to as the *habit* of faith, that is, an inclination of the mind disposing it to act in a certain way, namely to believe.[10] Yet he goes further still; faith is a constitutive quality of the mind whereby persons relate to their environment at all levels, e.g. to cultures, to other people, to God. So faith is not *something* we have, but rather a mode-of-being-in-relation to others and to the Other.[11]

Fowler constructs six stages of Faith Maturity. First, there is the *Intuitive-Projective Faith* stage in which for about the first six years of life a child receives faith from his or her parents in a very informal way. Second, at the *Mythic-Literal Faith* stage of the school years, faith is passed on to the young in the form of "stories" in which are enshrined Christian beliefs and the actions that must follow from them. Faith is accepted on the authority of those who recount the Christian myths. Third, at the *Synthetic-Conventional Faith* level, our faith, from the early teens even through adulthood for many people, comes from a sense of belonging to a particular cultural environment or group. We believe because the group believes; the reasons for believing are not objectively examined. If, of course, the cultural structures dramatically disintegrate, or if we are suddenly taken out of our familiar cultural setting, our faith is apt to move into crisis, e.g., religious who prior to Vatican II assumed that religious life was synonymous with certain accidental structures, such as set times for prayer and particular designs of the habit, often lost faith in religious life when these structures were removed.

Stage four is the *Individuative-Reflective* level of faith that is appropriate to the young adult. Here the cultural or authority imposed belief system of the previous stage is questioned, rejected or personalized. The polarity tensions within Christian symbols, e.g. love of self and love of neighbor, freedom and conformity, prayer and involvement in social action, are recognized, but the person tends to select one pole rather than the other. Religious, for example, who opt *exclusively* either for social action *or* for personal prayer time are at this stage. This is also a level popular among ideologists (and fanatics)—options are either "black *or* white." At this level symbols are intellectualized to provide ideas about life, but the critical affective dimension of symbols that disposes people to insights beyond the mere intellectual is poorly appreciated.

At the mid-life and beyond the *Conjunctive Faith* stage is possible. Here people are able to draw positively from opposite poles at the same time, e.g. prayer *and* action for justice; love of self *and* love of neighbor. Here one's faith enters into a new depth or integration and with this journey can come a deepening peace of soul, as one develops a growing intimate relationship with Christ. At this level symbols are reservoirs for intellectually understanding the purpose of life, but the affective quality of symbols becomes increasingly important for people; symbols offer insights, experience or intuitions that are unable to be grasped by the intellect. Yet a fundamental tension still remains: one's urge to give oneself fully to the Lord's concern for the poor, for example, is held back by a fear of what must be personally given up at the same time.[12]

It is rare that people reach the sixth stage of *Universalizing Faith*. Here the person reconciles the faith polarities in heart and in action; they make real and tangible "the imperatives of absolute love and justice" and they "exhibit qualities that shake our usual qualities of normalcy."[13] There is a driving selflessness, combined with a deep inner peace, in their compassion and action for justice, emerging out of a loving union with Christ. This intimacy with the Lord is of such intensity that with St. Paul they can truly say: "I have been crucified with Christ, and I live now *not* with my own life but with the life of Christ who lives in me" (Gal 2:19f). They, e.g. St. Francis of Assisi, Thomas Merton, Mother Teresa of Calcutta, are thoroughly community-oriented while at the same time being strong, independent individuals. Because their lives so challenge the status quo, the world of compromises, "Many persons at this stage die at the hands of those whom they hope to change"; honor tends to come after death.[14] It is scarcely surprising that, as Fowler himself says, they are exceedingly rare people.

Fowler's approach is particularly helpful for two reasons: it sharpens the profile of what a contemporary refounding person may look like and, second, it highlights why tensions develop between the refounding person and other members of the congregation.

My personal view is that refounding people must be at least in stage five and moving toward stage six. And this means we are speaking about very exceptional and scarce people indeed. There is a faith integration and a burning zeal in their lives that sees through apparently insuperable barriers of custom, ideological polarizations, and permits them to enter chaos for the sake of the Lord without paralyzing fear.

The constitutions of religious congregations are often expressed in a language of the faith level of stage five, while incorporating ideals from stage six. Religious with a faith level at stage four tend to see the constitutions as enshrining unrealizable dreams or ideals; they can become cynical, even angry, when they are challenged to live out what they feel to be constitutions out-of-touch with the real world. Lacking an appreciation for the symbolic and mythical qualities of the constitutions, these religious fail to grasp the sense of divine mystery and vision in the words and expressions used. On the other hand, religious at stage three, as they lack a critical or reflective approach to reality, may feel that they are living out the ideals of the constitutions to even a high level of perfection.

Refounding people, on the other hand, take these documents, which incorporate the congregational mythology, realistically and strive to adapt them to an ever-changing world. If other religious reject their constitutions because it is thought that these contain ideals that cannot be, or are not expected to be, realized, it is not surprising, therefore, if they also are annoyed by, or reject, those "crazy" religious in their midst who actually strive to live the document's values. The goodness and zeal of refounding persons contradict their previous secure assumption that the constitutions with their mythical or visionary insights are not to be taken seriously.

In particular, religious with stage three faith fear the chaos that refounding people will initiate if they succeed in their efforts at revitalization; the predictable will be destroyed and this they cannot bear. They are simply unable to grasp the inner dynamism of Christ's message that calls Christians to keep adapting the faith to the ever changing pastoral needs of people.

Religious at stage four are disturbed by the apostolic faith/justice/prayer integration that refounding figures are personally able to achieve. For example, those who choose exclusively the social justice option and consider personal prayer an unnecessary luxury will find the lack of vigorous ideology in refounding persons intensely frustrating. The latter are viewed as spiritual escapists from the real world or compromisers whose way of life "holds back the social justice revolution." Christian compassion and charity are considered to be symptoms of weakness.

I was once present at a lecture given by Mother Teresa of Calcutta and she was rudely criticized by a cleric in the audience: "You, Mother, are holding back the justice revolution with your works of compassion. You are stopping the people from becoming angry with their poverty and their dying. You should be attacking the sources of injustice!" She gently replied, ignoring the arrogant tone of the questioner:

There is no justice *or* compassion in Jesus, but only justice *and* compassion. We need one another. While you work in social action, I will show the love of Jesus to the unwanted who cannot wait for the revolution. I never look at the masses as my responsibility. I look at the individual. I can only love one person at a time. I can feed only one person at a time.

These words and her example illustrate a key quality of stage six—its subversive character that "often strikes us as arising from a kind of relevant irrelevance."[15] In a world which asserts that scarce resources should not be squandered on people who have no hope of recovery, it all sounds so "irrelevant" or "wasteful" to take care of the dying—to feed, wash and value them as people loved by the Lord! Yet, what could be more relevant to a materialistic world than an expression of concern for the dignity of *every* person, especially of those who are bereft of all human power! The cleric who gravely doubted Mother Teresa's "usefulness for the revolution" was certainly not in stage six. He was more at home in stage four; his faith had become so thoroughly intellectualized and out of touch with the subversive quality of Jesus' love for the poor in all times.

C. Spiritual Qualities

In a particularly relevant Vatican document, *Mutual Relations* (1978), it is said that three qualities must be present for a founding (and, therefore, a refounding) grace to be authentic: it must be evidently from the Holy Spirit, the person must have an earnest desire to be conformed in love "to Christ in order to give witness to some aspect of his mystery," and there must be "a constructive love of the Church, which absolutely shrinks from causing any discord in her."[16] I will explain each of these points more fully.

1. Gifts of the Holy Spirit

St. Paul enumerates these gifts: "love, joy, peace, patience, kindness, goodness, trustfulness, gentleness and self-control" (Gal 5:22). Note the reference to patience and self-control. The prophetic figure must quickly recognize that culture change, and therefore congregational change, is slow, if it is to become deeply rooted in the hearts of people. Hence, the need for enormous patience and self-control if people are to be motivated to enter into, and to be sustained in, the conversion process.

Manipulative or arrogant actions are foreign to a refounding person. Jesus is often depicted as asking people what they would wish of him, even though it would have been obvious to him what the need was. He wanted to respect the freedom and dignity of people, rather than force his unrequested powers on them. On entering Jericho, Jesus said to a blind man: "What do you want me to do for you?" (Lk 18:40). Or, to the sick man at the pool of Bethzatha: "Do you want to be well again?" (Jn 5:7). Notice also his sensitive relationship with the two disciples on the road to Emmaus; he did not impose himself on them for the evening, but rather "he made as if to go on" (Lk 24:28). They freely made the decision to invite him.

A refounding person needs to be trusting; otherwise he or she is a cynic, for cynicism is a chronic state of distrust and it is antithetical to the openness necessary within a person for creativity. To the cynic, experiments are futile, for "we have tried all that before and nothing ever works." Cynics know the answers without having gone deeply enough into the issues even to know the questions to be asked. Look at how Jesus relates to Peter. So often Peter shows such enthusiastic support for Jesus but just as frequently he breaks the trust placed in him, yet Jesus continues to trust Peter, even to the degree that he is willing to place him at the head of his disciples.

The refounding person struggles to be gentle, for he or she experiences in his or her own life the merciful way in which the Spirit is forgiving and does not push, but actively waits for a response however long delayed it may be. The gentle person is prepared to wait, to sow the seed of conversion, to encourage whatever interest, though it be hesitant, that others may show in the refounding process. One senses this gentleness of Jesus in his conversation with the woman at Jacob's well in Samaria. He gently leads her through a reflective process, avoiding harsh condemnations of her marital condition. In the end, she and many others were converted to him (Jn 4:1–42).

Yet even the greatest and most wonderful gifts of the Holy Spirit are surpassed by love. Hence, the hymn to charity in St. Paul's chapter 13 of his First Letter to the Corinthians has such a pivotal placing between chapters 12 and 14, which contain descriptions of the charismatic gifts: "If I have the gift of prophecy, understanding all the mysteries there are, and knowing everything . . . but without love, then I am nothing at all" (1 Cor 13:2).

The most powerful testimony to the presence of the gifts of the Holy Spirit will be the leadership shown through the personal example of the refounding person in imitation of Christ. Through the power of example the congregational prophet expresses his or her servant role in leadership: "I have given you an example so that you may copy what I have done to you," he says to the surprised disciples after he has washed their feet.

I tell you most solemnly,
no servant is greater than his master,
no messenger is greater than the man who sent him (Jn 13:15–16).

So often it is not what a reformist says that has the lasting impact, but how he or she lives what is being proclaimed.

2. *Union in Christ: Rejection/Suffering*

There are two dimensions to this quality of union in Christ. First, there is in the true refounding person the earnest desire to rediscover and relive the founding myth of the congregation and to reapply it, not in a static way, but dynamically to the new needs of the time. They believe deeply that the founding myth or charism stresses some particular dimension of the redemptive mystery, some unique insight, that the Church is seen to need for the fullness of its life.

Second, at yet a deeper level, there is the quality of willing conformity with the mystery of Christ's love: his life, death and resurrection. And this means inevitably that the authentic refounding person is called to suffer, often intensely, in union with Christ. The authors of *Mutuae Relationes* explain this point succinctly:

> The true relation between genuine charism, with its perspectives of newness, and interior suffering, carries with it an unvarying history of the connection between charism and cross, which, above every motive that may justify misunderstandings, is supremely helpful in discerning the authenticity of a vocation (*to found or refound*).[17]

Refounding persons, as did so many of their founding predecessors, experience considerable pain and suffering, particularly from members of their own congregations. Some cannot abide the "perspectives of newness" of the apostolic thrusts that the reformer proposes. Others who are trapped in the chaos stage, especially if they have escaped into denial, do not always want to be reminded of their situation. They get a twisted kind of identity from "enjoying the chaos." For them the risks of the demands that conversion would place on them seem far more threatening than the problems of the present congregational chaos. Others do not appreciate being challenged by people they feel they know so well; hence the words of Jesus: "I tell you solemnly, no prophet is ever accepted in his own country" (Lk 4:24). Some complain that scarce resources are being given to the refounding person when they should be used to maintain the apostolic status quo. Others are envious of his or her gifts and of the attention given them, while others, with no ill will, just do not grasp or appreciate the qualities of the would-be refounding person and they are fearful of the uncertain world he or she is calling them to.

In brief, the refounding person can expect to be subjected to all kinds of neutralizing reactions, such as were described at the end of Chapter 2. Plans are presented to provincial or chapter committees and repeatedly analyzed, and requests made for more and more unnecessary clarifications and details with the unexpressed hope that the reformer will eventually withdraw the ideas and no longer "cause trouble" to people. Frequently, if the congregational prophet dares to persist in his or her vocation, the opposition turns to rejection, marginalization or "banishment to the grim periphery" of the congregation.[18]

In terms of the threefold category breakdown of people involved in a change situation (as described in Chapter 2), "pathfinders," "problem-solvers" and "implementers," the would-be refounding person faces rather special tensions since Vatican II. (See figure 5.2) Prior to the Council, the creativity of the congregational pathfinder/founding person was rarely permitted to endure for very long, especially if the semi-monastic model of organization was quickly imposed on the founding myth.* Then the preferred dominant congregational figure became the logical, rational, present-oriented problem-solving superior who would favor creativity of the traditionalist and adaptationist kind only, that is, whatever would sustain the apostolic and structural status quo.

Congregational pathfinders of the reforming, future-oriented type, in the sense described in this chapter, were definitely discouraged; and religious subjects, the "implementers," were there to receive the decisions handed down hierarchically from the problem-solving superiors and to implement them without question in the "spirit of obedience." My own impression is that some very creative people in congregations with foreign missions attached to them, e.g. in Africa, Asia, Oceania, frequently volunteered for these challenging regions prior to Vatican II. They felt stifled by the lack of creative pastoral opportunities in the settled home provinces, with their very staid and predictable apostolates. Others may have become "problem religious," with rather individualistic tendencies, as they found it particularly difficult "to fit in" with the "normal and right ways of doing things."

Following the Council, a much-needed purification of the religious life founding myth occurred, though it has tended to be confined to only

*See above, Chapter 4, pp. 70ff.

one category of the people involved in the myth, namely, the "implement-ers." Religious were encouraged to enter into a consultative/participative form of decision-making, though superiors, or those formally in charge, having listened to all sides, were then to make the final decisions. The new Code of Canon Law has endorsed this approach: "By their (i.e. superiors') reverence for the human person, they are to promote volun-tary obedience. They are to listen willingly to their subjects . . . without prejudice to their authority to decide and to command what is to be done" (Can. 618).

The collegial or consensus approach to decision-making is now also becoming increasingly common in communities, i.e. decisions are made by majority vote. This has many benefits, but when it is abused, congrega-tional pathfinders suffer as they did prior to Vatican II; the would-be reformist can be suffocated by having to be present at meeting after meeting to explain details of a project that really cannot be fully articu-lated to individuals whose primary concern may be with their own needs. The gatherings are even more tedious if participants behave in ways that appear "groupy" or too emotionally demanding on one another. One form of religious life oppression becomes substituted by another—the analytical, present-oriented status quo superior is supplanted by the con-sensus, sometimes emotionally draining, over-egalitarian and inward-looking group. (See figure 5.2)

The group for its part becomes annoyed because the reformer has not the time to spend in frequent meetings or discussions that are inward-looking, or because he or she is unable to provide all the details of the proposed project. Members of the group are also apt to feel uncomfort-able in the presence of the reformer, since the latter's ideas about the "mission out there" threaten their preferred world of security. So the pattern begins over again: opposition, rejection or marginalization occur. And the congregation loses a chance to begin the process of refounding.

Rejection can also lead in the refounding person to feelings of intense loneliness, a sense of abandonment. Recall the loneliness of the Old Testament prophets: "I never took pleasure in sitting in scoffers' com-pany; with your hand on me I held myself aloof" (Jer 15:17). The prophet is apt to alienate the wicked as well as the pious, the cynics as well as the believers, yet the prophet cannot stop being what he or she is—the one to challenge, to defy despair or compromises and to push aside fear and numbness.

The way to union in Christ is the road of suffering. Pride is the source of a deceptive experience of self-sufficiency. So a shattering failure, or rejection by one's own congregation, can precede for a refounding per-son an ultimate jump into a more perfect faith, a faith that moves one

Time of Congregational Founding	CONGREGATIONAL INTRAPRENEURS (Founders/ Foundresses)	+	Problem-solving Superiors	+	Religious
Second Generation Congregation (to Vatican II)	Congregational Intrapreneurs	+	PROBLEM-SOLVING SUPERIORS	+	Religious
Post-Vatican II	Congregational Intrapreneurs	+	Problem-Solving Superiors	+	RELIGIOUS
Refounding Congregations	CONGREGATIONAL INTRAPRENEURS	+	Problem-solving Superiors	+	Religious

Figure 5.2. Changing Roles within Congregational Cultures

into the darkness of belief and away from one's own false securities. The archetype of rejection and loneliness is Christ himself. He experiences in Gethsemane a mysterious and intense feeling of abandonment and in-credible darkness: "A sadness came over him, and great distress" (Mt 26:37). Those who should have been closest to him, Peter and the two sons of Zebedee, had as yet no ability or grace to enter into the depth of Jesus' sadness. And Jesus turned in his abandonment to his Father in prayer.

For the reformer prayer is at the very center of life; in prayer the congregational prophet discovers the inner weaknesses, the absolute need for God, and the inner God-given strength to battle against the urge to give way to discouragement and apathy. In loneliness the prophet feels drawn to speak to Christ as a friend who also experienced such terrible darkness: "No wonder then if I cannot keep silence; in the anguish of my spirit I must speak, lament in the bitterness of my soul" (Job 7:11). And in prayer there is found hope, the source of apostolic enthusiasm: ". . . fear and trembling descend on me. . . . For my part, I put my trust in you" (Ps 55:5, 23).

At times there is a strong urge to escape the prophetic responsibility. The constant rejection of Gospel dreams and innovative plans for action, loneliness and even marginalization within the congregation are heavy burdens for a refounding person to carry, the more so when people outside the congregation eagerly request help and affirm his or her creative gifts. One such person commented to me:

> When I return to my community after helping other congregations, I feel like a stranger. No one is interested in what I am doing, for they are so afraid. Yet, I yearn to help them. I am tempted to flee, but I know deep in my heart this is not what God wants of me.

Jeremiah would well understand this comment. He found his task almost an intolerable burden:

> You have seduced me, Yahweh,
> and I have let myself be seduced;
> you have overpowered me:
> you were the stronger.
> I am a daily laughing-stock,
> everybody's butt . . .
> The word of Yahweh has meant for me
> insult, derision, all day long.
> I used to say, "I will not think about him,
> I will not speak in his name any more" (Jer 20:7–9)

Yet, despite this powerful experience of rejection, Jeremiah does not flee. He remains faithful to Yahweh: "Then there seemed to be a fire burning in my heart, imprisoned in my bones. The effort to restrain it wearied me, I could not bear it" (Jer 20:9).

3. Constructive Love of the Church: Avoidance of Discord

The authentic refounding person avoids *deliberately* causing conflicts or taking ideological or confrontational positions on topics that would lead to polarizations within the ecclesial community and within the religious congregation. As I have explained above, because the congregational prophet passionately loves the Church and his or her congregational charism, it is almost inevitable that there be tensions, difficulties and even conflicts with ecclesiastical and/or religious superiors and their communities. The document *Mutuae Relationes* acknowledges this fact:

> Every genuine charism implies a certain element of genuine originality and of special initiative for the spiritual life of the Church. In its surroundings it may appear troublesome and may even cause difficulties, since it is not always and immediately easy to recognize it as coming from the Spirit.[19]

The prophet perceives how the mission of the Church, or congregation, should be realized at a particular time and place. Others come to this intuition only slowly. Hence, the negative reactions are not always due to ill-will. The great Carmelite reformers, St. Teresa of Avila and St. John of the Cross, underwent painful ill-treatment and rejection by the religious they were calling to reform. However, even good people did not always understand the dreams of this remarkable pair. Intense conflicts emerged between the two saints and members of their respective congregations and also with the ecclesiastical authorities. Yet the key point is this: the true prophet does not consciously and deliberately cause the conflict. The latter emerges as a consequence of the efforts to invite fellow religious to a reconversion process.[20]

A practical question arises: What must a religious do when his or her religious authorities reject what he or she considers to be a refounding insight? I suggest the following steps.

a. Return to a Deeply Prayerful Discernment Process

The insight must be rechecked, as it were, with the Lord. The discernment will be conducted in deep faith, without anger or cynicism, for the aim is: What *is* God's will? Practical questions like the following need to be asked:

* Has sufficient information been given to superiors?
* Have superiors been given time to reflect on the proposals for action?
* Were the right procedures followed in the presentation?
* Has there been sufficient prayerful reflection on the project?
* How authentically honest is my concern for the refounding project? Am I seeking power over others, my own prestige?
* Am I genuinely concerned for a dialogue?
* Am I seeking the advice of a wise and knowledgeable spiritual director, one who can test with me the authenticity of my motives and the presence of the Holy Spirit?

b. Renew Request

If, after discernment, the person feels that he or she must renew the request, then it needs to be done with all the necessary qualities, e.g., patience, respect.

c. Go Higher

If the insight is still rejected, and if the person in a spirit of faith discernment still believes in the proposal, then the petition needs to be discussed with higher superiors, e.g. superior general. It might also mean, if it has not been done already, presenting the proposal to official legislative bodies of the congregation, e.g. provincial or general chapters.

d. Submission to Decisions

If the insight is still not accepted, and if the person still feels that he or she has a legitimate refounding charism, then the following options are open to them. The person can in faith discernment finally conclude that the proposal is not what God wishes for the congregation. Or the proposal is seen to be what God wishes, and there is some hope that the congregation will eventually be open to the proposal, but the timing of its presentation to the congregation needs to be delayed until the congregation is more disposed to receive it.

If there are no grounds to hope that the congregation is open to the proposal, then the refounding person may then decide to hold back indefinitely. On the other hand, if the proposal is considered sufficiently urgent and serious, the religious may decide to have the proposal tested by hierarchical authorities, e.g. the Congregation for Religious. This is a highly exceptional approach.

What Vatican II says of extraordinary gifts applies equally to the charisms of refounding persons:

> Judgment as to their genuineness and proper use belongs to those who preside over the Church, and to those whose special competence it belongs, not indeed to extinguish the Spirit, but to test all things and hold fast to that which is good.[21]

The touchstone of authenticity of the prophetic gift has always been the humble submission of the prophet to the final judgment of the Church or the appropriate congregational authorities, regarding his or her charism. This is the prophet's personal witness that his or her message is true.[22]

The discernment required, in what can be a long and personally agonizing process, must be conducted always at the level of deep interior faith. By "interior" I mean the willingness to use or to sacrifice all created things in the service of the love of God. Thomas Merton is right: "Christian asceticism leads us into a realm of paradox and apparent contradiction. . . . Our ability to sacrifice ourselves in a mature and generous spirit may well prove to be one of the tests of our interior prayer."[23]

The tragedy of some would-be prophets, whose first inspiration is highly relevant, is that they failed when patience, even humility, was required in order to participate in the long and slow process of discernment/

dialogue evaluation of their proposals. Refounding is ultimately the work of the Lord. He may well wish that the insights of the prophet be rejected for the present. He may wish that other people even take up the proposals after the prophet is dead.[24] And, to repeat a point made earlier: no matter how brilliant and authentic the prophet's proposal for reform is, the Holy Spirit will never pressure anyone to accept it against his or her will; the freedom of the individual is respected at all times.

e.   Withdrawal: New congregation or reform within a tradition

Religious life does not demand an absolute commitment, that is, an individual for legitimate reasons can request even in final vows a formal dispensation. There are examples in history of religious who discern that their task is to withdraw from their congregation in order to found an entirely new one, e.g. St. Peter Julian Eymard withdrew from the Society of Mary (Marist Fathers and Brothers) to establish the Congregation of the Blessed Sacrament. Mother Teresa of Calcutta left the Bengal Mission of the Loreto Sisters in order to begin her own congregation.

In history there are also cases in which the aspiration for the revitalization of an already existing charism can be realized by the congregational prophet only by establishing a new reform congregation. For example, this was a consequence of the Carmelite reform movements under Sts. Teresa and John of the Cross. The obstacles to the reform within the then existing Carmelite congregations were seen as insurmountable, so that the axiom, "The new belongs elsewhere," meant that independent congregations had to be established if the survival of the reform was to be guaranteed. So convinced of this was St. Teresa that she even sought the aid of King Philip II of Spain: "I am quite clear that, unless the Discalced are made into a separate province, and that without delay, serious harm will be done: in fact, I believe it will be impossible for them to go on."[25]

In a certain sense this is a refounding process, since the prophet aims to re-establish a new reformed congregation *within* a particular existing tradition. It is asserted that no new charism is being created. This must be seen as a legitimate option for congregational prophets, especially if they correctly discern that it is the only way that God wants the reform movement to occur. Various traditions, e.g. Franciscans, Carmelites, are far more open to this type of refounding than others. For example, this type of refounding is not possible within congregations in which the form of government is an integral part of the original charism, as is the case with the Society of Jesus. In such congregations the reform movements must either be led by the central government or legitimized by it. I do not believe there can be, for example, a separate congregation called the "Congregation of Jesuit Reform" or some such title.

Summary

Many religious congregations are in the stage of chaos. They are benumbed or paralyzed, uncertain about how to find apostolic direction and energy to face a world that is in revolutionary change. Such a stage, if rightly used, can be marvelously enriching, a pentecostally creative experience for individual religious and for the congregations as a whole.

To move out of chaos we need, as did the Israelites of old, *prophetic* refounding persons. Jesus Christ is *the* great prophet, the absolute source of our revitalization. But as prophets are still necessary in the Church, because they challenge us to live again the purity of the salvation message and make it relevant to today's world, so also are refounding prophets needed within religious congregations. They call us back to the purity of the founding myth of the congregation and point out the ways in which the inner power of this myth can be applied to apostolic needs *now*.

Congregational prophetic reformers are people born anew by the power of Christ and by a reliving of the faith founding experience of their respective congregations. Seized by the Spirit, they yearn to adapt the inner heart of the founding experience to the new pastoral/spiritual needs of today. And they invite others to join them in their task. They have a faith-stubbornness, and a humility that comes from an awareness of their own failings and their utter dependence on God, that ultimately can carry them through inevitable periods of opposition, rejection, even marginalization within their congregations.

Refounding is a gift of the Holy Spirit. Individuals and congregations can reject this gift and, if they do, there can be no refounding. It is a gift to be vigorously and enduringly prayed for:

> Some have lost their way in the wilds and the desert,
> not knowing how to reach an inhabited town . . .
> their courage was running low.
> Then they called to Yahweh in their trouble
> and he rescued them from their sufferings,
> guiding them by a route (Ps 107:4–6).

Chapter 6

Out of Chaos:
The Role of Religious Superiors

"So give encouragement to each other, and keep strengthening one another . . . you must think of what is best for each other and for the community." (1 Thes 5:11, 15)

St. Paul offered this advice: "To want to be a presiding elder is to want to do a noble work" (1 Tim 3:1). The task of a religious superior is a "noble" one, but, as a friend said recently, "No one in his or her right mind would ever freely desire the job of being superior in this post-Vatican world!" His sentiments would find confirming nods among many present-day religious. "It all seems such a thankless task," said another religious. Yes, one does not take on the duty of a superior these days to be thanked.

Yet, hesitant though religious may be to assume this "thankless task," the fact is that the role of superior, especially the major superior, is of critical importance in the refounding of a congregation. If a major superior is against refounding, then he or she can effectively hinder or prevent a person from exercising the refounding charism. In this chapter, therefore, I will:

- briefly reflect on the theology of a superior's role and the contemporary problems of being a superior;
- describe what is expected of a superior in the refounding process.

Superiors: Challenges and Theological Reflections

As we are told often by the writer of the Acts and St. Paul, there were in the early Church apostles, prophets and teachers, and others referred to as "helpers," "rulers," and "those over you in the Lord." As the communities of believers grew in size they searched more and more from among their own members for leaders to assume key duties. Hence, we read of elders, bishops, deacons, and pastors (see Acts 14:23; 1 Tim 3:12, 8, 10; Tit 1:7). The primary duty of these people is to be of service to the body of Christ in order that it may fulfill its mission within cultures. They are to be the "nerves and connecting tissues of the body, the servants of the servants of God."[1]

This description of leadership within the Church can be applied also to the task of the superior within religious congregations. If the office of leader as "a servant of the servants of God" is so noble, why would many religious today agree with my friend's grave hesitancy to accept willingly the duty of superior in contemporary times?

Difficulties Confronting Superiors

The task of the superior today is not a popular one for particularly these reasons:

a. There is confusion about the nature and function of religious life. (See Chapter 4 above) If the meaning of religious life is uncertain, so also is the job description of the superior.

b. Individuals of leadership ability hesitate to be involved if communities have become *excessively* relational ("groupy"); they feel they cannot spend long hours at sharing sessions that are strongly inward-looking and possibly emotionally draining.

c. Where memories of abuses by authoritarian superiors of the pre-Vatican hierarchical model remain vividly alive, there is a strong resistance to any form of authority, no matter how necessary and well supported theologically it might be.

d. Communities, provinces and congregations, instead of being as they once were "mono-cultural theologically and behaviorally," today comprise what are equivalently several different cultures or sub-cultures that may be polarized because of radically divergent values held on to ideologically and with deep emotion. A pluralism in value systems is creative and challenging *provided* people of different value orientations are open to learn from one another. By value I here mean "a conception, explicit or implicit, distinctive of an individual or characteristic of a group, of the desirable which influences the selection from available modes, means, and ends of action."[2] Values are the force behind behavior patterns or, as Brian Hall writes, they are the "units of information that mediate our inner reality into full expression in our everyday lives."[3]

To illustrate how values can differ dramatically among religious of the same congregation, I discovered in an in-depth study of a clerical province of three hundred male religious[4] that:

- On the nature of the *Church* 20% hold pre-Vatican II values ("The Church is a perfect, religious society and the only true way to salvation"), 45% Vatican II ("The Church as the People of God is a sacrament of unity") and 34% post-Vatican II ("The Church as a pilgrim is the prophetic critic of society and culture").
- On the nature of *salvation,* the province is markedly divided: 41% pre-Vatican II ("The Church is the medium of salvation"), 31% Vatican II ("God's grace of salvation is equally at work within all peoples") and 27% post-Vatican II ("All religions are means of God's saving grace.)
- As regards *religious life* values, there are also significant differences, e.g. 8% hold to a pre-Vatican II view that the vow of obedience means that the religious should "sacrifice his personal goals and actions for the goals and actions of the congregation"; 26% opt for a very human relational stand, that is, that one should *only* coordinate one's life with that of the congregation, thus permitting the individual to downplay the importance of any serious commitment to the common good; 65% choose the Vatican II view that "the religious should coordinate and if necessary sacrifice personal aspirations and actions for the common good."
- Overall I estimated in this detailed survey that up to a third of the province tend to have diocesan priest values, rather than those of religious life.

This example highlights the enormous difficulties that major superiors may have to contend with today. Fortunately, religious in the province described above are not ideologically polarized along value orientation lines. However, problems for their superiors are still considerable. How does the major superior, of a province like the above, help plan apostolic teams in which participants are committed to a common vision when views about such key issues as Church, salvation, and ministry are so different? Or how does the superior foster the growth of religious life communities, when a significant section have yet to be converted to religious life values? With such different value orientations among religious surveyed, the superior would need to become an expert in animating cross-cultural relationships!

Today religious are less likely than before to express openly their theological and religious life value differences.[5] Some religious life subcultures have learned to work together or have separated to work in different geographical sections of a province. An atmosphere of peaceful co-existence, referred to in Chapter 4 above, often prevails, for people are weary of "battling to have their values accepted by others," but the problems of being a superior in an atmosphere of ideological polarization, even though it may not be so vocally expressed as before, are immense and frightening to the faint-hearted. How does one respond to individuals who reduce obedience to only human relational values? How does one stimulate a group to face the demands of mission creatively that is primarily inward-looking and concerned with their own needs and not those of the common good, or will not acknowledge at any point a superior's role in decision-making but only what a majority of community members agree to?

e. On the assumption that religious do share common values, superiors wishing to sponsor and support congregational pathfinder/prophetic initiatives are confronted by communities, which are especially favorably disposed to implementers and, to a lesser degree, problem solvers. A good deal of creative action does require participation, particularly at the implementation stage,[6] but if implementers do not themselves have minor refounding gifts, then it is difficult for them to appreciate what the refounding person is trying to say and do. They can become obstacles to refounding and thus the task of the superior is made yet more complicated.

f. Our congregational cultures, prior to Vatican II, were traditionalist and adaptionist, not reformist, in allowing creativity. We simply have little or no history of reformist creativity after the deaths of our founding persons; administrations commonly built controls to avoid risks and to keep all policy decisions at the top. We lack models of reformist creative action so that new superiors dreaming of being future-oriented are unsupported by a tradition of refounding. This feeling of not knowing what to do can be terrifying and is not encouraging to religious to assume wholeheartedly the task of a reforming superior.

g. The contemporary superior's duties increasingly require his or her presence at death rituals, e.g. funerals of congregational members, arrangements to close houses, rather than at life-creating ceremonies, e.g. professions, ordinations. For some these duties are too depressing.

Theological Reflections on the Role of Superior

The superior has competency in three areas of authority: in teaching, sanctifying and governing, and in exercising these functions, superiors are to stress, according to the values of Vatican II, the consultative/participative approach.[6]

1. Office of Teaching

By this I mean that "religious superiors have the competency and authority of spiritual directors in relation to the evangelical purpose of their institute."[7] That is, superiors must know and be willing to explain personally or through others the charism or mythological values of the congregation. These values form a critically important measure of what the congregation should be doing apostolically.

2. Office of Sanctifying

This is the office of pastoral service to one's fellow religious. Superiors are to "foster perfection in what concerns the increase of the life of charity according to the end of the institute, both as to formation, initial and on-going, of the members and as to communal and personal fidelity" to the values of religious life and the congregational charism.[8] The challenge is to encourage, even though resistance can be considerable, the on-going conversion of individuals and communities. One danger that superiors must avoid is the assumption that new chapter documents, or brilliantly composed circular letters or mission statements, about the need for prayer/conversion or updated structures are in themselves *the* major forces to effect refounding. It is an easy temptation to give way to, when a superior finds the efforts at calling religious personally to reconversion so lacking in positive response.

3. Office of Governing

Superiors have the duty of "ordering the life of the community, of organizing the members of the institute, of caring for and developing its particular mission."[9] Their first obligation is the corporate welfare of the congregation (or province or community) and that means being future or mission, not maintenance, oriented.

The pitfall to be avoided in the exercise of this office is the temptation not to see the importance of keeping up the struggle for structural changes in the service of reform, e.g. developing support systems for refounding people. The superior can become so frustrated by the resistance experienced, that he or she refuses to do anything further and personally escapes, inwardly claiming, as Henri Nouwen writes, that "all the conflicts of the world find their origins in the human heart . . . (and) the only real place to start changing the world is to start in the center of their own inner life."[10] Or the superior concentrates only on the office of sanctifying, but he or she speaks in such generalities about the need for inner conversion that no one feels in the least threatened. In both cases the superior avoids the frustration, but the process of refounding is hampered by these escapist reactions.

Elsewhere[11] I have explained how I believe the superior should go about fulfilling these three offices. In brief, assuming that the primary overall thrust of the superior is to foster the future-oriented, creative involvement of religious in the development of themselves and the congregation, I suggested two key action-principles:[12] the "Hands-On, Value-Driven" approach,* that is, being out in the field in close personal contact with the religious concerned, listening and challenging them with the values of religious life and the congregational charism, e.g. values of apostolic creativity, flexibility and charism, e.g. values of apostolic creativity, flexibility and mobility; the "Loose-Tight" approach, that is, delegating one's authority as widely as is possible, but calling people to be accountable for how they use this delegation according to the values mentioned above.

As far as the major superior personally is concerned, I believe that he or she *must* be as free as is possible from the practical demands or details of maintenance duties. One provincial I know gives eighty percent of his official time to mission, that is, creativity for refounding, and only twenty percent for maintenance activities. Over a period of time he has educated his province to the values behind this allotment of time, for at first many religious opposed what he was planning to do, believing that the provincial alone should hear their problems. Two full-time elected councillors work with the provincial as a team and deal with most maintenance matters, including a sizable percentage of the personal visitation of the religious in the province. Religious find the provincial frequently with them, relaxed, alert, actively listening, challenging their ideas about the future and calling them to be apostolically and personally accountable according to the congregational values. In the past this was not the case, so they now wonder why the administrative restructuring had not been done earlier!

Action for Refounding: Guidelines

The superior is to be involved in refounding in short and long terms. Each will now be explained.

Action in the Short Term

"Survey the path for your feet,
and let all your ways be sure." (Prv. 4:26)

1. Commitment to Refounding

Superiors, to be effective in refounding, must be thoroughly committed to it. Notice, it is the same primary condition behind all successful involvement by management in fostering intrapreneurial activity within

*See Chapter 2, p. 41.

corporate business cultures. Religious congregational refounding is no exception to this requirement. To test one's level of commitment to refounding here are some key questions:

- Am I prepared to give up a policy of primarily *reacting* to problems as they emerge in the stage of chaos and instead develop a future-oriented administration in which challenges are anticipated?
- Am I fully convinced that ultimately individuals refound congregations, not committees, not chapters?
- Am I prepared to keep working at the refounding process, even though I know that there will possibly be attempts by my congregation to reject my efforts, even to marginalize me?
- Do I recognize that the process is a *faith* venture demanding of me an ever-deepening union with Christ?

Without faith my involvement remains merely human, and no matter how energetic my work may be and how well aided I am by the latest findings in the social sciences, it sinks to the level of a purely human action; whatever may appear to be my achievements, they are the works of time and not of eternity. It is therefore to the faith dimension that I now turn, before we look at what the social sciences can offer us.

2. The Discovery of Refounding Persons: Role of Discernment

Commonly it is said that God will raise up prophets no matter what happens. So, why worry about going through the process of discernment or struggling to build up a favorable congregational cultural support for them? Moreover, the argument continues, in the process of congregational repression and stubbornness on the part of superiors, the true prophet grows in humility and holiness; then, when God wishes it, a very saintly prophet will emerge and he or she will have a far greater influence on the congregation and the Church than would otherwise have been the case.

The argument is dangerously and tragically simplistic. Repression of the Spirit, because of my negligence and laziness, is objectively morally wrong. Despite the fact that I claim to stand up for truth, which is at the heart of the Gospel message, I nonetheless scandalously proclaim to my congregation, by my refusal to enter into a discernment process, that truth does not matter. This is condemned by St Paul:

Never try to suppress the Spirit or treat the gift of prophecy with contempt; think before you do anything—hold on to what is good and avoid every form of evil (1 Thes 5:19–22).

Jesus is blunter. He attacks the scribes and Pharisees for hypocritically persecuting the prophets:

> Alas for you, scribes and Pharisees, you hypocrites! You build the sepulchres of the prophets . . . saying, "We would never have joined in shedding the blood of the prophets, had we lived in our father's day." You are sons of those who murdered the prophets . . . I am sending you prophets and wise men . . . some you will slaughter and crucify, some you will scourge. . . . I tell you solemnly, all of this will recoil on this generation (Mt 23:29–36).

These are powerful, terror-inspiring words. They give no room for complacency on the part of congregational leadership. What right have we nonchalantly to allow people to suffer, "for the sake of improving their holiness so that they might be better prophetic instruments," because of our own culpable negligence to enter into a discernment process? This approach sounds "perilously close to sanctifying evil means for a good end."[13] God alone knows just how many potential congregational prophets with their innovative ideas have been "slaughtered" by being silenced or marginalized, and thus prevented from exercising their ministry to their religious communities and the Church. If this is still happening, then surely "I tell you solemnly, all of this will recoil on this generation" (Mt 23:36).

Another danger to watch is to approach the discernment process half-heartedly, that is, being too ready to call this or that person a congregational prophet. It can be unfair to the people concerned and harmful to the congregation, for very serious mistakes can be made: "Beware of false prophets who come to you disguised as sheep but underneath are ravenous wolves. You will be able to tell them by their fruits" (Mt 7:15f).

As a superior, committed to the corporate future of my congregation in its service of the Church, I have a serious obligation to discover who, if any, are being called by God to lead us out of chaos. We can find the authentic prophet through the discernment process, which is the prayerful reflection on a human situation in the light of faith; it is not a method of short-circuiting faith, but rather it is a way of choosing what God wants of us. We theologians, administrators and social scientists can provide all kinds of carefully documented evidence about this or that person, but we are still limited. We must relate to a God who is humanly inconceivable, unpredictable, yet merciful, in his ways.

An essential requirement for my involvement in discernment is my own conversion to the Lord.[14] This means that I must discover and root out all the attitudes, ignorance and prejudices which obstruct my openness to the Holy Spirit. So, I turn to whatever can help me, including the social sciences if necessary, to find out what may be obstructing the discernment process. (See figure 6.1) Conversion has been defined and referred to several times in this book. But, because it is a grace so crucial to the superior's role in the refounding process, I wish to delve still more deeply into it. (See figure 6.1)

The process of conversion is a journey into detachment. "A man," writes St. John of the Cross, "who is in darkness does not comprehend the light, so neither will a person attached to creatures be able to comprehend God."[15] Darkness covers the chaos of my attachments, my secret desires for power over others or my many vanities, so I must enter into it and uncover this inner confusion and chaos that I really do not want to look at for fear of having to do something about it all. This cannot be done by my own powers alone, for they cannot be trusted, but only with Christ who is the Light. By entering into my own inner darkness, I find my own personal anomy or lack of direction in life. Listen to the paradoxes of St. John of the Cross:

> In order to arrive at possessing everything,
> Desire to possess nothing.
> In order to arrive at being everything,
> Desire to be nothing. . . .
> In order to arrive at that which thou knowest not,
> Thou must go by a way thou knowest not . . .[16]

Other medieval mystics, some modern poets and existentialists share a common insight: the confrontation with one's inner darkness/chaos is the condition for one's creative discovery of life's meanings. No modern poet is able to express better the nature of this assault on one's inner chaotic darkness of attachments than T.S. Eliot. Adapting St. John of the Cross, he writes:

> In order to possess what you do not possess
> You must go by the way of dispossession,
> In order to arrive at what you are not.[17]

This darkness Eliot describes at one point as the "wasteland"; its qualities are: a deep sense of disappointment and hopelessness, a feeling of chaos, the conviction that the meaning has evaporated from life, and a feeling of terror as one stumbles on one's own hollowness. He distinguishes "hollowness" from "emptiness." If the journey inward leads us to acknowledge that God alone can fill our hollowness, then, Eliot says, we become truly "empty" people, for we have emptied ourselves of all that is

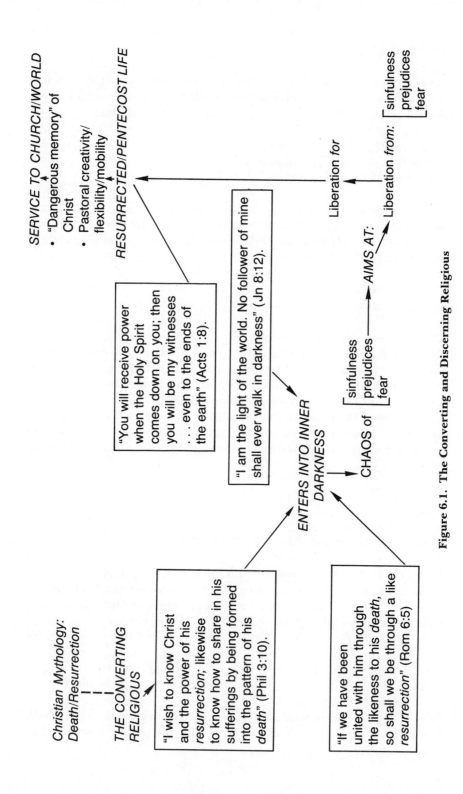

Figure 6.1. The Converting and Discerning Religious

not of God. The movement from being hollow people to empty people is his description of the conversion process; the ascetic emptiness is a condition for spiritual rebirth or a deep, intimate union with Christ:

> Descend lower, descend only
> Into the world of perpetual solitude . . .
> Internal darkness, deprivation . . .[18]

The "descend lower" imperative is the call to enter the journey of conversion, the faith voyage into one's inner hollowness. One emerges purified and strengthened from the wasteland, marked with joy and the laughter of freedom:

> Even while the dust moves
> There rises the hidden laughter . . .[19]

The imperative to "descend lower," as the prerequisite for conversion and discernment, so movingly expressed by Eliot, is to be found powerfully uttered by the prophet Jeremiah in his call to the people of Israel. It is a call, however, that he himself painfully interiorizes. Not only did he accept the duty of being Yahweh's mouthpiece to the Israelites, but he went further. He embraces the challenge to bear in his own life the weight of Yahweh's sorrow at his people's sins. Petrified with fear, because he is desperately aware of his own inner chaotic inadequacy, he cries out in agony:

> A curse on the day when I was born. . . .
> Why ever did I come out of the womb
> to live in toil and sorrow
> and to end my days in shame (Jer 20:14, 18).

In this cry Jeremiah does not deny his call to be a prophet, but he affirms it from the very depth of his inner self. For the more he is aware of his own inner poverty, his inability ever to continue preaching conversion with his own strength, the more he falls on his knees to beg Yahweh for help. Yahweh will provide the inner resources. He will fill the void of his own hollowness; this gives him a deep abiding consolation no matter what happens: "But Yahweh is at my side, a mighty hero. . . . Sing to Yahweh, praise Yahweh, for he has delivered the soul of the needy from the hands of evil men" (Jer 20:11, 13).

The theme of acknowledging one's inner powerlessness as the condition for God's protection is at the heart of many psalms. For example, sense the psalmist's self-discovery of inner poverty and the consequent immediate recognition of his need of God:

> Lay your scourge aside,
> I am worn out with the blows you deal me. . . .
> Like a moth you eat away all that gives him pleasure—
> man is indeed only a puff of wind!
> Yahweh, hear my prayer.
> Listen to my cry for help,
> do not stay deaf to my crying.
> I am your guest, and only for a time,
> a nomad like all my ancestors (Ps 39:10-12).

This dramatic petition, springing from a deep awareness of personal need, is to be repeated by the Savior himself both in the garden of Gethsemane and on the cross itself:

> And a sudden fear came over him, and great distress. . . .
> "Abba (Father) . . . take this cup away from me.
> But let it be as you, not I, would have it" (Mk 14:34-36).
> My God, my God, why have you deserted me?" (Mk 15:34).

In the midst of our own congregational chaos we have a choice: *either* we recognize our inner wasteland of confusion and anxiety, that is, we acknowledge our inner poverty and our corresponding need for God, *or* we fall victim to self-misery, despondency and/or denial, thus refusing the chance to experience the God-offered conversion. Christ himself, in his life and passion, is the exemplar of the inner journey into powerlessness or dispossession as the way to creative resurrection in the Father. He wholeheartedly accepts the experience of desertion, abandonment and crucifixion—salvation chaos—in order to embrace both humanity and God.[20] He entered our wasteland of confusion to lead us out of our confusion; he truly became, in Eliot's language, the "empty man," not the "hollow man," that he might express solidarity with us: "His state was divine, yet he did not cling to his equality with God but *emptied* himself to assume the condition of a slave. . . . But God raised him on high" (Phil 2:6-9).

The suffering, dispossessing and rising Christ is the regeneration myth of the human race. We *relive* this myth when we accept our total emptiness and absolute need of God. Only then are we open to hear what the Holy Spirit is asking of us. "Remember," writes St Paul, "how generous the Lord Jesus was; he was rich, but he became poor for your sake, to make you rich out of his poverty" (2 Cor 8:9). We cannot face our inner nothingness, if Christ had not first become poor; discernment then becomes a positive experience of discovery, for we become rich out of his poverty. Without Christ the inner journey into our own hollowness, as Eliot poignantly reminds us so well, can produce a sickening fear and desperation. It can lead to a madness.[21]

In brief, the way to refounding for superiors (and for all religious) is the way of dispossession—the entering into our inner chaos of confusion, attachments, hollowness—to find in faith that God is to be the absolute in our lives. We become totally open to him. We become "empty people," disposed to hear *him* speak. Conversion for discernment is a gift and must be prayed for with all the earnestness we can put into the task. Take the Old Testament, especially the penitential psalms. There we have a prayerful yearning for conversion emerging out of a deep sense of sin, suffering, inner chaos. There is the stab of conscience, the shame of inward dirtiness, intense sorrow for sin, and the feeling of being lost and alone. However, all these miseries are joined with prayers for mercy, forgiveness, and a chance to begin all over again:

> God, create a clean heart in me,
> put into me a new and constant spirit;
> do not banish me from your presence,
> do not deprive me of your holy spirit (Ps 51:10-11).

3. Placing the Refounding Persons

If refounding persons are discovered through discernment, the superior's task is officially to sponsor them, that is, make it structurally possible for them to use their God-given gifts for the best service of the Church and the congregation. The following guidelines may be helpful if the superior is to exercise his or her charism of administration wisely and courageously:

a. In fulfilling the duties of "sanctifying" and "ordering" the community, the superior must discern what prophetical ideas are to be put aside, at least for the time being, not because they are untrue, but "perhaps because they are too true, too holy, too abrupt and sudden for a profitable, mature, unifying and strengthening action within a community."[22] The superior is concerned that the prophetic person have the best possible impact on the community, and for this to occur it may be necessary to delay this or that aspect of the prophetic insights until the community is somewhat more at ease with the vision.

This guideline must not be taken as an encouragement for the superior to do nothing, but only to exercise supernatural prudence for the sake of the common good. Sheer willful stubbornness and jealousy on the part of members of the community do not, I believe, justify delaying any refounding project.

b. Do not underestimate the congregational cultural resistance to the prophetic project. Hence, "the new belongs elsewhere" axiom is to be applied.* That is, a prophetic project should not *normally* be placed in the midst of existing works, where prophetic people would be under constant critical assessment by members of the community and required to waste invaluable energy "apologizing" for what they are doing.

However, by way of exception to this guideline, refounding persons are to be placed in the recruitment and initial and on-going formation programs, for it is in these areas that such people can have a significant impact in inculcating values that are crucial for congregational revitalization.

c. Discern with the congregational prophets whom they consider to be minor refounding persons. Recall that these people do not have the primary refounding gift, but are to be the key project supporters of the refounding prophets.

d. Do not overburden refounding people with administrative duties, for they need to be free of all undue pressure to allow their creative imaginations to work. For this reason, I do not think that a provincial can normally be a major refounding person, for the former's task is already a full-time administratively absorbing commitment. I envisage that a superior general can have the charism, because his or her task in the post-Vatican II Church most often involves few time-consuming administrative responsibilities.[23]

e. Don't expect of refounding persons many details of what they propose to do and why. They won't know. They have a vision and a plan for implementation, but the details of the plan often need to be worked out as the project proceeds. Superiors with problem-solving qualities, e.g. concern for logical, detailed and rational planning, must take very careful note of this guideline. And the superiors need to protect congregational prophets from over-demanding implementers in the congregation who may wish to be consulted on every detail of the refounding persons' project and who may wrongly consider themselves to have at least minor refounding gifts.

f. Allow refounding persons to develop informal support systems in or outside the congregation, i.e. these people will feel the urgent need to share and test their insights with people they feel they can trust and whose diverse disciplinary skills challenge them to think carefully through their plans for action. If the congregation is small, they are unlikely to find within it the wide range of backgrounds and interest they so need. If the

*See above, Chapter 2, p. 40.

congregation also happens to be overly relational in its community life, it will be too inward-looking and threatened to be of much stimulating support to refounding people.

Action in the Long Term

"Where there is no vision the people get out of hand" (Prv 29:18)

If, in the long term, superiors are not working to build congregational cultures based on values supportive of refounding people with their challenging ideas and actions, then I strongly suspect that there is little hope for the future of the congregation. Our basic assumption is that individuals must not be so fettered by a culture of controls, so mired in a cake of custom, so handicapped by an ethos of negativism, envy, intolerance, and poverty of apostolic opportunity, that they do not feel free to react to changing conditions with innovative Gospel strategies of evangelization. Nor are creative candidates attracted to join a culture unsupportive of innovation.

Superiors must act at two levels to build a congregational culture that is supportive of on-going creativity and innovation: at the structural and attitudinal levels, the latter being far more difficult than the former.

1. Facilitating Structural Change

There are three categories of structural change that should usually be the responsibility of superiors and/or the appropriate chapters:

a. Remove Burdensome Structures

There are structural changes to be made within existing apostolates in order to remove excessively burdensome administrative obligations from religious, thus freeing them for personal and apostolic creative action. These are structures that can *only* be removed by superiors and/or chapters.

Example

> A highly qualified formator was given charge of a large number of candidates and told to reform their religious life formation, as well as the overall academic and financial structures of the huge institution. The major superior complained from time to time that what she had asked for was not being done

with the speed she desired. Within a short period of time the formator suffered severe burnout and had to be withdrawn. Her major superior commented: "I wrongly thought she was a refounding person. She had not the strength for it." In fact, the major superior had asked this formator to do what the former alone could and should have done, namely, reform the financial and academic structures by appointing people skilled in those tasks, leaving the formator with the onerous duty of formation alone.

Regretfully I see far too many examples of this kind—the repeated overburdening of capable persons, and the impossible is expected of them with superiors refusing to take the responsibility for what they alone have the authority to do. This practice of demanding more and more work from skilled people is gravely unjust to them and effectively stops them from contributing to the refounding process. If major superiors consistently do this, the matter is so serious that provincial chapters should either "censure" them for neglecting their duties, or, through their own authority, introduce restructuring processes to free creative and innovative religious from the impossible burdens asked of them. In the case given above, neither the provincial chapter nor the superior general and her council, who knew what was happening, intervened when in fact one or the other should have done so.

b. Systematic Abandonment of the Irrelevant

To help develop a future-oriented thrust within the congregation there needs to be the systematic abandonment of what is apostolically irrelevant. The aim is to remove resources from present unnecessary activities in order that they can be made available to support the re-founding process. The following criteria for assessing whether or not an apostolate is relevant may be helpful:

- Is it responding to urgent pastoral needs?
- Does it reflect the faith/justice priority of the Church's mission?
- Does it allow for creative pastoral action?
- Is it in accord with the congregation's charism?
- If the apostolate is irrelevant, are the personnel capable of being assigned to more urgent pastoral tasks?

The process of withdrawal from an established apostolate can be an intensely painful one, but it must be done if the project no longer fits the criteria. Too often congregations withdraw resources simply because they are finally pressured by events to do so. Superiors act creatively if they encourage a discernment process within an apostolate while the personnel involved are able to make a responsible decision unpressured by events.

c. Initial Formation Structures for Creativity

Superiors have the authority to establish formation structures and programs, under the direction of suitably chosen and professionally trained formators, that can foster over time positive value changes within the congregation.

This also means insisting on adequate screening of candidates. When congregations are struggling to survive, the temptation is to weaken the requirements for admission into the congregation in order to raise the number of entrants. This is a dangerous short-sighted policy and can be *gravely* unjust to the candidates, to the formators who must eventually spend long periods of precious time discouraging those who are unfit for religious life, to the congregation and to the Church.

The stark reality is that you decide, in a large part, on the quality of your congregational culture by the type of people you recruit. If a superior wants candidates who have above average needs for security and affirmation, low tolerance for ambiguity, little creative potential, then he or she is building a congregation that will *not* reproduce in the future a culture supportive of on-going refounding. The superior is fostering congregational suicide! If the congregation wishes to be creative, it recruits candidates with innovative potential, or else it does not recruit at all. The truth is: a congregation exists first and foremost not for its own survival, but for the mission of Christ and the service of the Church. And the criteria for this purpose are set by Christ and his Church.

d. Establishment of International Teams

Historically, international apostolic teams of the same congregation have encouraged vigorous creativity pastorally and in religious life itself. Raymond Hostie notes that "Cistercians, Norbetines, Dominicans, Carmelites, Jesuits and Piarists, all emerged from groups whose members belonged to three nationalities, even four or five. . . . Heterogeneity is a necessary condition for activating effective fermentation."[24]

Four conditions must be met if creativity is to emerge from within an international group.[25] First, those invited to join the teams must be capable of living internationally and of developing teamwork. Not *everyone* has the ability to live and work in an international team; there can be heavy demands on the psychological and spiritual resources of individuals as they are called on to face up to the requirements of constant adaptation to new cultural pressures, both from within the team itself and from the country where they work.

Second, members of teams must be given adequate spiritual and human preparation in order that they can fit into challenging international and intercultural situations. Members need the chance to deepen, preferably together, their grasp of the founding mythology of the congregation. They need linguistic skills, but also an awareness of key anthropological conclusions into the nature and power of culture, culture change, and the role of foreign catalysts in culture change. In their training programs members will need to have adequate periods of living in cultures very different from their own. They will need to experience the shock of being "at sea" in a culture that is unfamiliar to them; they will need to discover for themselves the richness of being humble and dependent on other people whose culture they do not know or understand. Their own cultural biases and prejudices will need to be challenged; otherwise an insidious ethnocentrism will govern their relations with other team members and the people they hope to serve pastorally.

Third, in the structuring of an international team, as far as is possible, no one culture should predominate. If one cultural group does predominate, it is likely to over-influence attitudes and policies of the group. If a culturally balanced team is impossible, the predominant cultural group must be especially sensitive to avoid obstructing the emergence of creative supranationalism in the team. By *supranationalism* I mean the ability and the willingness of individuals or groups to strive to identify with cultures and needs *beyond* the frontiers of their own country's culture in ways that are both critical and non-exclusive. This identification with cultures is not blind or uncritical, for the weaknesses, as well as the strengths, of cultures are recognized. The identification is not exclusive. That is, supranationalists are open to still other cultures beyond those with which they are immediately concerned. As the world is fractured by ideological conflicts, pathological forms of nationalism and intercultural tensions, it is "groaning in travail" (Rom 8:22), desperately in need of reconciliation across and within national frontiers.[26] Inasmuch as many religious orders are stamped with an international character, the Church rightly expects of them bold religious life and evangelical initiatives in response to today's critical need for supranationalism, and international teams with the right qualities are able to do this.

Fourth, it is wise to keep the numbers of team members and of the teams themselves small, e.g. three or four teams of three members each, within the country where they are working. Any larger and the tendency will be for the teams to unite into a self-contained, security-forming group. The sense of urgency to keep going out to people within the culture in which they are working may well be reduced if the numbers are any greater. Similarly, if the group is any larger it might tend to an overpowering force hindering the personal growth possibilities of recruits from the local culture.[27]

2. Facilitating Attitudinal Change

In their role as facilitators of attitudinal change, superiors have two aims: to help people to become less obstructive of creative change agents or refounding people and to encourage within religious an openness to use whatever talents they have in the service of the Church.

a. Calling Religious to Conversion

This is a priority, and possibly the hardest task of the superior: the call to individual and corporate conversion. It requires considerable spiritual sensitivity if the calls are to be made on the most effective occasions. In times of congregational chaos, superiors are apt to feel inadequate for the task of spiritual animation. I am personally convinced that many religious today are yearning to be led and to be spiritually challenged. All we need is a little courage, humility and trust in God. The following practical suggestions may help.

b. Visitations/"Rites of Passage"

My impression is that the superiors either themselves or through their delegates are often embarrassed about annual visitations of their religious. One said to me: "I just do not know what to do or say, so I keep to generalities and only see them briefly." I think many superiors avoid visitations entirely because they do not know what to do. A notice like the following might appear on the community board: "The provincial is here for a few days only. He is available if needed." The notice is equivalently saying: "I have to be here and will see you if you absolutely need to. Otherwise, keep away!" Not at all encouraging! Sadly, an important pastoral chance to call one's brothers and sisters closer to Christ and to the process of refounding is being missed.

What should the superior, or his or her delegates, do on visitation? First, arrange appointments with *all*, so that individuals feel they have a right to see you and you have the obligation to meet with them. Second, I do not think there is much that the superior need say—in fact the less the better! The superior's primary skill is positively to *listen*, to challenge and question.

While it is not the task of the superior to inquire into the inner spiritual life of the religious or to pressure him or her to do so in any way, unless the constitutions of the congregation (supported by Canon Law) require it, the superior should feel free, for example, to invite religious to share how they see their own life in relation to the institute's charism, gently challenge them to creative action and the support of refounding persons, and possibly invite them for a period of spiritual renewal. Since we religious are hesitant to praise or thank one another, the superior should make a point to thank the religious for some creative apostolic action—however small it might be—over the past year.

By "rites of passage" I mean such experiences as grave personal sickness or suffering, retirement or sad bereavements. People are especially vulnerable to pastoral care at such points, but superiors can again avoid them if they do not know how to handle these potentially creative experiences.

Example

Brother X, who has serious cancer, is expecting that his superior will be able to offer him some much-needed spiritual counseling. But the superior, though sensing the need, does not know what to do. He visits regularly and talks at the patient with a false cheerfulness: "Don't worry; you will get better quickly! Now, this is the latest news about the school we are building . . ." and so on. Brother X is grateful when the superior finally leaves, for it is exhausting being talked at! The superior cannot relate to the sick person simply because he personally has refused thus far the call of the Lord to "pass through the gloomy valley" to discover truly that "Yahweh is (his) shepherd" (Ps 23: 4, 1).

Brother X does finally experience a deep reconversion through the pastoral care of a religious sister, who had in her own life rediscovered the compassionate mercy of God in a time of great personal suffering and darkness. He recovers and is now a highly successful provincial in animating his province to renewal and refounding. However, he is not a good maintenance administrator, as was his former provincial superior, but no one particularly worries about this, for he appointed others to take care of that side of administration.

---

c. Provide Space for Religious To Discover Themselves

There are many ways through which this can be done, depending on the willingness of the religious themselves, e.g. in directed retreats individuals are confronted personally to face their own inner selves; or pastoral exposure programs, in a culture dramatically different from one's own, may be helpful in uncovering one's own spiritual and human inade-quacies.[28] If religious show any personal interest in writing or reading poetry, in art or music, give them every possible encouragement. If religious are encouraged to use their imagination in these or other such ways, then they are likely to be not only more relaxed, but disposed to be creative and innovative in their vocational lives.

In a survey I conducted of one clerical religious province, two thirds of the superiors, and over fifty percent of the remaining religious, com-plain that the members of their communities "watch far too much televi-sion." I was not surprised, because for several generations the initial and on-going formation programs of the province had discouraged religious from pursuing hobbies or developing an appreciation of the arts. I am certain that this is a significant factor behind the viewing of "far too much television" and the emergence of an admitted boredom and dull-ness in their communities.

d. Training Professional Critical Observers

The role of a social scientist, e.g. cultural anthropologist, social psy-chologist, is to articulate a people's hidden attitudes, prejudices or pat-terns in change. He or she can help a group ask difficult and awkward questions about themselves, e.g. about the relevance of this or that apos-tolate, about their denial of chaos, their failure to confront injustices within their cultures. If these culture critics have a strong faith dimen-sion, then they have the ability of helping religious to acknowledge the existence of chaos and the need for the refounding process.[29]

Superiors, however, need to release suitable individuals for this ser-vice to their own institute and other interested congregations, have them trained to *full* professional standards in specialized areas, e.g. the sociol-ogy of religious life, social justice education, and then support them in what can be a demanding and lonely apostolate.

e. Foster the Discernment Process in Decision-Making

It takes faith and spiritual courage to confront chaos. A discernment process, as we have seen, helps to foster the faith and courage needed. The process is not a substitute for research discussion or debate, but it allows space for people to ponder the material in an atmosphere of faith.

If superiors encourage the process in their own work, then others may themselves become more comfortable with it and be prepared to use it for chapters, key meetings in the province and even in their own per-sonal lives. Thus, over time the congregation will become more open to reflect in faith on what hinders pastoral creativity and refounding.

f. Informal Brainstorming

Congregations have many formal avenues for people to be consulted or to participate in decision-making, e.g. councils of superiors, chapters. Often, however, such groups do not reach religious who are really creative thinkers or innovators, but who have been marginalized to the boundaries of the congregation through no fault of their own. Superiors would do well at times to call these people informally together in groups. This is a method to tap creative ideas, to support creative people and symbolically to educate the province as to what the congregation's value system or priorities should be.

g. Use Symbols and Tell Stories about Innovative Actions

Recall that people communicate primarily through symbols and myths (that is, narrative symbols or stories). Statistical reports and surveys of provinces are valuable educational instruments, but ultimately the use of symbols and stories is the major power force in aiding people to grasp what is really important to any group. Jesus used this technique of story telling in parable form; so have countless writers down through the centuries, e.g. Shakespeare, Lewis Carroll (*Alice in Wonderland*), Jonathan Swift (*Gulliver's Travels*). The messages they sought to convey remain ever fresh because of the event or story style through which they were conveyed. And I agree with the insight of Tom Peters: "The best leaders, especially in chaotic conditions (effective generals, leaders of revolutions), almost without exception and at every level, are master users of stories and symbols."[30]

Major superiors do not need to be a Swift, a Carroll or a Douglas MacArthur to use this effective technique of communication. If they really believe in the importance of apostolic creativity, then they will collect incidents *no matter how small* in which religious of their province(s) are shown to be pastorally innovative. And they will devise ways to relate these stories, e.g. through regular newsletters, at celebration rites in honor of religious. Religious will hear, and be more likely to remember, what the theory about pastoral innovation means the more they hear or read from the provincial about actual incidents of apostolic creativity.

Example

Religious in one section of a Third World nation are vigorously involved in large-scale socio-economic development programs, which are heavily dependent on outside financial aid. Because

of the size of the programs and the over-dependence on outside help, the projects frequently fail, but the major superior
makes no reference to the failures in his letters to the province
and falsely gives the impression that all is well.

He suddenly discovers that development programs in that
part of the country *must* be small and involve the people at all
stages. He finds a religious sister in the same region, whom
others either did not know or considered useless because she
conducted a very low-key and locally financed home-craft
project for girls. Recognizing that she understood the true
nature of development, he regularly wrote about her work in
his newsletter to his province, providing very human incidents of the long-term success of her work, e.g. the growth in
self-confidence of the girls through the discovery of their own
abilities to create from material around them.

The story contained powerful symbols of what innovative apostolic development should mean in that part of the country:
small, maximum participation of the people at all stages, minimal dependence—if any—on outside aid.

Hence, here is a practical exercise for major superiors: Do I in my
communication with my province or congregation present symbols and
stories of creative apostolic life? If not, what can I do immediately to
remedy my neglect?

Summary

Refounding is not a search for an increase in vocations. That may happen, but it is primarily a question of the revitalization of Gospel quality
living. We need prophetic, refounding persons to lead us through this
process of revitalization; God may or may not give us such people.

My hunch is that many brilliant, creative and innovative ideas of potential refounding persons do not just fade away; instead they are crushed
to death by highly analytical, logical and rational problem-solving major
superiors and by their administrations over-burdened by the demands of
maintenance.

Superiors, especially major superiors, have a critical role in preventing this happening. Their primary duty is to discern the presence of
these congregational prophets, how best they should be used for the
good of the Church and the congregation, and then support them in the

fulfilment of their vocation. This demands of superiors at times considerable risk and courage.

It is an adventure of faith requiring nothing less than a 180-degree
shift in the way superiors, and their councils, see their present congregational chaos and how best to get out of it. This requires a ceaseless attack
on one's own misguided attachments and inner darkness; otherwise
there can be no discernment. Then the power of this prayer of the
psalmist will have meaning for superiors:

> Put your hope in Yahweh,
> be strong,
> let your heart be bold,
> put your hope in Yahweh (Ps 27:14).

They will then experience the thrill of being helped out of chaos by the
Lord:

> I waited and waited for Yahweh;
> now at last he has stooped to me
> and heard my cry for help.
> He has pulled me out of the horrible pit,
> out of the slough of the marsh (Ps 40:1-2).

Chapter 7

Chaos and Denial: Facilitating and Obstructing the Refounding Person

"Listen! Imagine a sower going out to sow. . . . Some seed fell on rocky ground where it found little soil and sprang up straight away, because there was no depth of earth; and when the sun came up it was scorched. . . . Some seed fell into thorns, and the thorns grew up and choked it. . . . And some seeds fell into rich soil and, growing tall and strong, produced crop; and yielded thirty, sixty, even a hundredfold."

(Mk 4:3–8)

In previous chapters I have explained the roles of the congregational prophets and their superiors in the process of refounding. In this chapter I will concentrate on congregational cultures, that is, on aspects that aid the refounding process, but *particularly* on values and customs that "scorch" or "choke" refounding persons and stop them from fulfilling their vocation. In this I follow the example of Jesus himself who often described and even condemned people and their cultures, e.g. the Pharisees (Mt 23:1–36), because they cultivated values and customs that deafened them to his prophetic words, thus encouraging them to continue to deny their own inner chaos and need of his salvation. And so we have the dramatically presented parables like the seed that falls upon different kinds of ground (or culture) (Mk 4:3–8), the wicked vine-growers (Mk 12:1–12), the unmerciful servant (Mt 18:23–35), the guest without a wedding-garment (Mt 22:11–14), the foolish virgins (Mt 25:1–13), and the good Samaritan (Lk 10:30–37).

Refounding persons are the right people, in the right places, at the right time. They are the "right people" because they have the qualities required for leading a congregation out of chaos. They are in the "right places" because they receive within the congregational culture or "soil" at least minimum support from superiors and others; that is, the culture is sufficiently open or free from denial to hear the call of the refounding person. The time is "right" because the pastoral needs of people in a changing world require the vision, ideas, and processes envisioned by the prophet.

In this chapter I will:

- describe four models of culture and why some are more or less open to agents of change than others;
- clarify two variables: power and obedience;
- apply the models and variables to the analysis of congregational cultures.

Models of Cultures: Insights of Mary Douglas

Readers may wish, before studying this chapter, to read again Chapter 1 on the nature of culture and how the human person fears chaos or the loss of meaning, because here I wish to expand in more depth points raised there.

Mary Douglas, a leading figure in symbolic and anthropological approach to religious ritual and belief, looks at culture from the viewpoint of everyday life: food, bodies, jokes, dirt, material possessions, and speech. She sees that the human body is used to symbolize the body politic, the social structure. Powers and dangers are concentrated on the margins of society—in the anomalous, the marginal, whatever threatens us with chaos or meaninglessness. And reflecting social fears and dangers, it is the bodily orifices and substances, e.g. excreta, blood, nail clippings, hair, that threaten and pollute individuals and society. "The social body constrains," she writes, "the way the physical body is perceived. . . . The more the social situation exerts pressure on persons involved in it, the more the social demand for conformity tends to be expressed by a demand for physical control."[1] That which threatens conformity is considered socially polluting.

An analysis of Soviet ritual illustrates her insight. So great is the control over the body and dislike of most body processes that the first impression is of body symbolism being non-existent in Russian ritual. But, as one specialist in Russian society notes, only body movement resulting from loose control—wild or ecstatic movement, organic processes, trance, unconventional appearance—is excluded from ritual. Body movement which expresses very careful control and precise coordination in the movement of a number of human bodies, in contrast, is especially valued and frequently presented for public display and involvement, e.g. mass military parades.[2]

"Dirt," for Douglas, is a highly significant pointer to how people see their culture and those people who threaten it in any way. Dirt is matter out of place, or, in other words, that which is dirty, unclean or deviant, is that which does not fit into its appropriate category. For us Westerners, shoes are not dirty in themselves, but it is dirty to put them on the supper table. If we put them on the table, we feel in some way or other that the table has been polluted; we have broken our cherished classification that shoes belong on the floor, for they are "clean" there. Food is not thought to be dirty in itself, but it is certainly dirty to place cooking utensils in the bedroom. The fact that shoes *should* be on the floor and not on the table, or that pots and kettles should not be in the bedroom, means that what is dirty or clean is defined not just cognitively but morally. It is a question of right and wrong.[3]

Finally, ritual has a critical role in the maintenance or changing of social relations. "Ritual," she writes, "is pre-eminently a form of communication . . . (Ritual) forms, like speech forms, (are) transmitters of culture, which are generated in social relations and which, by their selections and emphases, exercise a constraining effect on social behavior."[4] Friendship with a distant friend cannot be maintained without such rituals as letters of sympathy, telegrams of congratulations, or the occasional newsy letter.[5] The rituals she has in mind are so often of the simplest kind, e.g. cleaning, tidying the house or the desk, placing shoes where they should belong. Individuals, for example, who dare to break rigid dress codes in Russia or similar highly structured cultures risk ritual expulsion to the margins of society.[6] Court trials and imprisonment of such people are "tidying up" operations. Order is restored and chaos once more averted.

To understand change, or resistance to change, in rite, symbol, and myth, Douglas has developed a typology that permits her to examine social relations analytically in any social context.[7] In her formulation of the typology, Douglas uses two variables, "group" and "grid." The "group" variable connotes the degree to which people are restricted in their social relations by their commitment to a social unit bigger than the individual. Restriction is low when people are able to negotiate their way through life on their own initiative as individuals, neither restricted by nor dependent on a single group of other people. Group strength is highest when individuals give considerable time to relating to others in the social unit to which they must give allegiance and which they depend on for support.

The "grid" is the set of rules that relate one person to others on a ego-centered basis. The rules establish restrictions on *how* people interact rather than with whom; for example, they may interact on the basis of ascribed status, e.g. hierarchical roles, or on the principle of equality of human persons. Grid is strong whenever roles are established according to explicit social classifications and low when ascribed status roles are very unimportant.

With these variables, Douglas constructs the following four models of culture, which I will then adapt to religious congregations: (See figure 7.1)

1. Strong Group and Strong Grid Culture

In this model, change takes place *extremely* slowly. Intense loyalty to the group and the grid (traditional symbols and structures) is expected, and rituals that celebrate and reinforce identity and unity are of fundamental importance. There are built-in mechanisms that force a reforming person, who dares to question the group's interpretation of the founding myth, to conform to the status quo, or, if that fails, to be ritually marginalized as something "dirty" or "polluting" from the group into some harmless position.

This model is helpful for the understanding of many behavior patterns in the pre-Vatican II Church. Boundaries were extremely clear, for Catholics were defined in opposition to Protestants, who were seen as threatening the body of Christ. Internal administrative structures and statuses were rigidly hierarchical and unchanging; rituals were highly formal and impersonal, often reinforcing a sense of spiritual elitism.

2. Strong Group and Weak Grid

Here group awareness is strong, but since the internal system (i.e. grid) of behavior patterns is weak, the individual is able to reflect on, and be critical of, the internal structures of that culture. There is considerable concern, however, to guard the boundaries of the culture. Questioning the values that give the group its identity is not permitted, so whereas the group often tolerates remarkable individualism, any behavior that threatens group identity is forbidden. Whoever questions the group's boundaries or identity is branded a "defector," a "traitor." Relevant action is taken to control or expel such people.

Douglas, as we have explained, sees ritual as creating order by marking the margins that divide the pure from the impure; that which is impure is polluting and dangerous and must be kept at bay. The degree to which a person is anxious about bodily pollution depends on the degree to which the group is worried about penetration of its social boundaries. Accordingly, a minority group, the Israelites, felt its bound-

	Strong Group & Strong Grid	Strong Group & Weak Grid
Orientation	Maintenance	Maintenance
Power	Unilateral & Position Power in Group and Grid	Unilateral & Position Power in Group
Obedience	To Group and Grid	To Group
Provincial	Position Power Strong	Personal Power in Grid and Position Power in Group
Innovation	Potential Poor	Potential Good

	Weak Group & Weak Grid	Weak Group & Strong Grid
Orientation	Considerable Mission Potential	Very Good Mission Potential
Power	Weak in Group and Grid	Position Power in Grid
Obedience	To Personal Insights/ Feelings	To Grid
Provincial	Personal Power	Position Power in Grid and Personal in Group
Innovation	Potential Considerable	Potential Very Good

Figure 7.1 Typology: Innovation Potential in Provinces/Congregations

aries endangered and thus designed the elaborate levitical taboos to prevent the margins of the body from being contaminated by polluting substances.[8]

3. Strong Grid and Weak Group

Here people are individualistic, but less so than in the previous model. A society is divided up into segments for a variety of reasons, but these segments are not permanently divided, since they are united at other levels to form new and more inclusive segments when certain common needs require this. Total unity is fragile and, like all levels of unity at any stage in the society, it disintegrates once the reason for the unity disappears.

In brief, there are factors within the society that encourage people to form opposing groups, but there are counterbalancing factors that draw people in these groups together at other levels. Suspicion or potential/actual conflict or feuds divide the segments and are put aside only when common needs demand unity for survival. A feud can be defined as relations of mutual animosity among intimate groups in which a resort to physical or verbal violence is anticipated on both sides.[9] Past injustices or misunderstandings are recalled to remind all concerned that the "out-group" simply cannot be trusted to work with the "in-group."

There may be an official leader in such a society, but the real power rests in the various segments, the lowest segment having the most power over its members. Skilled leaders may be able to hold segments into an effective unity for a period of time, but the unity is apt to break down once its need disappears or a more powerful political manipulator wins the temporary allegiance of the segments. Oft-repeated rhetoric supportive of total unity is apt to so confuse the observer that it is thought that real unity exists, when, in fact, such is far from being the case. Finally, since group boundaries are fluid and group pressures minimal, the concept of pollution is rarely present, that is, charges of disloyalty tend to be leveled only against those who attempt to break from within the smallest segments in the society.

In Papua New Guinea, for example, there are no chiefs by birth. People become leaders, agents of change, by manipulating support from a variety of disparate groups. They remain powerful only as long as they can continue to respond to the self-interests of the supporting segments. The contemporary Filipino society resembles this model also. It is a highly fragmented, plural society, divided between uplander and lowlander, rich and poor, leftists and rightists, Christian and Muslim, between those of one ethnic, linguistic, or geographic region and those of another. It readily splits into many opposed segments once common self-interests or a more powerful force is removed. Within the United States there is a noticeable bias in favor of this model, a point made recently by sociologist Robert Bellah and others. Americans, it is claimed, favor the need for individual freedom so much that they have difficulty making and sustaining their commitment or loyalty to the group.[10]

4. Weak Group and Weak Grid

In this model people are even more individualistic than those in previous models. Neither society nor social networks have much control over individuals. The cult of individual self-fulfillment is popular, since there are no particular obligations of any sustained nature to society. Society exists to satisfy my personal needs; relationships with other people are thus very fluid. An unstable hippie culture of the late 1960s is an example of this model.[11]

From the point of view of the innovator or pathfinder, this type of culture is particularly favorable. Negative pressures, either from the group or network of internal structures, are minimal. It comes close to the chaos that was described in Chapter 1. Provided individuals have become sufficiently dissatisfied with their lack of belonging and identity, there is growing potential here for a leader to articulate a vision for a new cultural integration or an attempted return to some assumed former golden age, e.g. as is the case with the Lefevre movement.

Further Classifications: Power, Obedience and Mission

Leadership is the process of influencing the action of an individual or a group in an effort to achieve a goal in a given situation. Leadership is an effort to influence, but power is a leader's *potential* to influence. Power allows a leader to encourage others to obey or to have some sway over them.[12] Of the many types of power three major kinds are helpful in this analysis. First, *position* power is power that is derived from the position one has within an organization or culture, e.g. the United States President has position power derived from the office as legitimized in the Constitution. There are various kinds of position power, e.g. *coercive*, because people are forced to act out of fear of punishment, *reward*, because the person who has the power is able to hand out or hold back benefits depending on whether or not people do what is asked of them.

The second broad category of power is termed *personal*. This is the ability to influence because of the personal gifts that the leader may have, e.g. *expert* power is the ability to influence because of one's skills at animating others, *information* power is derived from knowledge one possesses and others need, and *referent* power comes from one's attractive personal characteristics as a leader. A third, and important, distinction is between unilateral and reciprocal power. In *unilateral* power, the person or group refuses to receive influence from others; dialogue in these circumstances is impossible. In *reciprocal* power, individuals or groups are open, not only to giving but to receiving influence from others, e.g. ideas, experiences, compassion.

Love is at the heart of the power of God. For this reason, the power of Christ, our Savior, is not coercive, but personal and reciprocal: "Yes, God loved the world so much that he gave his only Son, so that everyone who believes in him may not be lost but may have eternal life" (Jn 3:16). He seeks to lead by a divine-human sharing, first within himself through the incarnation, then through his salvific act of redemption. He, who is marginalized by society and is crucified on a cross, is the very contradiction of the coercive power of the human oppressor and sinner. His complete self-giving "is the power of his arm" and through his power "he has pulled down princes from their thrones and exalted the lowly" (Lk 1:51-52)[13] He seeks to draw us to himself *freely* through his own powerlessness:

> Now sentence is being passed on this world;
> now the prince of this world is to be overthrown.
> And when I am lifted up from the earth,
> I shall draw all men to myself (Jn 12:31–32).

The more we are open to hear and respond to the needs of others, especially the poor, the more we become one in this powerlessness of Christ himself. We share then in his self-emptying power of leadership. Christ is for us religious, as he is for all Christians, the exemplar of how power is to be used, not through coercion but through love.

To obey means in biblical language "to hearken" to the expression of someone else's will, to respond to it and to comply with it. It always denotes a willingness to listen and to do what other people say, as in the case of Mary, who listened to the angel of the Lord. Her obedience involved questioning, listening, and acting in faith. Christ fulfills the mission given him by the Father by repeatedly listening to him, reflecting and acting: "Take this cup away from me. But let it be as you, not I, would have it" (Mk 14:36).

Every religious community, in a spirit of loving discipleship, binds itself to be obedient to God, that is, to searching and listening to him in order to discover his will through reflection on the Gospels, constitutions, the needs of the poor, their superiors' requests. When a religious community fails to listen and act, because it places barriers to Christ's love as expressed through the Holy Spirit, then there is disobedience to the Father.

Models of Religious Provinces

The following models are based on the above anthropological analysis and the concepts of power and obedience to mission described above. (See figure 7.1) They are models of religious provinces, but with relevant modifications they apply to individual communities within provinces or to an entire religious congregation. Anthropological models exist to facilitate our understanding of complex realities, and they contain emphases or trends only. Details are omitted. In reality it can happen that, while one model predominates, there are indications that aspects of other models are also present but as yet are not strong enough to "threaten" its continuance.

1. Province: Strong Group and Strong Grid

This province is maintenance-oriented. There are strong pressures from the group and the grid to maintain the status quo with its symbols and apostolates. People deny that the pastoral needs of people are changing dramatically or that the founding myth of the congregation has anything new to say about the need for reflective and critical pastoral listening. At important gatherings of the province, e.g. chapters, the values that support the status quo are ritually re-expressed and re-inforced in speeches, in legislation or in the type of congregational culture hero who is praised.

The province is especially opposed to refounding persons. Either people see no need for them, or they are considered highly threatening to the status quo and so their "polluting" influence is ritually neutralized, e.g. through social or geographical marginalization such as an appointment to a distant community or even to another more accepting province "on special assignment." Those outside the province, e.g. bishops or general administration officers, who raise questions about the pastoral relevance of the status quo are either carefully prevented from airing their views in public, or are severely castigated for daring to criticize "with so little knowledge of the situation."

Power is unilateral inasmuch as the province refuses to listen to what God might be saying through lay people, bishops, general administrators and the founding myth of the congregation. Power is also coercive and manipulative, for individuals are forced to comply with the status quo and do not feel free to question in public what is happening. If they dare to do so, they are likely to be marginalized in one way or another. Religious obedience is interpreted as submission to the group's traditions; the wider ecclesial dimension of obedience is ignored.

Because this is a hierarchically structured province, with its emphasis on clearly defined statuses and roles, community life and interpersonal relations are impersonal and formal. Communities are not intellectually stimulating since religious are not encouraged to read or study anything that might threaten the status quo.

The provincial, who is chosen for his or her analytical problem-solving skills, is aware that power lies in the group's boundaries and the apostolic grid, and so reinforces the continuance of this power. This is done through the use of position power to appoint "safe" people to key positions and marginalize those who threaten the status quo. Candidates are recruited, provided they have the qualities to maintain the province's traditions, and their formation is controlled by the provincial by giving them only formators who will reinforce the traditions.

Of the four models, this is the most resistant to change. Only a sudden disaster, e.g. a dramatic and sustained drop in vocations or the withdrawal from religious life of significant people in the province, seems capable of loosening the power of the congregational culture so that religious are confronted with the effects of their own long-hidden denial. Congregations that approximate to this model are less evident now in Western nations, but they do continue to flourish in many Third World countries.

If perchance a mission-oriented provincial is chosen to lead such a province, despite the pressures that would be against him or her, there are significant things that can be achieved in favor of mission. Through the use of personal and position power he or she is able to place mission-oriented religious into key positions; initial formation programs can be opened to ecclesial influences and pastoral needs. Religious communities are able to be exposed to information and workshops that may challenge them to listen to what God is saying. To be effective the provincial would need to work slowly, for a vigorous reactionary movement could easily swing against his or her efforts, thus undermining what is being attempted.

2. Province: Strong Group and Weak Grid

This province also is maintenance or status-quo oriented. Group pressure to maintain a sense of belonging to the province is high, far more so than to the wider congregation. However, as the grid is weak, that is, there is little obligation for religious to relate to one another within the province or even to live in community, individualism is very strong.

Members of the province enjoy being together on occasions, e.g. for recreational activities. They may even assume that this coming together indicates a vigorous community life, but in fact the commitment stops there; there is no move to develop apostolic team life based on ecclesial or religious life needs. In a survey of three hundred missionaries I found that seventy-eight percent claimed they had a sense of belonging to their province, but few lived in community even though circumstances had so changed that a number could have done so. Not surprisingly sixty-seven percent felt that individualism interfered with the emergence of apostolic team work; seventy-five percent admitted that they had become so used to living alone and experiencing their own independence that they would find it impossible to now live in community.

As in the previous model, potential refounding persons are considered threats to the status quo, that is, to the continuation of a thriving individualism and a notable lack of religious life accountability. Power rests within the boundaries, and consequently obedience is interpreted as being loyal to the group's identity, not to God speaking through the pastoral needs of people, ecclesial or religious life superiors.

In this model the maintenance-oriented provincial lacks an effective position power; only with extreme difficulty can the provincial move religious from one apostolate to another. It is accepted that the group has coercive power, because it demands that the status quo be maintained. The provincial can be likened to a club captain, organizing recreational or social events and attending necessary group rituals, e.g. anniversaries, funerals. Using whatever small residual position power remains, the provincial is expected merely to reinforce the status quo.

Potential for innovation in this model is good, because at least strong coercive power is confined only to the group and not also to the grid. A mission-oriented provincial may discover one or two refounding persons in the province and encourage them to form new religious life communities and/or apostolic teams based on the charism of the congregation and the pastoral needs of the ecclesial community. The provincial will also invite willing religious to undertake periods of personal renewal and updating, hoping that over a period of time there will develop a group of reconverting religious increasingly open to question the status quo.

Following the survey of missionaries mentioned above, the provincial of the province initiated a vigorous program of personal renewal for the missionaries. At first, few accepted the offer, but as the years passed more and more admitted their need for renewal and were given time off. For example, a significant number participated in the Ignatian Spiritual Exercises and/or theological updating. I visited the province ten years after the survey had been completed to find a positive atmosphere, e.g. small communities and/or pastoral teams had been established in several parts of the province.

3. Province: Weak Group and Strong Grid

The province is maintenance-oriented and inward-looking, but it has very good potential for mission revitalization. The corporate identity of the province, or the sense of belonging to a group, is weak and the goals of the province are unclear. Its structure is segmentary, according to the pattern described above. It comprises traditional apostolates that operate as disparate, self-contained units, suspicious of one another's attempts to gain access to limited personnel or financial resources.

However, the segmentary apostolic units are prepared to form "alliances," or larger segments, within a province, in the face of a common danger. For example, at provincial chapters, when various apostolates feel that their existence is threatened, they form a common voting alliance to ensure their continuance. Once the threat to their existence is over, they return to their separate, self-contained identities and mutual suspicions.

Power lies in the grid, i.e. with the traditional apostolates or segments of the province. Obedience is interpreted primarily as loyalty to this or that apostolate, not to the province or the congregation as a whole. Would-be refounding persons, who dare to raise questions about the state of denial in the province, are condemned for their "dangerous disloyalty to this or that apostolate and for their disobedience to the traditions of the province" and consequently are marginalized, but with less vigor than that characterizing marginalization in previous models.

A maintenance-oriented provincial assumes the "club-master" role, so that the province is not challenged to listen and respond to changing pastoral needs of people. Personal care of individuals takes precedence over dealing with the corporate pastoral health and the future of the province. A mission-oriented provincial, however, will approach the task of being provincial in similar ways to his or her counterpart in the previous model. The provincial will use position power to appoint possible refounding persons to key positions in the province, e.g. initial and on-going formation programs, and personal power will be exercised to convince religious of the need for reconversion.

In a survey of a small province of one hundred and fifty clerical religious in the early 1970s, I found that the province approximated to this model. The religious denied chaos, for though they most optimistically felt that the province had a future, they were not at all certain what the goals of the province were and did not seem too interested in working together to define them. They strongly refused to accept the implications of the dramatic drop in new candidates. In chapter after chapter delegates claimed that all their apostolates were relevant and must be continued; they kept asking that each apostolate have assigned to it newly ordained personnel, completely ignoring the fact that there were few if any able to be appointed. Professionally their self-image was poor and there was a grave need for spiritual and theological renewal.

After the survey was completed, a succession of mission-oriented provincials exercised both their position and their personal powers to help the province face reality. Creative people were appointed as formators to initial formation programs and individuals were invited personally by the provincial to experience personal renewal and updating. I visited this province several years after the survey had ended and the atmosphere had radically changed, e.g. the issue of personal and corporate reconversion had moved into central focus for the province, the professional self-image of individuals had improved, the segmentary structure of the province had for the most part broken down.

This segmentary type of culture commonly characterizes entire congregations today which were in pre-Vatican II days administratively highly centralized. The official rhetoric of these congregations is often powerfully supranationalist, as in general chapter documents or mission statements, but the reality strongly contradicts this rhetoric. Internationalism exists inasmuch as some members live and work in foreign lands, such as missionaries and general administrators. There may be a growing interest in the Third World countries inspired by the congregation's call to be at the service of the poor, but the *really* operative force is the desire for vocations to keep the provinces and the congregation alive.

Loyalty in the congregation is first and foremost to the *province* to which one belongs, not to the congregation or its spirit. Whoever encourages congregational supranationalism would be thought of as a "traitor" to the province. Cooperation exists between the provinces and with the general administration only when it is absolutely necessary—and even then for the advantage primarily of the province. The general administration, for example, is able to staff congregation-wide programs, e.g. international mission projects, only through a process of *bargaining,* not dialogue. A province is prepared to release *difficult* personnel for such work, but not talented members, for the province's first obligation is to its own survival. At international meetings of the congregation, provinces look first to their own rights and their interests, not to those of the congregation.

Suspicion and feud-like behavior color the province's relations with the general administration and with other provinces. Stories of past interference and misunderstandings on the part of general officers are gleefully recounted in order to maintain in the province a distrust of "interfering outsiders."[14] Consequently, provinces that relate to the congregation according to this segmentary model make it particularly difficult for refounding persons at the general administration level to enter and challenge them to face their denial. According to this model the superior general and his councillors do not have position power to command provincials to act in a particular way, but they do have personal

powers of animation which with patience can over time be used effectively in the cause of refounding. For example, on visitations of the
provinces they are able to discover potential refounding persons, challenge them to action and support them as best they can.[15]

4. *Province: Weak Group and Weak Grid*

This province has considerable potential for listening to what God is
saying about new pastoral needs and the relevance of the congregational
charism, since there are few group and grid pressures that demand the
maintenance of the status quo and the consequent marginalization of
reformers. There is, however, a general breakdown of corporate identity
and the goals of the province's mission are confused. Members hold back
from committing themselves wholeheartedly to any apostolate, and there
is the tendency for religious to drift from one apostolate to another,
never quite settling down in any. In other words, the province is in an
advanced stage of chaos. Individualism and a cult of self-fulfillment are
strongly present, and obedience is defined in terms of primarily what "I
personally feel should be done for my needs."

The general atmosphere of chaos, with its breakdown of the power
of group and grid, is conducive to the emergence of prophetic congregational figures, who aim to redefine and articulate the goals of the
corporate body and establish new apostolic networks in light of these
goals. He or she struggles to introduce an understanding of obedience
to God in mission that is foreign to individualistic and inward-looking
religious. Very careful discernment is needed, however, on the part of
reformers in order to be sure that those who follow them are genuine
minor refounding persons. If religious join the ranks of refounding
persons primarily for their own personal security needs, then there will
be conflict between them and the outward-looking, mission-oriented
reformers.

Mission-oriented provincials will use whatever little position power
they have to appoint refounding persons to suitable positions and then
support them in the face of opposition. The provincials' major type of
power, however, will be personal. Religious will need to be counseled to
turn aside from denial and chaos by entering into reconversion processes
and updating programs. This person-to-person counseling on the part of
provincials will be demanding on time and energy, especially if religious
experience considerable personal brokenness as a result of the chaos or
collapse of province-wide traditions, structures and identity. Yet there is a
marked potential for revitalization in this atmosphere. Over a period of

time, if this process of reconversion succeeds, there should develop not just a growing support for the refounding of the province, but all kinds of presently undreamed-of radical ways of living out the Gospel.

Summary

Over years, each religious community develops its own culture that either restricts or facilitates refounding. Most often the culture restricts refounding. Of the four cultural models discussed here, the most obstructive to refounding activity is the strong-group and strong-grid model. Religious here are so enmeshed in the primacy and what they consider to be the unchanging legitimacy of their corporate identity and traditional apostolates that they become deaf to what God is saying to them about mission in the Gospels, in the changing pastoral needs of people and in the evaluations of their general administration visitors and local bishops. A refounding person must suffer intensely in this denial-ridden type of province, for their words and example fall on very rocky ground indeed. The other three models of religious life culture are in varying degrees more open to the task of refounding.

When Jesus was transfigured on Mount Tabor in the presence of Peter, James and John, Peter did a very human thing: moved by fear he wanted to deny that this extraordinary event was breaking into his ordered, meaningful or predictable world. So, he started to talk about totally irrelevant things, hoping no doubt "to make Jesus normal once more." The Father refused to be distracted by Peter's human silliness and demanded that Peter be attentive: "This is my Son, the Beloved. *Listen* to him" (Mk 9:7).

We religious can be so like Peter. We will do everything we can not to hear Jesus speaking to us, so we surround ourselves with all kinds of congregational cultural supports and anxiously deny, when challenged, that they distract us from listening to what Jesus is saying to us. Yet, if we are to enter into the refounding process, there must be a listening to what Jesus is saying about his mission through the Gospels, through the cries and sufferings of people "out there," through the insights of our founding figures and through the visionary plans of refounding persons. If we dare to listen in faith, we must risk an active response:

> Everyone who comes to me and listens to my words and acts on them. . . .
> He is like the man who when he built his house dug, and dug deep, and
> laid the foundations on rock; when the river was in flood it bore down on
> that house but could not shake it, it was so well built (Lk 6:46–48).

Chapter 8

Congregational Chapters and Refounding

"Without the Holy Spirit the most convincing dialectic has no power over the heart of man. Without him the most highly developed schemas resting on a truly sociological or psychological basis are quickly seen to be valueless."

Paul VII[1]

In the years immediately following Vatican II, religious congregations in a burst of euphoria and hope spent considerable time and energy preparing for, and then holding, lengthy general and provincial chapters of renewal. Somehow, we thought, these chapters would give us the revitalized vision and reform we needed.

However, though the much-needed structural changes in such areas as government came from these legislative gatherings, the overall renewal we expected from these chapters did not materialize—despite the mountains of preparatory papers, minutes of study groups and then, finally, the finely worded and inspiring documents (now most likely gathering dust in archives). Many religious today are skeptical, even cynical, of chapters and their latest expressions—new constitutions and the mission statement. Now questions like the following are being asked: Are our expectations of general and provincial chapters too high? Are there attitudes and procedural methods that hinder or facilitate the work of chapters? Why have many policies and decisions of chapters remained unimplemented? What is the relationship between chapters and refounding?

In the pages that follow I attempt to answer these questions, especially since chapters, if used correctly, *can* play a key role in the refounding process. I will concentrate particularly on general chapters, though my comments will apply with only minor adjustments to provincial chapters. In summary, I will:

- define the nature and aims of a general chapter;
- evaluate, in the light of faith and sociological criteria, various comments by participants in general chapters;

151

- explain the important role refounding persons have in implementing the policies of general chapters.

Aims of General Chapters

Ideally, a general chapter of an institute, having "supreme authority in accordance with the constitutions,"[2] should be "a sign of unity in charity," and should be "a moment of grace and of action of the Holy Spirit in an institute. It should be a joyful, paschal and ecclesial experience which benefits the institute itself and also the whole Church. The general chapter is meant to renew and protect the spiritual patrimony of the institute as well as elect the highest superior and councillors; conduct major matters and issue norms for the whole institute."[3] There are two key emphases in this description: the apostolic calls to witness here and now and to plan for the future of the congregation. I will set out briefly what each call means.

1. Apostolic Call To Witness:

- the chapter is to be a faith experience, a cooperative action of both the Holy Spirit and the participants.
- the chapter is to be to the Church and to the congregation a vivid community expression of Gospel charity and joy; communion will arise out of a process of personal and corporate conversion.

2. Apostolic Call To Plan

- calling the congregation to be accountable to the ideals of the Gospel and charism; praising creative apostolic initiatives and correcting aberrations since the last chapter;
- establishing policies that relate the congregation's charism, apostolic life, personnel and financial resources to the ever-changing pastoral needs of the people of God;
- electing the highest officer and his or her assistants, on the basis of their abilities, to lead/inspire the whole congregation to conversion, faith/justice mission and the implementation of the chapter's policies/decrees;
- calling participants to commit themselves to lead within the provinces in implementing the policies/decrees of the chapter.

The two calls are complementary. One must not exist without the other. If all the chapter does is to formulate policies for the coming years, it is no different than a board of directors of a corporate culture which meets to plan and choose its executive officers. If, on the other hand, participants believe that all they have to do is "pray and live in charity" and overlook the need to prepare theologically and in every way necessary in order to make sound religious life/pastoral policies, then they gravely misunderstand the incarnational role of the apostolic Christian and so of their congregation; they are running away from serious obligations, taking refuge in a false spirituality or supernaturalism. (See Lk 6:46–49)

General Chapters: Views of Participants

This twofold challenge to chapters is a noble one, but is it realized in practice? To help readers answer this question by reflecting on their own experience, I first list some evaluative comments of participants of several chapters held from 1971 to 1985 (though the statements are not listed in a chronological order), and then assess the comments in the light of the ideals for chapters set out above. Readers may feel sympathetic with one or several of the evaluations given.

A. *Comments of Participants:*

1. "No outward conflicts, but too much pressure for consensus in all things. The time for divisions was over, we were told. The consensus covered over deep divisions; I and others became intensely angry. The chapter was not a reconciling event."
2. "The chapter was for dialogue, yet it was riddled with conflicts. Some group said they were out to bring reality into the chapter. They caused conflicts repeatedly, refusing to listen to contrary views. We agreed on nothing."
3. "I tried to raise the important initial formation issue but the emotional reaction and pressure of the group against it was so great I had to drop it. I was marginalized for trying."
4. "We had a good chapter, since we stressed the discernment process, downplayed debates and the study of reports."
5. "I feel unhappy about the chapter. One national group stopped the discernment process. 'We don't decide things by prayer! That's pre-Vatican piety, they said."

6. "Some participants held back from sharing their views, until they had the right moment for maximum impact; they would not listen to others. They used their silence as power to manipulate us."

7. "People say that there should never be conflicts, but only consensus on issues. This puzzles me. Perhaps discernment might help."

8. "I feel the chapter was an experience of grace. I did not feel the under-current of ideological pressure groups, power movements, national/cultural lobbying, that characterized our last chapter."

9. "There was hard-headed debate, but a spirit of listening, openness to reports of the world we must be evangelizing, an experience of reconciliation and sisterhood. I sense there was a deep conversion to the Lord in all of us. Discernment, research and prayerful preparation helped. Decisions are being now implemented."

10. "On occasions our chapter made self-congratulatory expressions or decisions that were so unreal. One thought the whole world was waiting on every word, yearning to be led by a dynamic congregation. We wrote a mission statement, but ignored priority of apostolic needs, anything that would have embarrassed us to face the poverty of our spiritual and human resources. We had warm, comforting liturgies, making us feel good. What an escapist experience!"

11. "We wrote many documents, including a mission statement. We felt we had done well because we did a lot of writing, but the real issue of conversion remains unconfronted."

12. "I was frightened by labeling of participants as 'rightists' or 'leftists.' To be called leftist by one group, there was nothing one could do wrong in the chapter. Groups, especially some national groups, spoke of 'winning or losing battles,' rejoicing when rivals were 'conquered.' "

13. "It was a prayerful chapter. We got to the painful issues, and made good decisions. Now several months later, participants are not interested in doing anything about the decisions. What went wrong?"

14. "Two small, but vocal, groups struggled to dominate or manipulate our chapter. One group wanted by force of law to restore the status quo, the opposite group wanted change to be imposed by law on all of us. Both were humorless and almost fanatical."

15. "One group strongly kept saying that we must work exclusively with the poor. For this, they said, is what Christ did and the Church demands."

Some of these comments are optimistic, but overall respondents are uneasy about the long-term effectiveness of their chapters. There is also concern in some responses about the use of the terms "consensus" and "conflict." Since this concern is justified, I will show that the two words can connote two different models of societies, which, if used without considerable caution, can block our ability to listen to the Lord in a discernment process. (See figure 8.1)

B. Consensus and Conflict Models of Society

Models of Society: What Do They Mean?

From time to time in this book I have referred to "models" of culture or society. Now is the time to look more closely at what "models" mean in the social sciences. A model, or ideal-type, analysis denotes a particular and popular method of sociological investigation of society and more recently of theological inquiry.[4] An ideal-type is an "exaggeration" or

Main Emphases	Consensus or Integration Model	Conflict or Coercion Model
1. Primary forces	Norms/values	Interests
2. Life in society involves	Commitments freely given	Coercion
is radically	Cohesive	Divisive
and is dependent on	Consensus, Solidarity, Reciprocity, Cooperative interaction, Dialogue	Rivalry, Ordered conflict, Hostile competition Feuding
3. Leadership comes through	Position legitimate power	Coercive power
4. Society tends towards	Holding to status quo	Change through conflict

Figure 8.1 Consensus and Conflict Models of Society

highlighting of certain features which tend to be present in society; once the type is constructed by the researcher, a concrete situation can then be better understood by means of comparison with the ideal-type. Ideal-types have been constructed, for example, of capitalism, communism, bureaucracy, and pre-Vatican II religious congregational governments.[5]

In summary, an ideal-type has the following qualities. First, it is not "ideal" ethically, but it is "ideal" in a logical sense. It is freely designed by the researcher in an effort to comprehend reality better by isolating, accentuating or emphasizing, and articulating the elements of a recurrent social phenomenon (e.g. bureaucracy) into an internally consistent system of relationships.

Second, an ideal-type in no way embraces *all* the details of the reality; the aim, as noted, is to highlight "significant" recurrent phenomena. This means that various aspects of society are not included in the model, because they do not fit its overall purpose or focus. Third, ideal-types are not hypotheses; they are not falsified, if they are not fully substantiated in a particular situation. They are research aids in the construction of hypotheses. Fourth, ideal-types generally are really scientific refinements of common sense. For example, the fact that people use the two models we describe below does not mean that they are trained social scientists. It may mean that they instinctively feel, for whatever reason, comfortable with the emphases that the models describe. Moreover, some models, such as the two we are to describe, have become popularized in all kinds of literature, so that the non-expert readily absorbs the language particular to the models and thus uses them in ways that may or may not be sociologically exact.

Finally, an ideal-type or model is not a caricature of reality. A caricature, when applied to a person, consists of a graphic *distortion* of the salient points of his or her appearance or habitual costume so as to excite amusement or contempt. Likewise, when applied to a society or group, there is the same deliberate distortion. An ideal-type does not distort reality, but only highlights particular emphases to facilitate a better knowledge of a situation. Of course, if an ideal-type is wrongly used, it can well become a caricature of society.

Consensus and Conflict Models: Explanation

Cooperation or consensus and conflict are two primary processes of social living. Consensus is that general agreement in thought and feeling which tends to produce order where there was disorder. Conflictual relationships can be categorized in terms of *competition* (mutually opposed efforts to obtain the same aims), *rivalry* (conscious competition between particular groups), or *conflict* (the struggle over values and claims to limited resources in which the aims of the opponents are to neutralize, injure or eliminate their rivals). Two commonly used ideal-types have been constructed around these two words: consensus and conflict.[6]

In the *consensus* model it is assumed that people generally agree on values and norms and that social life is basically stable because cooperation is rewarding. A spirit of interdependence pervades the society. Conflictual or tense situations do occur but they do not threaten the dominant consensus stress; conflict resolution, in which equilibrium or harmony is restored, is achieved through trust and dialogue and with the aid of legitimate leadership.[7] Reciprocal power is the dominant kind of power in this model. Major cultural change comes very slowly and depends on significantly large alterations in attitude and belief. The model therefore is conservative about change; many suggestions for rapid or dramatic change are considered unrealistic, because people generally hold so firmly to their existing attitudes, values and customs. (See figure 8.1)

In the *conflict* model, the key quality is the domination of some groups by others; it is assumed that actual or potential conflict is at the heart of all social relations. If consensus exists it is only a facade. Behind this mask of harmony the powerful, including legitimate authorities, in order to maintain their status positions, manipulate or oppress others through the use of coercive power. Change occurs by further exacerbating existing conflictual situations and through encouraging the emergence of new groups or individuals, who are able to challenge the power structures in a confrontational manner. Adversaries in conflicts generally judge the outcomes in terms of victories and defeats, wins or losses.[8]

Uses and Abuses of Consensus and Conflict Models

Most social scientists would avoid today adopting *exclusively* either model, but, depending on the nature of the particular group being studied, they would draw on the strengths of both ideal-types. Cultural anthropologists generally feel more comfortable with the consensus model; they discover that people may adopt the jargon of change, but remain at heart most unwilling to give up their security and sense of belonging. The process of facilitating change is more complex than just the encouragement of conflict, which may actually have quite the opposite effect.

Abuses of the models occur through:

a. the unscientific and exclusive application of one or other models to reality. For example, as is the case with mainline Filipino and Japanese cultures, the facade of consensus can hide deep conflicts and anger.[9]

The exclusive use of the conflict model blinds people to the existence of values held in common.

b. the desire to deny uncomfortable or embarrassing realities, e.g. to avoid accepting that there are values in common in a group one adopts exclusively the conflict model.

c. turning either model into an *ideology*. By ideology I mean here an action-oriented dramatic understanding of the person and the world. One is emotionally and totally gripped by an ideology and it becomes for its adherents a dogmatic faith, blocking out all challenges to its correctness; people believe in it, then they believe in believing in it.[10] The conflict ideologist divides the world simplistically into the "oppressor" and "oppressed" and allows no gray areas whatsoever. Whoever dares to doubt the analysis is emotively assigned to the category "oppressor" or "right wing."[11] Similarly, the consensus ideologist will tolerate only "harmony," so that even genuine conflictual situations are covered over. People who oppose the consensus ideologist are likely to be branded with titles like "leftist" or "marxist." Ideologists are apt to be fanatical, humorless people.

Consensus/Conflict Model Analysis and the Church

Interest in the conflict perspective in social relations revived in the 1960s. Prior to this the dominant social-science theories and models depicted societies most frequently as founded and maintained on consensus and cooperation. However, the political domestic and international upheavals of the 1960s focused attention on social conflicts and their attempted resolution through yet more conflicts. For example, as concern for world poverty grew, people used the conflict model to better appreciate how economic, political and military power could be used to impose unequal exchanges, which lead to a world system marked by dependency and poverty.

At the same time as the conflict model was being revitalized and refined among the socially concerned in the secular world, the Church began to experience the impact of the incarnational/social justice thrust of Vatican II. Papal social documents and synodal statements reflected this trend. Proponents of liberation theology pointed out that the philosophy of consensus was being twisted into an ideology in South America by the powerful minority to oppress the poor. Structural poverty must be tackled if justice was to exist. The South American bishops' conference in Medellín in 1968 shocked participants into an awareness of this fact, and thereafter the small seed of liberation theology sprouted and grew rapidly. On the wider international scene, Paul VI in his landmark 1971 document *Octogesima Adveniens,* his *Evangelii Nuntiandi*[12] of 1975 and the bishops' 1971 synod on *Justice in the World* pinpoint the causes of world poverty in terms of the sociological conflict model, but clearly rejecting both conflict and consensus ideologies.

In the late 1970s there developed among concerned pastoral workers what became known as Social Analysis. This is a sharpened, critical self-awareness of the ways in which we can be biased or limited in our own thinking of our social, economic, cultural or religious life context. Advocacy for the poor is a critique of conservative establishment, power, domination and wealth ideology. Identification with the poor and the oppressed is pictured as a "war waged on a more or less clearly identifiable enemy. The model is essentially a conflict one where the promotion of a good is inextricably linked to a fight with a known adversary."[13] Unfortunately, Social Analysis, when it is used by the amateur social scientist, can readily turn into a conflict *ideology* and thus be the cause of injustice rather than an instrument for its removal.[14]

In summary, in the main Church documents that helped establish and emphasize the preferential option for the poor:

1. The conflict/consensus models are used as instruments of social/power analysis.[15]
2. The limitations and the dangers of misusing the *conflict* model in particular are pointed out:
   • The model cannot embrace the transcendent; concern for justice must embrace the fullness of the Gospel message.[16]
   • The model must not be used to support violence or conflict ideology.[17] Nor should the conflict model be turned into an ideology that interprets the special option for the poor as embracing evangelically only one section of the population.[18]
3. Efforts at attitudinal or structural change that ignore our proneness to sin are doomed to failure.[19]
4. True dialogue between individuals or groups is based not on the ability to dominate, but on a spirituality of powerlessness born of charity; charity moves us to be open to others in order to respect and listen to them.[20]
5. Evangelizers must watch lest they use the models in an amateur, but ostensibly scientific, way to manipulate and oppress people.[21]
6. The commitment to social justice apostolate must come out of a deep spiritual conversion, nourished through prayer. Prayer leads us to understand how injustice is rooted in the sinfulness and selfishness of our hearts.[22]

Participants in the above evaluations of their general chapters refer frequently to discernment. As we have seen above, discernment is not so much a skill as a presence with the Lord. It is being a Mary, "who sat down at the Lord's feet and listened to him speaking" (Lk 10:38). It assumes conversion or the fact that the person has responded to God's grace and abandoned himself or herself to the Lord.[23] For communal discernment *every* person must have this relationship to God. Consequently, communal discernment will be strong or weak depending on how sincerely prayerful each participant happens to be.[24] Discernment does not dispense with the need to use every human method possible, e.g. sociological research, debates, to clarify the options that one must choose from.

Evaluation of Participants' Comments on General Chapters

It is not at all surprising that many participants in their comments on their general chapters used the terms "consensus" and "conflict" or their equivalents. During the period in which renewal chapters were being held (from 1967 to the present), the jargon of the consensus model was popular in the world of commerce, because of the emphasis on the human relations model in fostering a more participative involvement particularly of "implementers"; the language of the conflict model was being stressed in the political world. The Church, with its new openness to the world, absorbed and used, as we have seen, the language for the service of evangelization.

Participants, in their use of terms and jargon at congregational chapters, merely reflected what was happening in the wider world and within the Church itself. Unfortunately, as it is generally rare for religious to be trained professionally in the social sciences, it was inevitable that in the use of sociological models or analyses there would be failures to grasp the technical ramifications of the language used. This is evident, as we will see below, in the comments of participants.

In light of this background explanation, I analyze individually the participants' comments on general chapters.

Misuse of the Conflict Model (Comments 2, 3, 5, 6, 12, 14)

Deliberately or not people coerced other participants. Comment 3 points to the use of subtle, but effective, coercive power; the individual felt emotionally pressured to withdraw a matter of considerable importance to the congregation—initial formation. In comment 5 one national group refuses to cooperate in the discernment process, so the only option open is the use of power politics, pressure grouping, wins and losses. In comment 6 some manipulate the group through orchestrated silences; they will not risk sharing views in faith until they are in a position to dominate the group with their own decisions. Christian mutuality, or the use of reciprocal power, does not exist. In comment 15 there is an attempt to coerce through strong vocal pressure and ignorance of precisely what the Church is saying about the "option for the poor." In comment 2 individuals are thoroughgoing ideologists; they openly proclaim that nothing will be done except through conflicts initiated by them.

Misuse of the Consensus Model (Comments 1, 7)

In comment I participants were using consensus ideologically, though they may not have been aware of it. Obviously, they had experienced in the past the disruptive bitterness and failure of the conflict ideology and wanted to avoid it at all costs. However, they then misunderstood the meaning of consensus. People of comment 7 are searching to grasp the meaning of discernment.

Misunderstanding of Discernment (Comments 4, 9, 13)

Comment 9 would suggest that a realistic chapter was held; not so with chapters referred to in comments 4 and 13. A key presupposition in discernment is the willingness to do what God wants of us, no matter how distasteful it may be. The fact that "nothing has been done about the chapter decrees" shows that this effective willingness was not present.

Escapism/Denial (Comments 1–7)

Discernment demands that we admit our mortality and our utter dependence on God. The ideological insistence on either the conflict or consensus models is an escape from reality and it denies the fact that ultimately there can be no worthwhile change, unless it springs out of one's conversion to the Lord, to his love and meekness. The lack of humor and the touch of fanaticism are not signs of conversion (comment 14).

Refounding and the Implementation of Chapter Policies

By failing to implement the policies and decrees of renewal chapters, a congregation misses a graced chance to respond to the Father's call to be one with his Son in mission; it also leads to disillusionment, and even cynicism, on the part of the religious of a congregation who see nothing happening after a much-publicized chapter.

The obstacles to the implementation, however, are considerable. For example, chapters of renewal required of congregations a radical change in values and life style, that is, in the congregational culture. Chapter documents requested that congregations be especially devoted to the evangelization/justice needs of the poor rather than having a dominant concern for middle class and elite Catholics. Religious must even live in imitation of Christ and in solidarity with the poor. When people wrote these documents and voted in favor of them, they would have rarely appreciated the enormous attitudinal and structural changes that this value shift would demand of themselves and their congregations. The euphoria of the chapter room atmosphere often evaporated, when participants returned to the concrete realities of their provinces and to the fears of those who could see their predictable middle-class life style and their apostolates being now threatened.

Chapters normally would have had a high representation of problem-solving administrators or provincials among the participants. Hence, while these people would have agreed with the new policies, e.g. of concern for the poor, they often lacked the qualities of inspirational leadership that are crucial for their implementation. Nor did they have the experience of a tradition of imaginative and creative pastoral innovation to draw on within their congregations.

In addition, many congregations following their chapters of renewal were administratively decentralized. General administrations, now freed of bureaucratic burdens, were confronted with an identity crisis; with the demise of the authoritarian, problem-solving model of leadership at the center and with little interest being shown in them from the provinces, they simply did not know what their new role should be.[25] If they recognized that their task was to animate the congregation to interiorize the new visions of the chapters, they frequently lacked the expertise and qualities to know how to go about such a challenging task. These congregations effectively became headless and drifting during the critical years following the renewal chapters; provincial administrations, thrilled by their new-found autonomy, were left, however, without the much-needed inspirational stimulus and pressure from the center to face up to the implications of the vision statements of chapters of renewal.

I will now illustrate how two religious congregations, the Society of Jesus and the Society of Mary (Marist Fathers and Brothers), reacted to the refounding challenges presented to them in their chapters of renewal. The former congregation is administratively strongly centralized in consequence of its founding charism and the latter, like most congregations after their chapters of renewal, is decentralized.

Case-Study: The Jesuits

Fr. Pedro Arrupe was elected superior general on May 22, 1965, at the 31st General Congregation (chapter) of the Jesuits, six months before the closing of Vatican II. During that Congregation Fr. Arrupe told delegates what he would require of the revitalizing institute. Jesuits must face a world that demanded Gospel responses to "atheism, Marxism, ecumenism, problems of social and international justice"; Jesuits, in accordance with their charism, must be pioneers in fostering the interaction between the Gospel and cultures throughout the world, using, where possible, whatever assistance the human sciences could provide. He did not minimize the dramatic nature of the culture shift required of Jesuits: "Adaptation must bear on the structures, works, men, and mentalities. This operation is not easy!"[26]

Fr. Arrupe, after the Congregation had ended, moved rapidly in an inspirational way to confront Jesuits with its implications. In a letter to all Jesuits he articulated the obstacles to renewal and the need for a " 'pedagogy' to avoid the danger of falling into the extremes of unrealizable utopian radicalism or pusillanimous fear which presents those attitudes as impossible for us.... The implementation of the decrees ... demands of us before everything else a deep and clear affirmation of faith . . . a change of attitudes, of criteria, of ways of thinking, and of the standard and style of life . . ."[27]

Fr. Arrupe exercised leadership in a "hands-on, value-driven" manner in two ways: through letters to his institute on key issues of renewal which were followed up by visits, either personally or through his assistants, to Jesuits throughout the world during which the latter were challenged to interiorize the values of the renewing congregation. There were letters on discernment (1971), on obedience and service (1967), on poverty, witnessing, solidarity, and austerity (1968), and on the four priorities of renewal of Jesuit life (1971).[28]

In late 1974, the 32nd General Congregation opened and its central document was on faith and justice; the delegates clarified the implications of this document for the spiritual life, life-styles, apostolates and formation of Jesuits.[29] The "hands-on, value-driven" approach of Fr. Arrupe continued on after the Congregation, as is evident in his letters to Jesuits: for example, on the Genuine Integration of the Spiritual Life and the Apostolate (1976), on Apostolic Availability (1977), and on Inculturation (1978). He was equally prolific in communications explicitly on the Jesuit charism and its relationship to the contemporary apostolate.

Earlier in this book I stated that Fr. Arrupe will be considered in history as a major refounding person. As superior general, he had an extraordinary grasp of the contemporary secular challenges to the Gospel, a deep personal feeling of oneness with St. Ignatious Loyola as founder, the gift of seeing the practical implications of these insights for Jesuits, and a remarkable gift of being able to inspire people to follow him. Beyond the Jesuit congregation, Fr. Arrupe was able with remarkable generosity and energy to articulate for so many religious congregations what renewal really means in today's context.[30] Perhaps the secret of this man's refounding strength is to be found in his spiritual ability, in the face of personal suffering often intensified by considerable opposition at times to his reform movement from within his own congregation, to face death with remarkable equanimity and hope. Writing before his retirement and his sickness, he said significantly: "In reality, death . . . is for me one of the most anticipated events."[31]

Case-Study: The Marists

The general chapter of this clerical religious congregation (Fathers and Brothers of the Society of Mary) was held in 1969–70. After calling Marists to renewal, it applied the theory of the missionary document of Vatican II (*Ad Gentes*) to its own involvement in what had up to this stage been known as the foreign missions of Oceania, insisting on the need both to foster local leadership in the churches and financial and manpower self-reliance among Marists in their own evangelization work. At the time this was quite a demanding mandate. A second important thrust of the chapter was to call all Marists to face the problems of poverty and injustice in the Third World.

From the ending of this chapter until the beginning of the next in 1977, the general administration, unlike its Jesuit counterpart, suffered from an identity crisis referred to above. As from 1970 the congregation administratively was decentralized and "a certain attitude or mentality of mistrust of all central authority"[32] on the part of the provinces left the central administration paralyzed. It simply did not know what to do, e.g. canonical visitations were discouraged by provinces and if they did take place no one quite knew their purpose. Some time later, the general administration tentatively tried to *react* to major problems surfacing in the provinces, but there was no serious attempt to anticipate crises or to lead the provinces to face the pastoral and spiritual implications of the general chapter of 1969–70. The congregation drifted without leadership at the center and with the provincial administrations seeing little or no need for a general administration.[33]

With the election of a new superior general and administration in 1977, the style of leadership altered for two reasons: Marists generally were beginning to feel very *vaguely* that the center should give some leadership and, secondly, the new superior general was a person with gifts to challenge Marists to interiorize Vatican II and congregational values. A new policy of evangelization based on the institute's charism and on contemporary theological thinking slowly evolved, under the inspiration of the superior general. The provincials, in a spirit of dialogue with the general administration, accepted in 1980 this new approach.[34] Supported by the provincials, the superior general then moved rapidly to establish two new international mission teams in Brazil and the Philippines.

In 1983, the general administration, taking the initiative and again in dialogue with provincials, further refined the institute's policy of evangelization; its basic assumptions and guidelines were to apply on the global level, e.g. the emphases on personal and corporate conversion, the evangelizing power of religious community, pastoral mobility, flexibility and creativity, concern for the neglected and social justice, and the need to empower lay people to discover their own gifts of evangelization.

The style of leadership changed from a reactive one in the 1970s to a proactive or "hands-on, value-driven" approach. Members of the administration introduced systematic, purposeful personal visitations of all Marists in the world. The superior general, Fr. B.J. Ryan, sensitive to the contemporary apostolic relevance of the founder, courageously pointed to the obvious gaps between the founder's vision and the reality of Marist life, e.g. the founder did not want Marists running parishes, yet over a quarter are involved in this apostolate.[35] The themes of conversion, a deeper knowledge of the institute's charism, and emphases of the new global mission policy became dominant, though not always popular, themes in visitations. Provincials were increasingly encouraged to be accountable to the superior general in the carrying out of general and provincial chapter policies.

The problems that the general leadership faced appeared almost insuperable in 1977. For example, most provinces still related to one another according to the *strong grid weak group* model, which meant that they would positively interact and cooperate for as long as their own individual interests required. Provincial administrations were reminded on many occasions that the values of the congregation were foreign to such self-interested insistence on provincial independence.[36]

Mainly in consequence of this type of approach, the provincial administrations have begun *slowly* to cooperate with one another on the basis of Marist values and not self-interest.

I would consider Fr. Ryan to be a refounding person. Gradually and hesitantly the values he sought to inculcate are beginning to take root. By his style of leadership, he has shown that position power or authority to command is not necessarily the source of change, but rather today the leader needs personal power based on a solid grasp of the institute's vision, its values, the needs of the contemporary world and a gift of being able to communicate courageously and with inspiration. He recognized, like Fr. Arrupe, that to communicate values one must be out where religious are living and working.

As most congregations are now administratively decentralized, this example provides a helpful illustration of the type of person needed at the superior general level, and of what can be done with limited resources to encourage a congregation along the hazardous road of refounding.

Summary

General and provincial chapters are to be witnesses of charity to the Church and to their own institutes; they are to challenge their institutes apostolically to relate to changing pastoral needs of the world. In order to know these needs, participants must break through the barriers of their own prejudices and ignorance. An amateurish use of the social sciences, e.g. through the misuse of sociological models of analysis, only increases these barriers. Not only provincials, but also superiors general have critically important roles in the refounding of religious congregations.

St. Paul could never have been a trained social scientist, but he had a shrewd insight into how people can misuse power. He detested those who sought to divide the Church into exclusive, conflictual, unlistening power blocks that aimed to dominate one another—all in the name of Christ: "What could be more unspiritual than your slogans, 'I am for Paul' and 'I am for Apollos'?" (1 Cor 3:4). That approach, he insists, traps people and deprives them of their freedom and openness to the Spirit; it is a "second-hand, empty, rational philosophy based on the principles of this world instead of on Christ" (Col 2:8).

Paul then is condemning ideologies, or any action-oriented beliefs, which claim to legitimize the domination or manipulation of people. At root, "feuds and wrangling, jealousy, bad temper and quarrels; disagreements, factions . . . and similar things" are the fruit of "self-indulgence", which "is the opposite of the Spirit, and the Spirit is totally against such a thing" (Gal 5:20, 17).

The sign of the converting, therefore listening, person or group is love, for "Love is always patient and kind; it is never jealous . . . it is never rude or selfish . . . and is not resentful . . . (it) delights in the truth; it is always ready to excuse, to trust, to hope, and to endure whatever comes" (1 Cor 13:4–7). Such people will do all they can to discover God's will, for they take to heart the ever-pressing invitation of the Lord:

> Come now, let us talk this over, says Yahweh. Though your sins are like scarlet, they shall be as white as snow; though they are red as crimson, they shall be like wool (Is 1:18).

Chapter 9

Case-Study: Refounding
a Religious Congregation

All baptized in Christ, you have all clothed yourselves in Christ, and
there are no more distinctions between Jew and Greek, slave and
free, male and female, but all of you are one in Christ Jesus."

(Gal 3:27–28)

"All these joined in continuous prayer . . . including Mary the mother
of Jesus. . . . The faithful all lived together and owned everything in
common. . ."

(Acts 1:14; 2:44)

This is a case-study of one effort at refounding a clerical religious province according to a primary quality of the original founding charism,
namely, that priests and coadjutor brothers live together in charity and
in apostolic interdependence. Though it is too early to make any definitive assessment of the effectiveness of the refounding attempt, I think
that the process is slowly taking root, and, indirectly at least, it is having a
positive influence on the rest of the congregation in other parts of the
world.

A case-study, as a detailed perception of interconnected processes in
individual and collective experience, has three main characteristics. It
illustrates in a "flesh-and-blood" way theoretical principles and it dis-
cusses *particularities,* including individuals, rather than abstracted roles
of, for example, "agents of change," "refounding people." Also it is a
case *history,* because it records on-going processes in the relationship
between individual persons, the interaction of particular persons with
various institutions, and the stage-by-stage development and difficulties
of particular institutions. Those who read a case-study may, through a
process of reflection back on their own work, sense strengths and weaknesses there that a more theoretical analysis has not helped them to
discover.[1]

The refounding project began in 1969, under the leadership of an
Irish missionary Marist priest, Fr. Michael Bransfield, then forty-three,

in the Fiji Islands of the South Pacific. Fiji is part of the Oceania Province of the Society of Mary (Marist Fathers and Brothers), a congregation established by Fr. Jean-Claude Colin of Lyons, France, and approved by Pope Gregory XVI in 1836 for, among other works, "missions even in the remotest parts of the world."[2] The approbation of the congregation had been hastened once Rome knew that the founder was prepared to send men to distant and dangerous Oceania. With the fervor of a new congregation to encourage them, but with little knowledge of the physical or cultural environment of the region, the first Marist missionaries left for Oceania in 1836, becoming the pioneers of the Church in the southwest Pacific.[3] Today the province consists of three-hundred priests and brothers spread over a vast geographical area and involving nine separate mini-states or colonial dependencies.

I evaluated the project for the provincial administration first in 1971 and again in more depth in 1974–75; since then I was able to keep reasonably close contact until 1985. I approach the analysis here by explaining:

- the founder's vision of how brothers and priests should relate to one another;
- the chaotic state of relationships that developed between brothers and priests in the province, when local men were first recruited to the brotherhood of the congregation;
- an evaluation of the stages of refounding the province according to the original vision.

Founder's Vision: Apostolic Community of Priests/ Brothers

The founder's view on the role of brothers in the emerging officially clerical congregation seems to have remained for the most part constant, namely to look after the temporal and material aspects of the institute in order to allow the priests to exercise their sacramental ministry with greater ease. He wrote in 1833: "The coadjutor brothers in a special way are under the protection of St. Joseph, who ought to be their example in all their works; hence they are called Brothers of St. Joseph; their work is to prepare the food, take care and distribute the linen and clothes."[4] At that point he was still thinking of four branches: priests, brothers, sisters and a third order, all under the one superior general. However, not included in this description of brothers are the teaching brothers founded by Blessed Marcellin Champagnat, a Marist priest and early associate with Fr. Colin. These latter brothers were considered to be part of the slowly growing Society of Mary, but would later be formed into a separate congregation, Marist Brothers of the Schools (FMS).[5]

Many years later, in 1870, the founder reiterated his original view of the major purpose of the coadjutor brothers: "The second grade is that of lay brothers, whose vocation in the Society is to take the part of St. Joseph in the Holy Family, that is to help the priests in temporal matters, and to look after business issues."[6] Despite the clarity with which the founder defined the task of coadjutor brothers, nonetheless he seems to have had in mind the possibility also of allowing some to be involved *directly* in apostolic work within a missionary situation. For example, in 1847 and 1848, seven novices made their profession as "catechist brothers" before going to the South Pacific, "where to all intents and purposes, they became coadjutor brothers." On the other hand, it is thought that he might have had in mind to establish there a special group of brothers for catechetical work quite distinct from the coadjutors.[7]

The founder's view of the role of the coadjutor brothers was far bigger, however, than that of temporal assistance to the priests and, perhaps, the possibility of direct apostolic work. Relationships of radical Gospel mutuality had to prevail between priests and brothers in Marist communities. The brothers were not to be thought of as servants to the priests, but as co-workers in the one congregational mission. The model of Marist community life is that of Mary in the early Church: "May the closest bonds of charity unite us always, may we truly be but one in heart and soul. The Society of Mary must *re-create* the early days of the Church."[8] Brothers and priests were to be one "in heart and soul."

Fr. Colin forthrightly condemned all forms of clericalism, that is, any sign of social class elitism among the Marist priests whether it be expressed toward the brothers or laity, an evil all too evident he believed in the churches of Europe of his day. Elitism struck at the heart of his vision that Marists "re-create the early days of the Church." For example, in 1838 he angrily commented: "In the beginning, people did not want the brothers to eat with the priests, but I would never agree to a separation. I opposed it with all my strength."[9] Writing to Marist missionaries in Oceania in 1840, he sharply reminded his priests: "Those who are your companions and who are often called brothers—may that word keep its full meaning for you; love them as brothers. . . . I am sure that out there as well as over here, the brothers are looked upon as members of one body."[10] In 1843 he asserted that "there is no difference between us and the brothers. They take the same vows, and apart from that, what difference could there be? Are we not all from the same clay, made of the same matter?"[11] In brief, the interdependence of priests and brothers expressed in charity and work was to be a prophetic expression of the eschatological myth of the congregation, a testimony that people of vastly different backgrounds can live and work together through the power of the Gospel.

In the 1960s the scope of the apostolate of the brothers was reviewed and general chapters explicitly interpreted the founder's mind to mean that brothers could assume a direct apostolate, that is, their work need not be confined to temporal or material works of the congregation. The official reasons given for the interpretation, however, were pragmatic and no reference was made to the charism of the founder; the "education and talents of those who apply to be brothers" had greatly improved since the founder's time and "the door is to be left open for full utilization of the brothers' capabilities."[12] The lay dimension of their vocation was stressed particularly in the general chapter of 1969–70, and it was agreed that "when the Church is asking the laity to become more directly involved in the apostolate, we too must make possible . . . their (brothers') participation in apostolic tasks, and give them the necessary formation for this."[13]

Into Chaos: Local Recruitment and Loss of Brothers

In 1953 it was decided to recruit local Pacific Islanders to be brothers and a novitiate was established in the heart of an elite Sydney suburb, Australia, geographically and culturally remote from the jungles and lagoons of New Guinea, Fiji, and other then colonial territories in the South Pacific. The experiment was disastrous. It was reported to the provincial chapter of Oceania in 1969 that of the thirty-nine locally-born Pacific Island men who had been recruited into the congregation over sixteen years, only ten remained. "This means," said the Provincial, "that only a quarter have persevered and that the training and stability of our indigenous brothers constitute a serious problem."[14] A polite understatement! The statistics given do not include those who returned to the South Pacific before profession; and eventually most of the ten referred to eventually left the congregation. The reasons for the chaotic situation were not difficult to see:

1. Poor Screening and Recruitment

Practically no criteria were given to Marists in the field to assess the qualities of potential candidates. One missionary said to me: "I sent X to Sydney. He seems to be a good man and should make a good brother. As long as he learns to pray and is able to do the heavy work around the mission station, he will do well!" Like others who went to novitiate, this person had only a very limited primary education with the barest knowledge of English.[15]

2. Extreme Poverty of Training

The stress in the training of brothers was monastic and overly pietistic in style: "Keep the rules and learn to say your prayers" was the motto of the training program. By doing this they would successfully become, it was assumed, good servants to the priests in Oceania. No reference was made during the "formation" program to the diverse and complex cultures of the candidates nor to the poverty of their background education, for they were seen as unimportant for successful training.[16] No worthwhile technical training was offered them.

Little wonder that candidates suffered severe culture shock on arrival in Sydney from the distant islands in the Pacific and on return to villages after profession. Missionaries complained that they were "useless on the mission station for they had no skills, wanted to live like Europeans, demanding the privileges of priests, but refusing to work hard and even looking down on their own Pacific Islanders and the way they live. We really don't need them. They are more trouble than they are worth."

3. Paternalistic Attitudes of Superiors

The attitudes of the provincials in the early stages of this venture were culturally paternalistic and educationally naive. In this they reflected what most colonial officials thought of the Pacific Islanders at that time. The provincial in his 1960 report to the provincial chapter spoke of "our little natives," but at least he queried the effectiveness of the program, although he never doubted the value of training brothers in the heart of Sydney. His successor, while never doubting the value of the program, wondered if "a white superiority attitude or complex in some of our men" hindered the integration of the professed brothers into Marist life on their return to Oceania.[17]

4. Expectations and Attitudes of Missionary Priests

Priests expected at least skilled manual workers, but they did not receive them. While individualism was a strong quality of missionary life, it was not the only factor hindering the successful entry into Marist life by the newly professed brothers. The overall education gap between the brothers and priests was enormous so that, at least on the natural level, they had little in common to form the basis of a community life.

The refounder, Fr Bransfield, summarized in 1971 the pathetic situation that had emerged for brothers who still remained:

> Lip service has been paid to equality, especially since Vatican II, (though) equality has been extended in peripheral matters. However, in such fields as shared responsibility and true interdependence, with only a few exceptions, equality does not in fact exist.
>
> Yet during the training the brothers are told that but for sacramental matters, they are of equal worth with the priests in our Society. The very inadequacy of the training offered to them to date, in contrast with the large investment in the education of priests, clearly indicates that, during training, and consequently in later life also equality, does not exist. . . . The inevitable effect of the resultant disappointment and disillusionment is unhappiness and puzzlement and bitterness. . .[18]

Out of Chaos: Stages of Refounding the Marists within Oceania

This chaotic relationship that had developed between priests and brothers within the South Pacific was not unique to the Marists. In fact many clerical congregations throughout the world, which have brothers, have reported similar tensions. "Many coadjutor brothers," writes one commentator, "have heard their vocations defined and described only in terms of humility . . . (which) has sometimes been employed as a catch-all phrase to impel conformity."[19] Some Jesuits have complained that "some fathers disdained the brothers as members of an inferior class whose proper function was manual, even menial, work; and more than a few brothers felt humiliated, "second-class citizens."[20] This makes the refounding efforts of Fr. Bransfield of value, not just to the Marist congregation as a whole, but also to many clerical religious institutes in the Church.

Fr. Bransfield exemplifies many of the qualities that should characterize refounding persons: an awareness of people's pastoral needs and an ability to articulate them, a sensitive concern for the poor and for a faith/ justice integration in their favor, a creative pastoral imagination, an intuition into the inner heart of the founding mythology of the congregation, a stubborn and optimistic faith commitment to the project yet an openness to learn and have his work frequently evaluated, a warm sense of humor and an abiding commitment to Marist community. Especially during the early years of developing the project, his efforts were severely criticized at times by his confreres, but he took it all without complaint; he would visit and be with his confreres as often as he could. When I was asked by the provincial administration to evaluate his work in 1972, he was a most willing supporter of my assignment. He would say: "If you think I am wrong, then say so and I would not hesitate to withdraw from the project." There were several more evaluations later, but his attitude remained the same. Later, when he was appointed to another post, he did so graciously and with a remarkably detached spirit.

There are identifiable stages in the refounding process initiated by Fr. Bransfield:

Stage 1: The Pre-Establishment Planning

The refounder could see two clearly defined needs. First, the urgency "to establish a new relationship between fathers and brothers in the (Marist) province, a relationship of real interdependence, of appreciation of each one's contribution in a genuinely shared Marist apostolate to benefit the Church in Oceania in the areas entrusted to the Society of Mary."[21] This new relationship could be achieved only if the education and apostolate of the brothers could be updated "in accordance with the spirit of Vatican II . . . and in response to the needs of Oceania." "The ideal," he wrote, "of real community of life between priests and brothers must be based on mutual respect, and can only be achieved by increasing the competence of the brothers. The Society should put a similar effort into the training of brothers as it does for priests."[22]

Second, he recognized the widespread poverty in the rural areas of Fiji and the Pacific Islands in general, and, what was extremely rare at the time among experts, what could be done to remove the causes of the poverty.

Economists agree that *the* root problem of poverty affecting the majority of South Pacific people is how to improve agricultural production, but the social and economic obstacles seem insuperable. Gunnar Myrdal, in his classic study of the causes of Asian poverty, emphasizes that "the main resistance to change in the social system stems from attitudes and institutions. They are part of an inherited culture and are not easily or rapidly moved in either direction."[23] The same is true of the rural areas of the South Pacific Islands, where a new discipline at all levels and a new concept of leadership is necessary, if the cultural obstacles to poverty's removal are to be overcome.[24]

Experts and national Five Year Development Plans within the Pacific repeatedly assert that the leadership needed to combat negative cultural values will emerge only through rural adult education. Yet few ever define the qualities needed in the teachers for such education. Rene Dumont, an international expert on agricultural education, claims that *the* need is for people who may be called "low-key development extension workers" equipped with a very practical education and gifted with "a great deal of devotion." But the ultimate problem, he concludes, is "how to teach devotion."[25] In addition to devotion, however, two further skills are needed. No matter what technical skills, e.g. how to improve the quality of the soil, an extension worker may require, his or her most basic and primary quality is the ability to work with other people; this is a particularly difficult skill to teach and to learn.

Second, there is required the gift of genuine empathy for the people and their culture that the educator is wishing to serve. This means that the genuine grassroots teacher does not plan *for* people, but is prepared to sit *with* villagers for hours or even days questioning and searching with them for realistic answers to their problems, finally allowing the people to decide what they see as best for themselves.

The refounding genius of Fr. Bransfield is that he could see in a practical way how the two primary needs could be responded to and at the same time: the need to update the training of brothers so that they could help form effective apostolic communities with Marist priests and the need for "low-key rural multi-skilled extension workers" equipped with the gift of devotion to serve the needs of the poor. He creatively discovered how to construct, with the aid of low-key extension workers, a process of community rural education whereby people are stimulated and enabled not only to enrich the quality of their lives and that of their families and village, but to contribute more effectively to the social and economic progress of their country. The process he had in mind fitted the criteria that he considered should guide Marist apostolic involvement within the South Pacific Islands, for it would aim:

- to respond to the needs of the neglected in the rural areas;
- to be simple, that is, those participating would be able to grasp its aims and objectives, unlike many failed rural experiments in the South Pacific;
- to provide devoted, person-oriented teachers prepared to listen and to work with the poor;
- to foster the personal and corporate growth of neglected rural people.

The brothers would be offered, in addition to the necessary knowledge of Scripture, catechetics and associated subjects, the chance to be trained

as low-key multi-skilled community extension workers, and their training for this critically important task would take place not in the elegant,
middle-class suburb of Sydney, but within the rural areas of Fiji, with the
aid of the people they expected to serve. In 1969 this was still a rather
revolutionary form of religious life formation. He defined his intended
approach in this way:

> If the value of a training facility is to be secure, its members, though aware
> of the advantages for themselves, must be absolutely sincere in their desire
> to help the local people.
>
> As an apostolic community, Marists (must) attempt to empathize with the
> people in their environment, and beyond their horizon with those of the
> whole South Pacific. They wish to be open to them, meet with mutual
> respect and trust, be interdependent with them, and genuinely desire inte-
> gral development for them. Taking to itself the command to love our
> neighbors . . . the community must try to be at least as concerned about the
> well-being of people in its environment as it is about the growth of its own
> Marist students.[26]

He obtained permission from his superiors to transfer in 1969 the training program for brothers to an economically underdeveloped rural area
in Fiji, where the congregation owned land (called Tutu) virtually un-
used and without any buildings. Assisted by one experienced farmer, a
New Zealand brother, Kevin Foote, and a small group of brothers who
had survived the Sydney experience and local volunteers, he began the
building of what he called the Tutu Marist Training Center.

It quickly developed two sections: the novitiate (for candidates for the
priesthood and brotherhood from all parts of the South Pacific) and a
rural adult education wing, with the dual function of providing brothers
with spiritual formation, and with community change-agent leadership
skills in order to assist the development of a more productive and more
meaningful life for people in the rural Pacific.

In planning the implementation of this vision, Fr. Bransfield exemplified a refounder's gift of creative imagination. He recognized that *the*
weakness in so many rural education programs was their overstress on
institutional training. Candidates would spend months at schools learning about rural problems and how to respond to them, but on return to
their villages there was no one to guide them in the practical application
of their new knowledge. They would lose their enthusiasm and become
disillusioned because of their failures. So, he devised a method whereby
lay people would come to his proposed training center for about a month

and return to their villages for six weeks, a process that would continue for a period of one or more years.

During their time back in their villages implementing their knowledge, the participants of the training center would be visited by "low-key development workers." He envisaged that the latter, who in his planning would be brothers, would spend sufficient time in the villages not only to be with the participants of the center's program, but also to raise topics of major concern for change within the wider village community, e.g. traditional attitudes and customs obstructing development, problems arising from local land tenure systems. The programs he intended to offer were multi-faceted, that is, they would be concerned not only with agricultural issues, but with whatever was considered necessary to help people grow as persons, e.g. family life enrichment programs.

He recognized that his congregation did not have the resources to introduce these programs by itself, so he successfully turned to the government for financial and specialized teaching help. Brothers would be trained alongside lay people, and several would then assume the role so urgently needed, namely, to be multi-skilled extension workers.

Stage 2: The Initial Founding of the Project: 1969–1978

During this stage the initial apostolic purpose of the training center was definitely achieved; Tutu became an integral and vital apostolic catalyst for personal and corporate integral development within the area of Fiji that it served. Within a short period of time, several significant programs had been introduced and brothers were involved as either participants and/or educators themselves, e.g.:

- Comprehensive Village Development Programs for Young Farmers: Two Years
- Marriage Enrichment Programs: Six Months
- Block Courses on Specialized Topics
- Human Development Programs for Youth: Two Years

Visiting experts and villagers together praised what was happening, e.g. one educationalist wrote that "Tutu is exciting. . . . There is no place like it in the Pacific."[27] The uniqueness of the center within the South Pacific was seen by a noted commentator on socio-economic change in the region: "Perhaps the most important aspect of Tutu . . . is the effective integration of work with study"[28] or, in other words, the balance achieved between institutional and extension ("on-the-spot") training described above. Others have observed that the project has not "developed a highly sophisticated organizational framework with large-scale financial resources." If it had, "it could not have been as effective or identified closely with the people who have little finance and uncertain resources. One of its greatest strengths has been that it has evolved out of very close contact with the people it aims to serve. There was freedom to experiment and grow from the ground up."[29]

Fr. Bransfield from the beginning kept both provincial and civil government administrations informed and involved, although, like most founding or refounding persons, despite the clarity of his vision, he was not always able to provide detailed analysis of how the project was to be implemented. This commitment to accountability was demanding on time and energy, but he considered it crucial for the success of the movement. He was not a loner. His Marist provincial and councillors supported him during periods of at times sharp opposition from Marists throughout the province, but they could do this only because he deliberately kept them aware of what was happening. They also had become convinced that he was acting rightly. Despite the opposition from other Marists, he did all that he could to inform and involve them and obtained, sometimes after difficult debates, the support of successive provincial chapters. The approval of chapters was remarkable, for participants were most often of the problem-solving type, demanding cold-headed facts, rational arguments, and certainly not visionary intuitions.

In order to provide clear lines of accountability, as well as to guarantee protection from undue interference, Fr. Bransfield encouraged the provincial administration to have a constitution written for the government of Tutu. On the benefits of evaluation, an outside observer wrote: "One of the important attributes of Tutu has been that its staff have been highly sensitive to rethinking and evaluating as they have gone along. This has probably contributed to its success."[30]

In my first evaluation of the project in 1971, I stated that it could continue only if the province was prepared to support it with two people with the right human and academic qualifications: a cultural anthropologist to assist lay and brother participants to become sensitive to the positive and negative dimensions of their culture, and a director of the vital rural extension work. Those selected would need to agree with the basic thrust of Tutu and its underlying philosophy. Despite opposition from members of the province, the provincial administration appointed two of the province's most capable men to the project: Frs. Michael McVerry and Phil Callaghan, both of whom I would consider to be minor refounding persons. If the provincial administration had withdrawn these two men, in the early period of their appointment, because of pressure from the province, I believe that the project would have collapsed. This again illustrates the vital role played by the administration throughout the evolution of the refounding project.

In 1976 a group of eight academics, agricultural experts and religious were invited for a further evaluation by the Marist provincial administration. The report was positive, acknowledging the simplicity of the project, the enthusiastic support of lay graduates and village communities, the benefits of training brothers with villagers and of offering brothers the chance to become themselves effective village change-agents as extension workers, and that "the real worth of the spiritual training at Tutu is deep, and personal," but it called for a period of urgent consolidation, e.g. brothers and priests needed to cut back on their commitments and spend more time together, more attention had to be given brothers to aid them integrate prayer with their work, and the values and the goals of being a brother in the Society of Mary needed to be further clarified and articulated.[31]

In brief, Tutu, as an apostolic witness of the Church's, and Marist, concern for the integral development needs of neglected rural peoples in Fiji and in the South Pacific in general, had become within a short space of time a remarkable accomplishment. It had become a showcase of what could be done to involve villagers in their own growth with limited financial resources, a dedicated staff and clear goals. Its philosophy of community growth had proved successful: cultural change is slow, and it is to be realized in small and comprehensible steps and is dependent on the inner conversion of people through the questioning and affirming presence of empathetic village educators. The religious community had grown; a thoroughly international group of thirty or more brothers from all over the South Pacific resided at the Tutu Training Center, and in the novitiate candidates for the priesthood and brotherhood were being trained together as a totally new experience for the province.

However, the real test of refounding was yet to come: How would the province receive the first graduate brothers from Tutu? Was the province in fact ready and able to receive them?

Stage 3: The Missioning of Brothers to Marist Communities

In 1974–75, in the course of an extensive survey of the province to which the training center belonged, I discovered that there was at least verbally widespread support for Tutu. Marists were pleased that brothers were now being trained for the direct apostolate. However, because of the findings of the survey, I concluded that Marist priests were generally unprepared to have brothers live and work with them in community.

I recommended that if refounding was to be ultimately effective, "it is advisable for newly-trained candidates to form their own communities within regions with direct supervision from Tutu itself."[32] In other words, I was advising the province to accept what I consider to be a fundamental guideline for refounding: "the new belongs elsewhere."

I based my advice on the following realities: significant percentages of Marists admitted that priests related to brothers in "demanding and domineering" ways, that many doubted that "priests had the spirit of sharing the same vocation with brothers." Overall, I judged that most priests held to the class structure view of brothers, namely that they are to be the servants to the priests for manual work.

The obstacles to the emergence of communities of priests and brothers living radical Gospel mutuality came not just from the pervasive master/servant attitudes, as well as from memories of past difficulties and failures in relationships, but also from the problems that priests had in relating to one another. Priests generally recognized that the tradition of living alone as missionaries made them often unsuitable for community life. Many in the survey considered themselves "far too independent," "excessively individualistic," "too difficult to live with," "paternalistic toward the people," "not united in apostolic action."[33]

Brothers at Tutu were now being trained, as most of the ordained Marists in the province had not been, according to the founder's vision of apostolic community life, but it would take time and experience for these revitalized values to take deep root in the daily lives of brothers. Given the attitudes of the priests that were inimical to the development of community life, and the fact that it would be unreal to expect such attitudes to change suddenly despite the good will of the priests, I felt that the congregation would be exposing its brothers to an impossible situation. I claimed that it would be more prudent to allow them to form communities on their own and, through their example of lived Marist values, they would hopefully and gradually be able to win over the priests to the founder's vision of community.

In fact, a provincial chapter following the survey opted for a more suitable solution; it was agreed to set up communities for locally-born, newly ordained priests *and* brothers, that is, communities of those who had been trained together at least at the novitiate level in Tutu. If locally-trained priests could not be obtained, then priests who could empathetically relate to brothers would be assigned to these communities. The long established practice of Marist missionaries living and working alone was not to be continued for those coming through the province's own formation centers. New apostolic communities have been established since 1980 in the province, e.g. in Papua New Guinea, Vanuatu, Solomon Islands, Fiji, consisting most often of a young priest and brothers who strive to work and live together according to the original apostolic and religious life vision of the founder.

The guideline that the new should be established away from the old has been usually followed, for the aim is to allow these communities to evolve without undue pressure or scrutiny from outside; individuals and the communities themselves must discover how to continue to interiorize the values of the founder's vision and at the same time react with Gospel criteria to the culture they are working in.

Inevitably, there are "growing pains" within these communities. Sometimes the teams have become so absorbed in apostolic work that they have neglected the spiritual and human needs of the communities and their members; at other times superiors have lacked skills of community animation and accountability; sometimes there has been insufficient sensitivity on the part of administrators to the heavy adjustment demands on individuals when they are assigned to work in foreign cultures within international teams. Questions like the following should now be raised for discernment:

- Are the goals of being a brother within the Society of Mary sufficiently researched and articulated?
- Is the model of community life still too Western?
- How is poverty to be expressed in ways that can be understood by the people the communities serve?
- Are individuals being given sufficient skills for their apostolic work?
- Is the initial spiritual training program over-protective and are the criteria for entrance and assessment for profession adequate and being sufficiently applied?
- Are brothers being offered sufficient time and space to reflect on their experience of trying to live out the Gospel and the congregational charism personally and corporately within at times vastly different cultural settings?
- Is there sufficient emphasis being given to the on-going formation needs of brothers, e.g. a deeper training in the spirituality of the congregation?
- Are communities sufficiently aware of the need to maintain the refounding process through fostering the emergence of new refounding figures from within?

It is now time for Tutu to evaluate itself again, lest its founding mythology drift and be distorted.

The following was written by Fr. Bransfield in 1972, and for many then it looked like an impossible dream, but now within a relatively short space of time it is at least in part visibly being realized:

> So, based on true interdependence and solidarity, on faith in the Providence of God and on the innate goodness of people, on the absence of envy or jealousy and mistrust of each other, Tutu aspires to be an initiation for growth, growth among the members of its community, growth among the people in its environment, fostering growth throughout the South Pacific, growth that will eventually unite all in Christ and his Mother.[34]

Summary

A case-study involves a detailed review of a single example of whatever it is that the social researcher wishes to investigate. It may prompt further, more wide-ranging research, or it may be, as is the case with this chapter, that some theoretical analysis is brought to life or given flesh and blood.

The above case-study illustrates much of the theory presented in this book. First, there are the insights and the qualities of the refounding person. A priest religious in the South Pacific senses two quite different needs: the need to foster the emergence of communities of priests and brothers living in radical Gospel mutuality according to the founding mythology of his congregation; the need, as evangelizers concerned with the faith/justice yearnings of people, to respond to neglected rural dwellers in the Pacific Islands.

With creative imagination he sees how these two needs can be responded to at the same time, and moves to implement his insight in small comprehensible stages with the support of his major superiors. The refounder, while holding firmly onto his vision of revitalization, is nevertheless constantly open to evaluate his work with the help of others and to alter, if necessary, practical aspects of his project.

Second, the project is an application of the axiom, "The new belongs elsewhere," for it is established away from congregational pressures that might well have made it impossible to succeed. Without the sponsorship of the major superiors, however, the project would never have developed and the Marist congregation, together with the local Churches where Marist communities of priests and brothers now work, would have been apostolically so much poorer.

Third, the attempt at refounding has reached a crucial stage. There must now be an in-depth evaluation by all involved in the project of how the revitalizing process is being realized, in light of criteria based on the project's original founding mythology. Not to do so at this point would be to endanger the refounding process.

The case-study should be helpful to all who are interested in observing how a particular refounding process is working out in reality. In particular, the project is encouraging to all who are concerned about how to resolve in charity and justice the difficulties that are common between priests and brothers within clerical congregations.

Conclusion

"I am sinking in the deepest swamp,
there is no foothold;
Worn out with calling, my throat is hoarse,
my eyes are strained, looking for my God. . . .

Pull me out of the swamp;
let me sink no further. . ."

(Ps 69:2–3, 14)

In his poem *East Coker*, T.S. Eliot reflects on his own life between the wars and at first considers the twenty years wasted:

So here I am, in the middle way, having had twenty years—
Twenty years largely wasted. . ."[1]

As we look back over the last twenty years since Vatican II, we also may consider them from the point of view of religious life revitalization "largely wasted." Renewal does not seem to have worked, despite all our feverish activity. A mountain of disaster confronts us!

Eliot, however, does not really think that his two decades were wasted; during that period he journeys into his own inner dark and frightening self and out of this journey he creatively discovers what it really means to love him who is Light. "Old men ought to be explorers," he writes. So must we, now so much older and less resilient than in the euphoric years immediately following the Council. The last twenty years are not wasted; they are God-permitted, *if*, like Eliot, we now use them rightly.

Yahweh speaks to us: "I am going to lure her and lead her out into the wilderness and speak to her heart" (Hos 2:16). Refounding begins first by accepting this invitation of the Lord. We must enter into our own darkness or wilderness to confront our sinfulness and our utter need for God who is Light, for "that darkness would not be dark to you; night would be as light as day" (Ps 139:12).

The author of Psalm 69 is himself in total darkness and chaos; the familiar and secure world is falling around him: "The water is already up to my neck" (v. 1). He cries in anguish to the Lord until his "throat is hoarse" and his eyes "strained, looking for my God" (v. 3). Yet he does

184

not despair. He is flowing over with trust and hope. If it be the will of
Yahweh, he will be saved:

> Yahweh will always hear those who are in need,
> will never scorn his captive people" (Ps 69:33).

We religious have read this psalm countless times, but do we—as individuals and congregations—believe it so deeply in our hearts that we fall
on our knees and cry from our inner chaos and darkness to the Lord
with all the humility and hope so magnificently exemplified by this psalmist? Until we do so, the last twenty years' experience will remain largely
wasted. The lesson from Jeremiah has been read, carefully filed away
and stamped: "Not applicable!"

> "Look, today I am setting you
> over the nations and over kingdoms,
> to tear up and to knock down,
> to destroy and to overthrow,
> to build and to plant" (Jer 1:10).

The first requirement, therefore, for refounding is: our earnest willingness, personally and as an institute, to strive to put aside our kingdoms of
false security and to expresss our desperate need for the compassionate,
merciful Lord and for his gift of refounding. There is no substitute for
this condition; we cannot build or plant without the Lord. Perhaps many
of us are still denying the call by God to journey into our inner chaos or
murky swamp of false attachments, because we are petrified of discovering our own powerlessness and its implications for radical Gospel action.
Our passport to reality away from denial is possible only through radical
conversion to the Lord.

Second, refounding is the entering individually and as a congregation
into the heart of the Gospel message through the eyes of the founding
person to rediscover the power of the mission given us by the Father.
Then, energized by this power, we will see the desperate need the world
has for Christ—his justice, his love.

The third requirement for congregational revitalization is that there
be people in our midst who have the gift of refounding. We are in such
chaos as congregations that we need persons who, gifted by God and
with the spirit of the founding figures, perceive the chasm between the
Gospel and the world, and imaginatively and creatively are able to build
bridges across that chasm. Refounding persons are excited and energized by the power of the Gospel and the relevance of the founding

charism; they combine hope and a practical realism. They courageously yearn to turn the fear of the unknown, that their congregational vision and Christ-centered lives evoke in others, into a creative force in the service of the Gospel. They hope that others will join them in their task of adapting the founding vision to the demands of the present world. Not surprisingly, authentic refounding persons suffer in consequence of their gift; they can be rejected, ignored, marginalized by the very people they strive so earnestly to serve. In this they but follow the call of the Master: "I have given you an example so that you may copy what I have done . . . no servant is greater than his master" (Jn 13:15–16). In brief, refounding persons call us to an adventure in faith, namely that we place apostolic innovation on center stage in the post-Vatican II Church.

If these people do exist within our congregations, then the obstacles hindering or preventing the exercise of their gifts are enormous, if not at times devastatingly overwhelming. Our congregational cultures have in the past, and continue today, to emphasize values and customs that make us intensely suspicious of individuals with gifts of creative imagination and faith/justice Gospel radicality. This ignores the ecclesial importance of some people having gifts that others do not have. But, humanly speaking, it is so much tidier and more orderly if everyone is the same, no one with imagination and life-creating gifts standing above anyone else! Then, it is imagined, there will be no envy, no jealousy, no competitiveness, no frightening changes, no fear of the unknown. At the time of St. Paul Christians suffered the same very human, but paralyzing, disease— an overdose of behavioral uniformity or egalitarianism, and that apostolic innovator wrote eloquently against it:

> Instead of that, God put all the separate parts into the body on purpose. If all the parts were the same, how could it be a body? As it is, the parts are many but the body is one. The eye cannot say to the hand, "I do not need you," nor can the head say to the feet, "I do not need you." . . . Now you together are Christ's body; but each of you is a different part of it (1 Cor 12:18–21,27).

If the imprisoning, non-Gospel leveling or creation-choking values and customs are not cast aside to permit God-called refounding people to exercise their creative ministry, then there is little hope that a congregation will survive or be revitalized. It is equivalently committing congregational suicide.

Finally, congregational administrators, especially major superiors, must struggle to create an environment favorable for congregation refounding persons to emerge and to be sustained in their ministry. Their primary ministry is the corporate welfare of the congregation, and that means being future-oriented, "at war" with spiritual and apostolic mediocrity, first within themselves and then within their congregations or provinces.

Let me spell out what this vigorous challenge to mediocrity must involve. It means:

- believing, through the power of Christ, that the best way to be assured that religious life has a future is to invent it out of the chaos of our own personal and corporate nothingness.
- understanding that if a congregation is to survive, it must in the world of never-ending change be continuously refounding itself.
- not *necessarily* opening a new house or apostolate or uniting provinces; such actions may appear to be synonymous with revitalization, but in fact they may be obscuring the real obstacles to refounding and delaying its implementation.
- ceaselessly begging the Lord of the harvest that he send major and minor refounding people or congregational prophets, in the service of the Church, who ultimately with the Lord are the main agents for propelling the congregation into the future.
- doing everything possible to discover the presence of extremely rare refounding persons, positioning them for the most effective use of their talents, and protecting them from unnecessary interference from others.
- fostering any apostolic, reform-oriented creativity, even if it appears to be humanly small or insignificant, for from "a mustard seed . . . the smallest of all seeds on earth" comes "the biggest shrub of them all" (Mk 4:31–32).
- recognizing that there will be obstacles to the encouragement of creativity and refounding people; resistance at all levels is as certain as the existence of the pulling down effect of gravity; the prophets, Jesus himself, and all founding persons experienced it.
- remembering that the refusal, on the part of congregational leadership, to tolerate or condone congregational atrophy and values that suffocate creative refounding people is accompanied by its own privileged form of redemptive suffering: "You are a chosen race . . . to sing the praises of God who called you out of the darkness into his wonderful light" (1 Pet 2:9).

Then Peter got out of the boat and started walking toward Jesus across the water, but as soon as he felt the force of the wind, he took fright and began to sink.
"Lord! Save me!" he cried.
Jesus put out his hand at once and held him.
"Man of little faith," he said, "why did you doubt?" (Mt 14:29–32).

Notes

INTRODUCTION

1. *The Shape of the Church to Come* (N.Y.: The Seabury Press, 1974), p. 47.

2. See "Refounding Congregations from Within: Anthropological Reflections," in *Review for Religious,* Vol. 45, No. 4, 1986, pp. 538–553, and *Strategies for Growth in Religious Life* (N.Y.: Alba House, 1987).

3. Trans. Henry W. Longfellow (N.Y.: Charles C. Bigelow, 1909), p. 15.

4. "Pontifical Commission's Report to U.S. Bishops: U.S. Religious Life and the Decline of Vocations," in *Origins,* Vol. 16, 1986, p. 467.

5. Op. cit.

6. *The Emergent Church* (N.Y.: Crossroad, 1981), p. 113.

7. "Theological Reflections on Religio-Sociological Interpretations of Modern 'Irreligion,' " in *Social Compass,* Vol. 10, No. 3, p. 257.

8. "Pastoral Constitution on the Church in the Modern World," in (ed.) Walter M. Abbott, *The Documents of Vatican II* (London: Geoffrey Chapman, 1966), par. 62. In an address to the theologians of Spain, John Paul II said: ". . . the theology of our time needs the help not only of philosophy, but also of the sciences, and especially of the human sciences, as an inseparable basis for a response to the question, 'What is man?' Therefore, interdisciplinary courses and seminars should not be lacking in schools of theology" (*L'Osservatore Romano,* 20 December, 1982, p. 3).

9. Philip Hughes, *A History of the Church* (N.Y.: Sheed and Ward, 1949), Vol. 2, p. 430.

10. Ed. Frederic I. Carpenter, *Ralph Waldo Emerson: Representative Selections* (N.Y.: American Book Co., 1934), p. 90.

11. James Walsh (ed.) (N.Y.: Paulist Press, 1981), p. 121.

CHAPTER 1

1. *The Web of Government* (London: Macmillan, 1947), p. 4.

2. Lawrence Cada, Raymond Fitz, et al., *Shaping the Coming Age of Religious Life* (N.Y.: The Seabury Press, 1979), p. 6.

3. This is a modified definition of culture by Clifford Geertz, *The Interpretation of Culture* (N.Y.: Basic Books, 1973), p. 89.

4. For fuller explanation see Gerald A. Arbuckle, "Communicating through Symbols," in *Human Development,* Vol. 8, No. 1, 1987, pp. 7–12.

5. *The Sacred Canopy: Elements of a Sociological Theory of Religion* (N.Y.: Doubleday, 1969), p. 23.

6. Ibid. p. 24.

7. See Arbuckle, "The Philippine Revolution: An Initiation Rite," in *East Asian Pastoral Review,* Vol. 24, No. 2, 1987, pp. 119–136.

8. See Michael Barkun, *Disaster and the Millennium* (Syracuse: Syracuse University Press, 1986), pp. 186–199. The model of culture change used here is adapted from Anthony F.C. Wallace, "Revitalization Movements," in *American Anthropologist*, Vol. 58, 1956, pp. 264–281.

9. See Mircea Eliade, *Myth and Reality* (London: Allen and Unwin, 1964), pp. 187–193, and *The Myth of the Eternal Return or Cosmos and History* (Princeton: Princeton University Press, 1965), passim.

10. *The Symbolic Language of Religion: An Introductory Study* (London: SCM Press, 1970), p. 101.

11. *The Masks of God: Creative Mythology* (N.Y.: The Viking Press, 1968), passim.

12. See Bronislaw Malinowski, *Magic, Science and Religion, and Other Essays* (Glencoe, Ill.: Free Press, 1948), pp. 100f.

13. See Carl Jung, *Psychological Reflections: An Anthology of Writings*, (ed.) Jolande Jacobi (N.Y.: Harper, 1953), p. 314 and passim.

14. See comments by C.S. Kirk, *Myth: Its Meaning and Functions in Ancient and Other Cultures* (Cambridge: Cambridge University Press, 1970), pp. 341ff, and Percy S. Cohen. "Theories of Myth," in *Man: Journal of the Royal Anthropological Institute*, Vol. 4, No. 3, 1969, p. 340.

15. See Victor Turner, "Myth and Symbol," in *International Encyclopedia of Social Sciences* (Assen: Van Gorcum, 1977), Vol. 10, p. 579, and Cohen, op. cit., p. 341.

16. See Claude Levi-Strauss, *Totemism* (Boston: Beacon Press, 1963), p. 104; for critique see Edmund Leach, *The Structural Study of Myth and Totemism* (London: Routledge and Kegan Paul, 1967), passim.

17. See Victor Turner, *The Ritual Process: Structure and Anti-Structure* (Ithaca: Cornell University Press, 1969), pp. 96f.

18. Quoted in Alexander W. Reed, *Treasury of Maori Folklore* (Wellington: A.H. and A.W. Reed, 1963), p. 19; for a fine overview of primal mythology see Barbara Sproul, *Primal Myths: Creating the World* (San Francisco: Harper and Row, 1979), passim.

19. *The Sacred and the Profane* (N.Y.: Harcourt, 1959), p. 95.

20. See Leonard J. Biallas, *Myths, Gods, Heroes and Saviors* (Mystic, Conn.: Twenty-Third Publications, 1986), p. 24.

21. Ibid. pp. 258–282.

22. See Christel Lane, *The Rites of Rulers: Ritual in Industrial Society—The Soviet Case* (Cambridge: Cambridge University Press, 1981), passim.

23. See Fawcett, op. cit. p. 277.

24. See Turner, "Myth and Symbol", op. cit. p. 576.

25. 7 January 1985, p. 26.

26. Ibid. p. 20. See insights also by Christopher F. Mooney, *Religion and the American Dream: The Search for Freedom under God* (Philadelphia: Westminster Press, 1977), pp. 17–60.

27. *Time*, p. 23.

28. See Ian Craib, *Modern Social Theory: From Parsons to Habermas* (Brighton: Wheatsheaf, 1984), pp. 115–119. According to *The New York Times* (14 July 1985)

Rambo was favorably referred to at least a dozen times in the discussion on the aid to Afghanistan.

29. See B.S. Sproul, op. cit. pp. 27f.

30. Op. cit. pp. 100ff.

31. *The Sacred and the Profane,* op. cit. p. 95.

32. Op. cit., p. 101.

CHAPTER 2

1. *Thriving on Chaos: Handbook for a Management Revolution* (N.Y.: Alfred A. Knopf, 1987), pp. xif.

2. *Corporate Cultures: The Rites and Rituals of Corporate Life* (Reading, Mass.: Addison-Wesley, 1982), p. 176.

3. For overview of how "culture" is used in management studies see Gerard Egan, *Change Agent Skills in Helping and Human Service Settings* (Monterey: Brooks/Cole, 1985), pp. 277–287.

4. See Rosabeth M. Kanter, *The Change Masters: Corporate Entrepreneurs* (London: George Allen & Unwin, 1983), p. 37.

5. *Corporate Pathfinders: Building Vision and Values into Organizations* (N.Y.: Penguin, 1987), p. 4 and passim.

6. Ibid. pp. 210–219; for helpful analysis of different business cultures see Charles B. Handy, *Understanding Organizations* (Harmondsworth: Penguin, 1986), pp. 185–221.

7. Thomas J. Peters and Robert H. Waterman, *In Search of Excellence: Lessons from America's Best-Run Companies* (N.Y.: Harper & Row, 1982), p. 29.

8. See Kanter, op. cit. pp. 17–36.

9. Op. cit. p. ix.

10. E.g. see Craig R. Hickman and Michael A. Silva, *Creating Excellence: Managing Corporate Culture, Strategy, and Change in the New Age* (N.Y.: NAL, 1984), p. 31 and passim.

11. See Gifford Pinchot, *Intrapreneuring: Why You Don't Have to Leave the Corporation to Become an Entrepreneur* (N.Y.: Harper & Row, 1985), p. xiii.

12. *The Economist* (UK), 30 May 1987, p. 17.

13. Leavitt, op. cit. p. 134.

14. See Richard Tanner Pascale and Anthony G. Athos, *The Art of Japanese Management* (London: Allen Lane, 1982), pp. 85–139.

15. Hickman and Silva, op. cit. p. 23.

16. See helpful comments on imagination and creativity by Neville Smith and Murray Ainsworth, *Ideas Unlimited: The Mindmix Approach to Innovative Management* (Melbourne: Nelson, 1985), p. 11 and passim. For insights on the necessity of listening, see Tom Peters, op. cit. pp. 434–440, and Robert H. Waterman, *The Renewal Factor: How the Best Get and Keep the Competitive Edge* (N.Y.: Bantam Books, 1987), pp. 150–153.

17. See Michael L. LeBoeuf, *Imagineering* (N.Y.: Berkley, 1986), p. 7 and passim.

18. See *The Economist* (UK), 11 April 1987, p. 82.

19. See Everett E. Hagen, *On the Theory of Social Change: How Economic Growth Begins* (London: Tavistock, 1964), pp. 88–95; Silvano Arieti, *Creativity: The Magic Synthesis* (N.Y.: Basic Books, 1976), pp. 37–52.

20. "The Image of God and the Epic of Man," in *History and Truth* (Evanston: Northwestern University Press, 1965), p. 127.

21. Op. cit. p. 47.

22. See Bernice Martin, *A Sociology of Contemporary Cultural Change* (Oxford: Basil Blackwell, 1981), p. 159.

23. See Herbert A. Shephard, "Innovation-Resisting and Innovation-Producing Organizations," in (eds.) W.G. Bennis, K.D. Benne and R. Chin, *The Planning of Change* (London: Holt, Rinehardt & Winston, 1970), p. 525.

24. See Peter Drucker, *Innovation and Entrepreneurship: Practice and Principles* (N.Y.: Harper & Row, 1986), pp. 135f.

25. See Leavitt, op. cit. pp. 121–161.

26. See William G. Dyer, *Strategies for Managing Change* (Reading, Mass.: Addison-Wesley, 1984), pp. 175ff.

27. *Self-Renewal: The Individual and the Innovative Society* (N.Y.: Norton, 1981), p. xxi.

28. See Steven Probesch, " 'Intrapreneurship' Raising Doubts," in *New York Times*, 28 July 1986, p. 26; Michael Porter, "Corporate Strategy: The State of Strategic Thinking," in *The Economist* (UK), 23 May 1987, pp. 19–22.

29. See Drucker, *Managing in Turbulent Times* (London: Pan, 1980), pp. 43–72.

30. See Peters and Waterman, op. cit. pp. 278–291.

31. See Shephard, op. cit. p. 521.

32. See Gerald A. Arbuckle, "Economic and Social Development in the Fiji Islands through Credit Union," in (ed.) Neil Runcie, *Credit Unions in the South Pacific* (London: University of London Press, 1969), p. 91.

33. See Drucker, *Innovation and Entrepreneurship*, op. cit. pp. 161ff.

34. See Drucker, *Managing in Turbulent Times*, op. cit. p. 60.

35. Ikujiro Nonaka, as reported in *Asahi Evening News*, Tokyo, 17 March 1987. See comments by Waterman, op. cit. pp. 136–140.

36. Peters and Thomas, op. cit. p. 291.

37. Ibid. pp. 306–317.

38. See Deal and Kennedy, op. cit. pp. 72–74.

39. See Drucker, *Innovation and Entrepreneurship*, p. 154.

40. *The Interpretation of Cultures* (N.Y.: Basic Books, 1973), p. 45.

41. Gardner, op. cit. p. 45.

42. *The Denial of Death* (N.Y.: Macmillan, 1973), p. ix.

43. See William F. Ogburn and Meyer F. Nimkoff, *A Handbook of Sociology* (London: Routledge & Kegan Paul, 1964), pp. 139–158.

44. Jonathan Swift, *Gulliver's Travels* (N.Y.: Random House, 1950), p. 20.

45. See Roger M. Keesing, *Cultural Anthropology: A Contemporary Perspective* N.Y.: Holt, Rinehart and Winston, 1981), pp. 316–328; Stanley R. Barrett, *The*

Rebirth of Anthropological Theory (Toronto: University of Toronto Press, 1984), pp. 177–194.

46. Op.cit. p. xviii.

47. Cited by Smith and Ainsworth, p. 151.

CHAPTER 3

1. Anthony F.C. Wallace, "Revitalization Movements," in *American Anthropologist*, Vol. 58, 1956, p. 265.

2. See Thomas W. Overholt, "Prophecy: The Problem of Cross-Cultural Comparison," in (ed.) Bernard Lang, *Anthropological Approaches to the Old Testament* (Philadelphia: Fortress Press, 1985, p. 62 and passim.

3. See L.F. Hartman, "Chaos," in *New Catholic Encyclopedia* (N.Y.: McGraw-Hill, 1967), Vol. 3, p. 452; Barbara C. Sproul, *Primal Myths: Creating the World* (San Francisco: Harper & Row, 1979), pp. 7–11; Charles H. Long, *Alpha: The Myths of Creation* (Chico: Scholars Press, 1963), pp. 107–187; John L. McKenzie, *A Theology of the Old Testament* (N.Y.: Doubleday, 1974), pp. 173–202.

4. See Walter Brueggemann, *The Land: Place as Gift, Promise, and Challenge in Biblical Faith* (Philadelphia: Fortress Press, 1977), pp. 28–44.

5. See Victor Turner, "Betwixt and Between: The Liminal Period in Rites of Passage," in his *The Forest of Symbols* (Ithaca, N.Y.: Cornell University Press, 1967), pp. 93–111; see also Gerald A. Arbuckle, *Strategies for Growth in Religious Life* (N.Y.: Alba House, 1987), pp. 185–201.

6. Turner, *The Ritual Process: Structure and Anti-Structure* (Ithaca, N.Y.: Cornell University Press, 1977), p. 95.

7. See "Weariness, Exile and Chaos: A Motif in Royal Theology," in *The Catholic Biblical Quarterly*, Vol. 34, 1972, pp. 19–38; see also his "Kingship and Chaos: A Study in Tenth Century Theology," in *The Catholic Biblical Quarterly*, Vol. 33, 1971, pp. 317–332.

8. See "Weariness, Exile and Chaos: A Motif in Royal Theology," op. cit. p. 29.

9. Ibid. p. 38.

10. Eric W. Heaton, *The Old Testament Prophets* (Harmondsworth: Penguin, 1961), p. 79.

11. See Robert P. Carroll, *From Chaos to Covenant: Uses of Prophecy in the Book of Jeremiah* (London: SCM Press, 1981), pp. 31–58; Br. John of Taizé, *The Pilgrim God: A Biblical Journey* (Washington: The Pastoral Press, 1985), pp. 95–113.

12. *Justice in the World*, Synod of Bishops, 1971, par. 40.

13. See Bruce Vawter, *The Conscience of Israel: Pre-Exile Prophets and Prophecy* (London: Sheed and Ward, 1961), passim; Donald Senior and Carroll Stuhlmueller, *The Biblical Foundations for Mission* (London: SCM Press, 1982), pp. 55–82; Abraham Heschel, *The Prophets* (N.Y.: Harper & Row, 1962), pp. 3–26.

14. See Walter Brueggemann, *The Prophetic Imagination* (Philadelphia: Fortress Press, 1978), passim.

15. See Stuhlmueller, "What Price Prophecy?" in *The Way*, 1980, Vol. 20, No. 3, pp. 171–175.

16. See Heaton, op. cit. pp. 45–54; Stuhlmueller, *The Prophets and The Word of God* (Notre Dame: Fides, 1966), pp. 116–137.

CHAPTER 4

1. See explanations by Bernice Martin, *A Sociology of Cultural Change* (Oxford: Basil Blackwell, 1981), pp. 27–52.

2. *Life as Parable: Reinterpreting the Religious Life* (Quezon City: Claretian, 1986), p. 17.

3. See Andrew M. Greeley, *The Jesus Myth* (N.Y.: Doubleday, 1971), p. 11 and passim.

4. See Congregation for Religious, *Religious and Human Promotion* (Sydney: St Paul Publ. 1981), p. 17.

5. See Francis J. Moloney, *Disciples and Prophets: A Biblical Model for the Religious Life* (London: Darton, Longman and Todd, 1980), pp. 155–170.

6. See Leonardo Boff, *God's Witnesses in the Heart of the World* (Chicago: Claret Center, 1981), pp. 209–264; Alejandro Cussianovich, *Religious Life and the Poor: Liberation Theology Perspectives* (Maryknoll: Orbis, 1981), pp. 121–153; Jon Sobrino, *The True Church and the Poor* (Maryknoll: Orbis, 1984), pp. 302–337.

7. Congregations for Religious and Bishops, *Directives for the Mutual Relations between Bishops and Religious in the Church* (Vatican, 1978), par. 12.

8. *Followers of Christ: The Religious Life and the Church* (Exeter: Burns and Oates, 1978), p. 12.

9. "Religious Orders: God's Therapy for the Church," in *Theology Digest*, Vol. 33, No. 2, 1986, pp. 203–212.

10. See John M. Lozano, *Foundresses, Founders, and Their Religious Families* (Chicago: Claret, 1983), pp. 25–35, 61–64.

11. See "Decree on the Appropriate Renewal of Religious Life," in *The Documents of Vatican II*, (ed.) Walter M. Abbott (London: Geoffrey Chapman, 1966), par. 1.

12. *Western Society and the Church in the Middle Ages* (Harmondsworth: Penguin, 1970), p. 237.

13. *The Religious Orders in England*, Vol. 3. *The Tudor Age* (Cambridge: Cambridge University Press, 1959), p. 198.

14. See *The Life and Death of Religious Orders: A Psycho-Sociological Approach* (Washington: CARA, 1983), pp. 218–237.

15. "Vatican II and the Church's Response," in *Theology Digest*, Vol. 32, No. 4, p. 985.

16. *A Gospel Path: The Religious Life* (Brussels: Lumen Vitae, 1975), p. 101.

17. See Gerald A. Arbuckle, "Inculturation and Evangelization: Realism or Romanticism?" in (ed.) Darrell L. Whiteman, *Anthropologists, Missionaries and Cultural Change* (Williamsburg: Studies in Third World Societies, 1985), pp. 176–186.

18. Cited by Lozano, *Discipleship: Towards an Understanding of Religious Life* (Chicago: Claret, 1980), p. 53.

19. Jean-Claude Colin, *A Founder Speaks: Spiritual Talks of Jean-Claude Colin,* (ed.) Jean Coste (Rome: Padri Maristi, 1975), pp. 459, 321.

20. Ibid. pp. 363f.

21. See Hugh Laracy, *Marists and Melanesians: A History of Catholic Missions in the Solomon Islands* (Honolulu: University Press of Hawaii, 1976), pp. 11–88.

22. See Arbuckle, "The Evolution of a Mission Policy: A Case Study," in *Missiology: An International Review,* Vol. 14, No. 2, 1986, pp. 131–145, and "The Impact of Vatican II on the Marists in Oceania," in (eds.) James A. Boutilier et al., *Mission, Church and Sect in Oceania* (Ann Arbor: University of Michigan Press, 1978), pp. 275–299.

23. G.E. Bergeron, *Report to Bishop T. Wade,* 12 August 1940, Marist Archives, Suva, Fiji.

24. Karl Rahner, *Concern for the Church* (N.Y.: Crossroad, 1981), pp. 152f.

25. "Pastoral Constitution on the Church in the Modern World," Vatican II, Abbott, op. cit. par. 1.

26. See Arbuckle, *Strategies for Growth in Religious Life* (N.Y.: Alba House, 1987), pp. 5–10; Milton Viorst, *Fire in the Streets: America in the 1960's* (N.Y.: Simon and Schuster, 1979), passim.

27. *The Resilient Church: The Necessity and Limits of Adaptation* (N.Y.: Doubleday, 1977), p. 11.

28. "Dogmatic Constitution on the Church," Vatican II, Abbott, op. cit. pars. 39–42; see the reasons given for the confusion among the religious after Vatican II by the Pontifical Commission's Report to U.S. Bishops, "U.S. Religious Life and the Decline of Vocations," in *Origins,* Vol. 16, 1986–87, pp. 467–470.

29. "Dogmatic Constitution on the Church," Vatican II, Abbott, op. cit. par. 44.

30. See Lozano, *Life as Parable: Reinterpreting the Religious Life,* op. cit. p. 17.

31. It is reported that congregations in the United States "will require $2.5 billion to meet retirement costs not funded in the past." See *Origins,* op. cit. p. 78.

32. See George A. Aschenbrenner, "Quiet Polarization Endangering the Church," in *Human Development,* Vol. 7, No. 3, 1986, pp. 16–21.

33. See Gustavo Guitierrez, *We Drink from Our Own Wells: The Spiritual Journey of a People* (London: SCM Press, 1984), pp. 14ff.

34. Paul VI, Apostolic Exhortation *Evangelii Nuntiandi,* (Sydney: St. Paul's Publ., 1982), par. 28; see also Congregation for the Doctrine of the Faith, *Instruction on Christian Freedom and Liberation* (Vatican: 1986), pars. 61–70.

35. "The Dunciard," IV, 653–656, in *The Complete Poetical Works of Alexander Pope* (Cambridge: Houghton Mifflin, 1903), p. 250.

CHAPTER 5

1. See Anthony F.C. Wallace, "Revitalization Movements," in *American Anthropologist,* Vol. 58, 1965, p. 279.

2. See *Justice in the World,* Synod of Bishops (Vatican, 1971), par. 6.

3. "Essay on Man," 11, 10–17, in *The Complete Poetical Works of Alexander Pope* (Cambridge: Houghton Mifflin, 1903), p. 142.

4. See insights by Anthony Russell, *The Clerical Profession* (London: S.P.C.K., 1980), pp. 297–304.

5. "Decree on Ecumenism," Vatican II, in (ed.) Walter M. Abbott, *The Documents of Vatican II* (London: Geoffrey Chapman, 1966), par. 6.

6. "Ecclesiam Suam," in *Acta Apostolicae Sedis,* No. 56, 1964, p. 630.

7. See Gerald A. Arbuckle, *Strategies for Growth in Religious Life* (N.Y.: Alba House, 1987), pp. 46f.

8. *Foundresses, Founders, and Their Religious Families* (Chicago: Claret, 1983), p. 5.

9. See Carrol Stuhlmueller, *Thirsting for the Lord: Essays in Biblical Spirituality* (N.Y.: Alba House, 1977), p. 44.

10. *Summa Theologica,* 1a–2ae, qq. 49ff.

11. See James W. Fowler, *Stages of Faith: The Psychology of Human Development and the Quest for Meaning* (San Francisco: Harper & Row, 1981), pp. 292–303.

12. Ibid. pp. 184–198.

13. Ibid. p. 200.

14. Ibid. p. 201. I think Brian Hall enriches Fowler's insight as to the type of person at stage six. Hall speaks of the Prophetic Cycle in which a few people develop a perception of the world which is systemic and global; their values are primarily related to justice, global equality and concern for the world's poor. See *The Genesis Effect: Personal and Organizational Transformations* (N.Y.: Paulist Press, 1986), pp. 130f and passim.

15. Fowler, op. cit. p. 203.

16. Congregations for Religious and Bishops, *Directives for the Mutual Relations between Bishops and Religious in the Church* (Sydney: St. Paul Publ., 1978), par. 51.

17. Ibid. par. 12.

18. See Evelyn M. Woodward, "On the Grim Periphery: Reflections on Marginality and Alienation," in *Review for Religious,* Vol. 42, No. 5, 1983, pp. 694–711; for comments on the sufferings of founding persons, see Lozano, *Foundresses, Founders, and Their Religious Families,* op. cit. pp. 65–70 and David Hassel, "Prayer of the Paschal Mystery: Sorrow in the Risen Lord's Company," in *Review for Religious,* Vol. 42, No. 5, 1983, p. 679 and passim.

19. Op. cit. par. 12.

20. See comments by Sandra M. Schneiders, *New Wine Skins: Re-Imagining Religious Life Today* (N.Y.: Paulist, 1986), pp. 266–283.

21. "Dogmatic Constitution on the Church," in Abbott, op. cit. par. 12.

22. See Pedro Arrupe, *A Planet to Heal* (Rome: Center for Jesuit Education, 1977), pp. 40f.

23. *Contemplative Prayer* (N.Y.: Doubleday, 1969), pp. 72–74.

24. See Robert Aubert, "Prophets in the Church," in *Concilium,* Vol. 42, No. 5, pp. 679f.

25. Letter, 19 July 1575, in (ed.) E. Allison Peers, *The Letters of Saint Teresa of Jesus* (Westminster: Newman Press, 1950), p. 188.

CHAPTER 6

1. Arthur M. Adams, *Effective Leadership for Today's Church* (Philadelphia: Westminster Press, 1978), p. 83.
2. Clyde Kluckhohn, cited in Talcott Parsons and Edward Shils, *Towards a General Theory of Action* (Cambridge: Harvard University Press, 1951), p. 395.
3. *The Genesis Effect: Personal and Organizational Transformations* (N.Y.: Paulist Press, 1986), p. 23.
4. For a summary of some further findings, see Gerald A. Arbuckle, "The Impact of Vatican II on the Marists in Oceania," in (eds.) James A. Boutilier et al., *Mission, Church, and Sect in Oceania* (Ann Arbor: University of Michigan Press, 1978), pp. 275–299.
5. See George A. Aschenbrenner, "Quiet Polarization Endangering the Church," in *Human Development*, Vol. 7, No. 3, 1986, pp. 16–21.
6. *The Code of Canon Law* (London: Collins, 1984), Can. 618.
7. Congregations for Religious and Bishops, *Directives for the Mutual Relations between Bishops and Religious in the Church* (Sydney: St. Paul Publ., 1978), par. 13.
8. Ibid.
9. Ibid.
10. *Creative Ministry* (N.Y.: Doubleday, 1971), p. 78.
11. Arbuckle, *Strategies for Growth in Religious Life* (N.Y.: Alba House, 1987), pp. 91–152.
12. See Thomas J. Peters and Robert H. Waterman, *In Search of Excellence: Lessons from America's Best-Run Companies* (N.Y.: Harper & Row, 1982), pp. 279–291, 318–325.
13. Richard A. McCormick, "The Search for Truth in the Catholic Context," in *America,* 8 November 1986, p. 277.
14. See Thomas H. Green, *Weeds Among the Wheat: Discernment—Where Prayer and Action Meet* (Notre Dame: Ave Maria Press, 1984), pp. 177–187 and passim.
15. See (ed.) David A. Fleming, *The Fire and the Cloud: An Anthology of Catholic Spirituality: Basic Writings of the Great Mystics* (N.Y.: Paulist, 1978), p. 241.
16. *The Complete Works of St John of the Cross,* (trans.) E. Allison Peers (London: Burns, Oates and Washbourne, 1953), Vol. 1, p. 62.
17. "East Coker," in *Four Quartets* (London: Faber and Faber), 1959, p. 25.
18. "Burnt Norton," in ibid. p. 16.
19. Ibid. p. 18.
20. See Johannes Metz, *Poverty of Spirit* (N.Y.: Paulist Press, 1968), passim.
21. The Catholic novels of Graham Greene highlight this tension: without faith loss of reason is a real possibility for one who seeks to delve into one's nothingness. See Georg M.A. Gaston, *The Pursuit of Salvation: A Critical Guide to the Novels of Graham Greene* (Troy: Whitston, 1984), pp. 19–53 and K.C. Joseph

Kurismmootil, *Heaven and Hell on Earth: An Appreciation of Five Novels of Graham Greene* (Chicago: Loyola University Press, 1982), pp. 127ff.

22. Carroll Stuhlmueller, *Thirsting for the Lord: Essays in Biblical Spirituality* (N.Y.: Alba House, 1977), p. 30.

23. See Arbuckle, *Strategies for Growth in Religious Life,* op. cit. pp. 108–120.

24. *The Life and Death of Religious Orders* (Washington: CARA, 1983), p. 259.

25. See Arbuckle, "Beyond Frontiers: The Supranational Challenge of the Gospel," in *Review for Religious,* Vol. 46, No. 3, 1987, pp. 364–366.

26. See John Paul II, *Redemptor Hominis,* Encyclical Letter (Washington: USCC, 1979), par. 8.

27. See John Snijders, "Religious Life in the Young Churches," in *Review for Religious,* Vol. 42, No. 2, 1983, pp. 166–173.

28. See Arbuckle, "Seminary Formation as a Pilgrimage," in *Human Development,* Vol. 7, No. 1, 1986, pp. 28–33.

29. See insights by George E. Marcus and Michael M.J. Fischer, *Anthropology as Cultural Critique: An Experimental Moment in the Human Sciences* (Chicago: University of Chicago Press, 1986), pp. 113–164.

30. *Thriving on Chaos: Handbook for a Management Revolution* (N.Y.: Alfred A. Knopf, 1987), pp. 418–420.

CHAPTER 7

1. *Natural Symbols: Explorations in Cosmology* (N.Y.: Pantheon, 1970), pp. 12, 93.

2. See Christel Lane, *The Rites of Rulers: Rituals in Industrial Society—The Soviet Case* (Cambridge: Cambridge University Press, 1981), p. 224.

3. See Mary Douglas, *Purity and Danger: An Analysis of the Concepts of Pollution and Taboo* (London: Routledge & Kegan Paul, 1966), p. 48.

4. *Natural Symbols,* op. cit. pp. 20f.

5. See Douglas, *Purity and Danger,* op. cit. p. 48.

6. See Michael Binyon, "Why Jeans Threaten Sartorial Socialism," in *The Times* (UK), 16 January 1982, p. 7.

7. See Douglas, *Cultural Bias* (Royal Anthropological Institute, Occasional Paper, No. 35, 1978), passim; particular applications of her typology are in (ed.) Mary Douglas, *Essays in the Sociology of Perception* (London: Routledge & Kegan Paul, 1982), passim; see explanations by Gerald A. Arbuckle, "Theology and Anthropology: Time for a Dialogue," in *Theological Studies,* Vol. 47, No. 3, pp. 437–441, and Robert Wuthnow et al., *Cultural Analysis: The World of Peter Berger, Mary Douglas, Michel Foucault and Jurgen Habermas* (Boston: Routledge & Kegan Paul, 1984), pp. 77–132.

8. See Douglas, *Purity and Danger,* op. cit. pp. 54–72.

9. See Max Gluckman, *Custom and Conflict in Africa* (Oxford: Basil Blackwell, 1975), p. 2 and passim; also Jacob Black-Michaud, *Feuding Societies* (Oxford: Basil Blackwell), pp. 208–228.

10. See Robert N. Bellah et al., *Habits of the Heart: Individualism and Commitment in American Life* (N.Y.: Harper & Row, 1985), pp. 150f.

11. See Bernice Martin, *A Sociology of Contemporary Cultural Change* (Oxford: Basil Blackwell, 1981), pp. 136–152, 245f, and Philip Abrams and Andrew McCulloch, *Communes, Sociology and Society* (Cambridge: Cambridge University Press, 1976), pp. 45–49.

12. See Paul Hersey and Kenneth H. Blanchard, *Management of Organizational Behavior: Utilizing Human Resources* (Englewood Cliffs: Prentice-Hall, 1982, pp. 176–181.

13. See James P. Walsh, *The Mighty From Their Thrones: Power in the Biblical Tradition* (Philadelphia: Fortress Press, 1987), pp. 171–180 and passim.

14. See Arbuckle, "Beyond Frontiers: The Supernational Challenge of the Gospel," in *Review for Religious*, Vol. 46, No. 2, 1987, pp. 360–363.

15. See Arbuckle, "General Government: Its Leadership Role Today," in *Review for Religious*, Vol. 43, No. 6, 1984, pp. 831–840.

CHAPTER 8.

1. Apostolic Letter, *Evangelii Nuntiandi,* 1975, par. 75.

2. *The Code of Canon Law* (London: Collins, 1983), Can. 631.1.

3. Congregation for Religious, *Essential Elements in the Church's Teaching on Religious Life,* May 1981, par. 51.

4. See Avery Dulles, *Models of the Church* (N.Y.: Doubleday, 1978), pp. 19–37.

5. See Max Weber, *The Methodology of the Social Sciences* (Glencoe: The Free Press, 1949), passim.

6. See P.S. Cohen, *Modern Social Theory* (London: Heinemann, 1968), p. 167.

7. See Talcott Parsons, *The Social System* (London: Tavistock, 1952), pp. 297–325 and passim.

8. See Steven Vago, *Social Change* (N.Y.: Holt, Rinehart & Winston, 1980), pp. 39–44. The roots of the conflict model go back to people like Machiavelli and Hobbes. Karl Marx helped to refine the model, asserting that conflict leads to revolutionary change.

9. See comments by Ian Buruma, *A Japanese Mirror: Heroes and Villains of Japanese Culture* (London: Jonathan Cape, 1984), pp. 219ff.

10. See Antonio B. Lambino, "Ideology, Social Change and the Christian Conscience," in *Loyola Papers*, Ateneo de Manila University, 1976, No.7/8, pp. 11f.

11. See comments by Renato A. Ocampo and Francisco F. Claver, in *Pulso*, Institute on Church and Social Issues, Manila, Vol. 1, No. 1, 1984, pp. 7–16, 48–63.

12. See pars. 30–39.

13. John L. Seymour, "Social Analysis and Pastoral Studies: A Critical Theological Assessment," in *Pastoral Sciences*, Vol. 4, 1985, p. 58.

14. See Joe Holland and Peter Henriot, *Social Analysis: Linking Faith and Justice* (Maryknoll: Orbis, 1984), pp. 14–44.

15. See Congregation for Doctrine of the Faith, *Instruction on Christian Freedom and Liberation*, March 22, 1986, par. 42; also Donal Dorr, *Option for the Poor: A Hundred Years of Vatican Social Teaching* (Maryknoll: Orbis, 1983), pp. 175, 244–250.

16. See Paul VI, *Evangelii Nuntiandi*, par. 28.

17. See *Instruction on Christian Freedom and Liberation*, op. cit. par. 77.

18. Ibid. par. 68.

19. Ibid. pars. 38f.

20. Ibid. pars. 55–57.

21. See Paul VI, Apostolic Letter, *Octogesima Adveniens*, 1971, pars. 38f.

22. See Paul VI, *Evangelii Nuntiandi*, par. 15.

23. *Weeds Among the Wheat: Discernment—Where Prayer and Action Meet* (Notre Dame: Ave Maria Press, 1984), p. 64.

24. See John Futrell, "Communal Discernment: Reflections on Experience," in *Studies in the Spirituality of Jesuits*, Vol. 4, No. 5, 1972, passim.

25. See Gerald A. Arbuckle, "General Government: Its Leadership Role Today," in *Review for Religious*, Vol. 43, No. 6, 1984, pp. 820–823.

26. Pedro Arrupe, *One Jesuit's Spiritual Journey: Autobiographical Conversations with Jean-Claude Dietsch* (Anand Gujarat Sahitya Prakash, 1986), p. 26.

27. Cited by Thomas P. Faase, *Making the Jesuits More Modern* (Washington: University Press of America, 1981), pp. 338, 337. Faase analyzes the impact of Vatican II on the Jesuit culture.

28. See Arrupe, op. cit. p. 27.

29. See Faase, op. cit. pp. 45–82.

30. For example, see addresses by Pedro Arrupe to religious, *Challenge to Religious Life Today* (Anand: Gujarat Sahitya Prakash, 1979), passim.

31. *One Jesuit's Spiritual Journey*, op. cit. p. 103.

32. Roger Dumortier, *Report to the XXIVth General Chapter: The Facts and the Problems* (Rome: Padri Maristi, 1977), par. 234.

33. Ibid. par. 238.

34. See Bernard J. Ryan, *Concilium Societatis Mariae 1980 Wellington* (Rome: Padri Maristi, 1980), pp. 7–10, 21–23. See also Arbuckle, "The Evolution of a Mission Policy: A Case Study," in *Missiology: An International Review*, Vol. 14, No. 2, 1986, pp. 140–143.

35. See Ryan, *Where Does Creative Fidelity Call Us? Superior General's Report to XXVth General Chapter* (Rome: Padri Maristi, 1985), pars. 63–70.

36. Ibid. pars. 26f.

CHAPTER 9

1. See Maurice Glickman, "Case-Studies," in (eds.) Adam and Jessica Kuper, *The Social Science Encyclopedia* (London: Routledge & Kegan Paul, 1985), pp. 95ff.

2. "Omnium Gentium," in (eds.) Jean Coste and Gaston Lessard, *Origines Maristes (1786–1836)*, Vol. 1. (Rome: Padri Maristi, 1960), p. 875.

3. See Ralph M. Wiltgen, *The Founding of the Roman Catholic Church in Oceania*

1825 to 1850 (Hong Kong: Australian National University Press, 1979), passim; also Stanley W. Hosie, *Anonymous Apostle: The Life of Jean-Claude Colin, Marist* (N.Y.: Morrow, 1967), pp. 129–232.

4. *Antiquiores Textus* (Rome: Padri Maristi, n.d.), Fasc. 1, p. 78.

5. See Keith B. Farrell, *Achievement from the Depths: A Critical Historical Survey of the Life of Marcellin Champagnat 1789–1840* (Drummoyne: Marist Brothers, 1984), pp. 52–79, and Jean Coste, *Lectures on Society of Mary History: 1786–1854* (Rome: Padri Maristi, 1965), pp. 191–194.

6. *Antiquiores Textus,* op. cit. Fasc. 4, p. 59.

7. See Jean Coste, *Lectures on Society of Mary History,* op. cit. p. 190.

8. *A Founder Speaks: Spiritual Talks of Jean-Claude Colin* (Rome: Padri Maristi, 1975), p. 333.

9. Ibid. p. 53.

10. 21 September 1840, Marist Archives, Rome.

11. *A Founder Speaks,* op. cit. p. 207.

12. Joseph Buckley, Superior General, *Circular Letter,* 26 July 1962.

13. *S.M. General Chapter Decisions,* par. 29.

14. P. 1., Marist Archives, Suva.

15. See *Report of Provincial to Chapter 1960,* Marist Archives, Suva.

16. See Gerald A. Arbuckle, "The Evolution of a Mission Policy: A Case Study," in *Missiology: An International Review,* Vol. 14, No. 2, 1986, pp. 131–137.

17. *Report of Provincial to Chapter 1965,* Marist Archives, Suva.

18. Circular, August 1971, p. 4. Marist Archives, Suva.

19. W. Modlin, *The Brother in the Church* (N.Y.: Newman Press, 1967), p. 192.

20. George E. Ganss, "Toward Understanding the Jesuit Brothers' Vocation," in *Studies in the Spirituality of Jesuits,* Vol. 13, No. 3, 1981, p. 40 and passim; see also Pedro Arrupe, "Contribution of the Brother to the Life and Apostolate of the Society," in *Challenge to Religious Life Today* (Anand: Gujarat Sahitya Prakash, 1979), pp. 279–293.

21. *Tutu: Its Purpose and Function,* 16 October 1972, p. 1., Marist Archives, Suva.

22. Circular Letter, August 1971, p. 4.

23. *Asian Drama: An Inquiry into the Poverty of Nations* (Harmondsworth: Penguin, 1968), p. 1873.

24. See R.F. Watters, *Koro: Economic Development and Social Change in Fiji* (Oxford: Clarendon, 1969), p. 278 and passim.

25. "Green Revolution: Priorities in Melanesian Development," in *Catalyst,* 2nd Q., 1972, p. 26.

26. *Tutu: Its Purpose and Function,* op. cit. p. 1.

27. See *Report: Youth Education Officer* (South Pacific Commission, 1973), Marist Archives, Suva, p. 3.

28. Report of Ron Crocombe, 3 August 1974, Marist Archives, Suva.

29. Evaluation Team Report, *Education for Rural Development: The Tutu Experiment and Its Relevance in the Pacific* (Suva: University of the South Pacific, 1984), p. 3.

30. Ibid. 1st ed., 1977, p. 47.
31. Ibid. pp. 15–18.
32. Arbuckle and John Harhager, *Study Report: Sociological Survey—Marist Fathers, Oceania Province 1974–75,* Vol. 1, Marist Archives, Suva, p. 27/T.
33. Ibid. pp. 451/B–456/B.
34. *Tutu: Its Purpose and Function,* op. cit. p. 3.

CONCLUSION

1. In *Four Quartets* (London: Faber and Faber, 1959), p. 26.